KILLING *the* BIBLE

The Historic Characters Who Tried

W. Michael McCormack

Dedication

To my wife, love of my life, without whom this work would have never been.

© 2015 by W. Michael McCormack

All rights reserved. No part of this publication may be reproduced in any form without written permission from W. Michael McCormack. Requests for permission may be submitted by logging on to www.killingthebible.com.

ISBN-13: 978-0-692-56191-1
ISBN-10: 0692561919

Unless otherwise specified, Scripture quotations in this publication are taken from the HOLY BIBLE; NEW INTERNATIONAL VERSION® (NIV®). Copyright © 1973, 1978, 1984, 2011 by Biblica, Inc. Use by permission of Zondervan Publishing House. All rights reserved. Some Scripture quotations in this publication are taken from the Holy Bible; New King James Version (NKJV). Copyright 1982, Thomas Nelson, Inc. Use by permission. All rights reserved.

Some Scripture quotations in this publication are taken from the Holy Bible, English Standard Version (ESV). Copyright 2001, Crossway, a publishing ministry of Good News Publishers. All rights reserved. Use by permission.

Some Scripture quotations in this publication are taken from the Holy Bible, King James Version, (KJV) Copyright 1961, Dake Bible Sales. All rights reserved. Use by permission.

Printed in the United States of America

Contents

FOREWORD

INTRODUCTION

CHAPTER 1	THE BEGINNING OF THE ENGLISH PEOPLE	1
CHAPTER 2	HERE COME THE ROMANS	17
CHAPTER 3	BY THIS SHALL YOU CONQUER	41
CHAPTER 4	NEVER THE TWAIN SHALL MEET	67
CHAPTER 5	AND SO, THE CONTRAST BECOMES MANIFEST	95
CHAPTER 6	STANDING IN THE GAP	127
CHAPTER 7	HELL ON EARTH	147
CHAPTER 8	THE LIGHT AT THE END OF THE HORRID TUNNEL	163
CHAPTER 9	THE NEW TESTAMENT'S MAN OF LETTERS	179
CHAPTER 10	THE WITTENBERG DOOR	191
CHAPTER 11	EVERY PLOWBOY…	201
CHAPTER 12	BIBLE WORK GOES ON	221
CHAPTER 13	AMERICA THE BEAUTIFUL	235
CHAPTER 14	RUSTICS TO ALL THE WORLD	267

APPENDIX 1	HISTORICAL OUTLINE OF KILLING THE BIBLE	299
APPENDIX 2	POPULAR BIBLE VERSIONS	306
APPENDIX 3	ISLAM AND HER TENANTS	309
APPENDIX 4	THE FRUIT OF ISLAMISM	311
APPENDIX 5	A NEW PEOPLE FOR GOD	321
APPENDIX 6	BASIC BIBLE PRECEPTS	324

Foreword

This book documents what we believe to be God's true plan for his chosen people who have carried, and will carry, the message of THE KINGDOM to the world. Its scope is from the time that the plan began to be seen, even before Christ was born to Mary. Because we have said the words "his chosen people," some would say we are talking about Jews or Israelites. This is not so. This kingdom of God does not come through Jerusalem. In AD 30, Jerusalem rejected that privilege. Modern-day Israel continues to be an important place in biblical history, but it is not holy land any longer. It is a designated land for God's activity in the future of planet earth.

Similarly, the kingdom of God will be revealed as not going through Rome, but rather around it. Rome also remains a designated place for God's future activity, but it has never been holy ground in any way. Individual Christians and the true church of Jesus Christ have certainly lived and died there, but they were the holy saints, not the hierarchy we know as the Roman Church. Rome ceased to be eligible for kingdom progression in AD 66 with the swing of a sword on the Appian Way.

So, where has God designated a people for this crucial mission of carrying his message to the world? In his infinite creativity, he graciously tucked away a remnant on an island at the western edge of the Roman Empire—what we now know as the British Isles. Again, while God certainly had his faithful followers sprinkled everywhere, one group was tucked into a specially protected place. The theme of a remnant people is not new to Jews or Christians. In the Old Testament, we have numerous mentions of a people who would not bow to worship any other god but who their hearts and heritage told them was truly God. Remnant after remnant, for thousands of years, have been protected by the hand of Jehovah God. These were always a rustic people who shunned the spotlight, except where it could be turned to shine on God's marvelous works. These holy people have been destined to bring God's Word and will to a desperate world.

As we read, we will see that even the British Isles became, for a time, theologically cancer-ridden, requiring many years of spiritual chemotherapy. But the remnant of the rustic people boarded ships, beginning in the year 1620 and came to a new designated land, America. They anchored the holy cause of God to Plymouth Rock. A newly dedicated society emerged through the refining fire to take the message of Christ's sovereignty to the world. But the story does not end there.

Today, almost 400 years later, America is in danger of going the way of Jerusalem, Rome, and middle-age Britain. Millions of our children do not know the faith of their fathers and mothers under Christ. So, they do not know the joyful role they can play in the final act of the world's redemption. Millions more are dedicated to the Christian faith but, not knowing the true and documented history of God's movement in the world, they cannot effectively join it. Some wise man once said that "vision without practice is hallucination." Theological knowledge of the Bible which is devoid of the historical relevance of the faith may as well be hallucination.

Some would say that we argue for Britain and the United States to have privilege over others. We say that our insistence is not only for privilege but mandate. Our mandate has been and is to carry the Bible's message to a weary world. It should be our privilege to carry the mandate.

Psalms 11:3 says, "When the foundations are being destroyed, what can the righteous do?" The modern-day remnant needs a firm foundation in HISTORICAL Bible truth. The distinct outline of God's providential plan is written in the blood, toil, tears, and sweat of ancient and historical followers of God and, eventually, God in Christ. I believe that it is not too late to fulfill our destiny as God brings this fallen world to redemption. You have a part to play in this. Your eyes that read these words will rest in death or they will be transformed in "the twinkling of an eye." Time is swiftly passing for us to know the truth and use it to set ourselves and others free. In our day, as it has been in many centuries, there are those who would still kill the Bible. The two most useful ways are to ignore it by busying ourselves with temporal, earthly cares or to have so many translations, applications, and versions that seekers become confused as the Word of the Lord becomes commonplace. The third most useful way is to defame or degrade it by adding to it, as many of the major churches and cults have done through the centuries.

My prayer is that you will take this book and learn your heritage in Christ as you have never known it before. And that, in becoming aware, you will lead all whom you touch out of the darkness into his marvelous light.

In Him,
W. Michael McCormack
2015 AD

Introduction

God has always had a people on the earth. It has been touch-and-go many times. One could not be far off to think that Adam and Eve very nearly gave up when discovering that Abel lay dead in a field and Cain had run off because of his guilt. Now, instead of being invited back into the Garden of Eden, they seemed farther than ever east of Eden. However, they started over and birthed Seth, through whom the promise of redemption would eventually be fulfilled. Many of us know the story of the Bible from there. The stories of Noah, Abraham, Isaac, Jacob, Joseph, Moses, Joshua, Ruth, King David, and scores of others faithful to Jehovah God, speak to us down through the ages. They all lead to Jesus Christ and his true Church; redemption realized!

However, as early as the first century, even among the apostles themselves, there came disagreement about the terms of redemption. Was the gospel of Jesus received and salvation granted through faith alone or was something more required? The Bible we have today says that adding anything–good works, obeying the Law, etc.–makes Jesus Christ of no value to us. The apostle Paul wrote: "Mark my words! I, Paul, tell you that if you let yourselves be circumcised, Christ will be of no value to you at all" (Gal. 5:2).

With few exceptions, from those days to our time, mankind has had a need to get partial credit for our salvation. Our pride cries out for recognition. Slowly but surely, even with good intentions, mankind got off track and the "official" church became not the vehicle of the salvation solution, but often the arm of the Evil One. Our desire in writing this book is that the reader would be encouraged and vigilant in protecting and exclaiming **THE** gospel without compromise. If anything is added to the gospel—baptism, good works, sacrifices, prayers, attending church, earning grace, indulgences, receiving sacraments, works of mercy, taking communion, tithing—as a requirement of salvation, then it is no longer the pure gospel of Jesus Christ and the "good news" of having a redemption relationship with him. This is our treatise. The consequences for not accepting **The** gospel or believing "another gospel" are too great to ignore. It is truly a matter of life and death,—and eternity.

Those of us who are Bible-believing must gain the knowledge of its development in order to truly understand its importance and relevance today.

The Bible, as opposed to "religious systems" of all sorts, tells us the reality of our situation. All other attempts to save mankind, from whatever a church or spirit movement calls itself, are futile. If one doesn't want to open himself to what the Bible has to say, regardless of his religious persuasion, he should put this book down now and walk away. It will be a waste of time. He will be on the side of those who have, down through the ages, tried to kill the Bible.

The purpose of this study is to strengthen your knowledge of how we got the gospel of Jesus Christ in English and what part the development of God's Word, the Bible, played in the lives of the faithful and rustic folk called English—and American. It is my hope that those who have been or are being victimized by religion, in all its forms, will be released from bondage by knowledge of the truth revealed within these pages.

Why is this important for you? Because God wants you to join his mission in the world. Not some religious leader's or guru's idea of God's mission for you, but **his** mission for you. That message, of you on mission, will only come from the pages of the Bible as the Holy Spirit uses it as a foundation to speak to you and guide you in life. The Old Testament of the Bible refers constantly to the care of the poor, the widows, the orphans and strangers, - and the message continues throughout the New Testament. The strong must always seek to bless and raise the weak. This is part of the duty of the people of God. Jesus gave us the example. He was very much concerned about each person's spiritual relationship to God, but also about their physical and mental well-being. Our social mission is a "both/and" mission too.

But first, we must realize that Jesus' mission continued after his resurrection through building the Bible for his people. And, always, this process and progress came best through the unsophisticated, rustic people who had the humility to call upon God, Jesus and the Holy Spirit. Some of their story is here. I pray that it blesses you to read it as much as it has blessed me to write it down.

Semper Fidelis! (Always Faithful!)
W. Michael McCormack, 2015

This book is intended as a biblically mandated "positive rebuke" of the religions of man, especially those who pretend to speak for God and Jesus Christ but do not do *their* works. As we begin, let's see what this verse, our mandate, is really asking us to do. The original Greek gives some insight that points us in the direction we should go.

"Have nothing to do with the fruitless deeds of darkness, but rather expose them."
—Ephesians 5:11

ORIGINAL GREEK TRANSLATION

"And have no fellowship with the unfruitful works of darkness." In the original text, "Unfruitful works" has the meaning of "works of death and shame."

"But, rather even, expose them." The inflection in the Greek gives special intensity to the antithesis, meaning, "It is a duty and high obligation to reprimand them; not simply a negative separation, but positive rebuke by solemn and formal reproof."[1]

COMMENTARY (NIV)

If we do not expose them, we become partners with them.

And with that solemn call, grounded in love, let us begin our exploration.

---

1. Eadie, John LLD, *Commentary on the Epistle to the Ephesians*, (1883 reprint, James and Klock, 1977), 382.

CHAPTER ONE

THE BEGINNING OF THE ENGLISH PEOPLE

A Dramatization of the True Events in AD 1428

"This morning was little different than any other in the small, English village during the last day of the year. Foggy. Damp and chilling. However, over in the churchyard cemetery, there was furious digging, as though time would run out. The old, groaning year was AD 1428 and Pope Martin would finally have revenge on this heretic English man who had started such a heinous and damaging revolution. The pope's emissaries were standing by the six-foot-deep hole in their black robes and hoods, and there was a white-hot fire already burning just a few feet away between the graveyard and the river. The diggers were poor Englishmen, just making a living. The hooded monks encouraged them with threats: "Hurry, Hurry, you fools." They were not of hardy British stock, and the weather caused their bodies to shiver as they peered into the black hole.

Thunk, thunk, the shovels hit the wooden top of the coffin. There were smiles all around. "Quickly now," the holiest hood commanded. Soon, the simple oak casket was hauled onto the ground and the top pried off. The diggers were ordered to lift the remains out of the cold boards and throw them into a plain, burlap bag.

The fire was stoked so as to be the highest temperature. It was throwing off sparks, and the rising flames lit up the morning sky as the group neared with the bag. "*Farlo!*" (Do it!), again came a command; this time the holy hood was in such a hurry that he lost himself and spoke in the language of the papists. And with that, the bag was hurled into the middle of the flame to be consumed within minutes. It burned and smoked as it was stirred from a distance, with a ten-foot pole, as was customary. No "holy one" would dare take a chance at touching the heretic's bones.

With the sunrise, spectators came to the scene of the papal work group. As the morning star was gone and the running of the river began to glisten under the first rays of daylight, more parishioners arrived to see what had been advertised as final justice and a lesson to those who would rebel against His Holiness. As the crowd slowly reached several dozen and the fire died down, the friar of the parish was ordered to take a shovel and scoop up all the ashes into a large copper pot. The fire was out but it still looked alive as the ash particles, lighter than air now, smoked out of the cauldron.

The holy hood spoke again, this time in more of a monotone, as the pot was carried via other ten-foot poles through its handle rings and held, quivering, over the river's edge. "His Holiness, Martin the Fifth, decrees and ordains that from henceforth the name of this heretic shall never be spoken except to learn from his heretical deeds, which are never to be repeated."

Without further delay, the pot was tipped and the ashes were scattered into the River Swift. As they hit the water, they were immediately consumed by the current and taken downstream. There was only a "hiss" as dying embers met their end. The container was thrown in after them, –as it was now defiled, and the poles were cast in as well. The service was over, and as drizzle turned into a soft rain, the silent crowd dispersed to their homes for late breakfast, and the hooded priests disappeared.

As ordered by the hierarchy, the parish priest supervised the diggers in their last task of the morning, the removal of the headstone. It was pried out of the earth and thrown into the stony field behind the chapel, but flipped as it hit the hard ground and lay with the name upright. The etched words were still easily visible. The name read, John Wycliffe, and when he died, December 31st, 1384. Forty-four years ago to the very day.

What was the awful crime of this man? Had he been a murderer, a vile robber, a leader of mutinous armies against the church? No, but he was hated just the same. He had started the demise of the most notorious system the Devil had ever devised, and had sparked the Reformation that now threatened to split and gnaw the edges off of the Holy See. How had he done it? John Wycliffe had committed the sin of translating the Holy Bible from Latin into English so that his people could read it for themselves and hear the words of Jesus in their own tongue for the first time. He had encouraged them to memorize the Lord's Prayer and to pray directly to the Father of all Creation as their *ABBA*, Daddy. For this, Wycliffe was threatened with burning at the stake, but his powerful friends shielded him,—until this dreary, digging day.

John Foxe, author of the foremost book listing martyrs of the Christian faith, wrote these words in his remarks about the burning of the bones of John Wycliffe. He likened the ashes of John to the Word that flowed to the people of God: "And, like the River Swift which runs into the Avon and the Avon into the Severn and the Severn into the Bristol Channel which empties into the oceans of the world, so did the proliferation of God's Word go to the ends of the earth."

On that great day, when the trump shall sound and the dead in Christ shall rise first, Brother John will recompose into a heavenly body from a thousand ocean waves and rise to meet his Lord and Savior in the air. The Morning Star of the Reformation joining hands, at last, with his Bright and Morning Star.

John Wycliffe

Reading this bizarre story, we must ask, how did it come to this? How began the story that brought on this behavior? We now know that the process began over two-thousand years before this despicable grave-robbing day.

The Beginning of the Story

At the end of the parable of the tenants, Jesus remarked to the Jewish leaders, "Therefore I tell you that the kingdom of God will be taken away from you and given to a people who will produce its fruit" (Matt. 21:43 NIV).

Who would these people be that would receive the "kingdom of God" that the Jews were not worthy of? We have a clue in the Greek text of the passage. When Jesus says, "a people," the Greek language reveals that they would be a "rustic people," simple people, open and transparent folk, not afraid to believe. This is our first clue as to where to look, not in the sophisticated cities of the old world with lots of pride and prestige to lose, but in the simple counties and small towns of the "new world." Our second clue from Jesus lies within the meaning of the word, *fruit*. In the Greek, the inflected suggestion about the fruit of the kingdom is that the core of this fruit is the sovereign movement of God in the world. In other words, these rustic people would be given the responsibility of establishing a nation, and subsequent nations, which would have, as their calling, to tell the world about the movement of the Sovereign God in the world. That is originally what the Jewish nation was designed to do, but failed. Finally, we need to analyze the word "kingdom." From the time of the prophet Daniel to the Apostles Paul and John, the Holy Writ tells us that the kingdom of God, "the kingdom," is God in action; the place where what God wants done is done. It broke forth for Christians the day that Jesus was born.[1]

In his omniscience, God had, even when Jesus spoke these words, been preparing a particular people in secret for hundreds of years. The initial plan was for this crucial action, this movement, to come through Britain and principally with their influence. This happened in history. Then, loyal Christian followers brought the work of the kingdom to their obeying "rustic" descendant nation; America. These two nations represent the core of the fruit of the kingdom and its movement in the world. But we are getting ahead of ourselves. Chapter one is how we believe it began in the heart of God more than a thousand years before Jesus came as a baby. Let's trace our rustic heritage from the time of Noah!

Gomer's People

"Modern scholarship has undeniably discovered that English gets its alphabet from the evolution of the Ancient Hebrew, the language of God."[2]

When Noah's three sons departed the ark, they were driven to establish their own families. When the dispersion of Babel occurred, Noah's eldest son's clan departed to the west and north through what we now call northern Turkey. Japeth's descendants also settled in the hills and mountains of the Adriatic and on the northern shores of the Black Sea. From there, they migrated into Eastern Europe. Through the decades and centuries of familial undulation, many tribes grew into the peoples of Russia, Germania, and the European lowlands.[3]

The family that we specifically want to follow is the tribe of the eldest son of Japheth, Gomer. Gomer is a very interesting name. We find that the core Hebrew meaning of *Gomer* is "perfect," and the pictorial meaning is that Gomer is "perfected for a sure and certain purpose." The people of Gomer and his son, Ashkenaz, travelled into what is now Holland, Belgium, and France, which Europeans eventually would term Gaul, by the time of Christ. Ashkenazi tribal descendants fashioned sailing vessels and used them to travel across the narrow channel to the isle of Brytagne (Britannia). Within several hundred years, they had populated much of southern England and Wales and were called Cymric Celts as reported by other tribes who eventually visited them. Why Cymric Celts?

It seems that, through the linguistic years, Grandfather Gomer's family name had managed to evolve from the main sounding letters of **GoMeR** (no vowels, as it is in Ancient Hebrew) to **CMR**; pronounced Simmer. This is from whence we get Cymric.[4] And the term Celt comes from *Ceile* meaning "God" in Ancient Welsh. Putting them together we have—the "Gomer of God" people; the Cymric Celts. So, putting it all together, this

Brythonic island nation was populated by the lineage of Gomer, the perfect people to reveal the kingdom and bear its fruit. We have evidence of this recorded in the ancient Welsh document called the Myvyrnian Archaiology, under the heading of the Welsh Historical Triads. "One of the three social tribes of the Isle of Britain was the Cymry, that came with Hu Gaddarn of justice and peace…these three tribes had sprung from the primitive race of the Cymry."[5]

It is important to mention Gomer's brothers because some of their descendants will enter into the discussion later. Japheth had seven sons: Gomer, the eldest; Magog, who settled in southern Russia; Madai, settling in Medea or northern Persia; Javan, settling Greece and its islands; Tubal, settling central Europe; Meshech and Tiras, (not clear where they settled) probably the far East. The lineage of Javan should particularly capture our attention because the Javanites eventually became known as the Hellenists in ancient Greece.

> "Our [Greek] language came from the East,
> our wisdom from the West." —Plato

Ancient manuscripts give us ample evidence to suggest that the "wisdom men" mentioned by Plato, the philosophers who passed through the Grecian cities, were from the tribes of Great Grandfather Japheth, Grandfather Gomer, and Father Ashkenaz. Socrates and Plato garnered thoughts from them and created the foundation of their philosophy. As his quote above tells us, Plato was able to trace the fact that the Greek language came from northern Turkey to the east (Japheth's first settlements), but the foundations of their wisdom came from the west. Was it "the west" of Italy and Rome? No, the Italian Etruscans were still a developing civilization during the Greek's rise to dominance of the world under King Phillip and his more famous son, Alexander the Great. Much less were they able or willing to send wandering philosophers to other nations.

So, where was this area that the "philosophers" came from in the west? It was the northwest, from Gaul and Germania, where Ashkenaz and Gomer had travelled and their children had settled. It seems that great philosophers and wanderers had travelled from central Europe through the Adriatic and into Greece.

To give us some biblical perspective, all of this British foundational movement was during the same time as the second son of Noah was also settling the Fertile Crescent. The Shem-ites (Semites) were moving into the Promised Land for the first time under the leadership of God, through the family of Terah. And, biblically important, coming to settle through Abram, great[(4)] grandson of Shem, who would eventually be called Father Abraham. Ham, the third son of Noah, and his descendants were populating northern Africa and points south. But theirs is a different story for another time. Its best account is from the first book of the Bible, Genesis.

THE DRUIDS OF BRYTAGNE

"In the Bible, legend and history have met and fused."[6] —J.R.R. Tolkien

It may seem strange to introduce into this discussion the Druidic religion. However, it became of tremendous importance to the development of Christianity in the British Isles. Bear with me as we introduce ourselves to the Brytagnic Druids. What if I were to tell you that Britain's Celtic Druidism was used by God as fertile spiritual and cultural ground for Christianity in the cradle? Well, that is exactly what we are about to surmise.

This Cimry Celt strand of Druidism taught as follows:

Main Tenant = "The universe is infinite, being the body of the being who, out of himself, created it, and now pervades and rules it. The essence of this being is pure mental light and, therefore, he is called DU-W; the one in whom is no darkness at all."

If this sounds familiar, read 1 John 1:5:

"This is the message we have heard from him and declare to you: God is light; and in him is no darkness at all."

The Cymric Druids preached that DU-W has a triple nature. He is the creator of the past, the savior of the present and the renovator of the future. The three positions were the personages of Celi, Yeshu, and Taran.[7]

This was the divine trinity whose symbol was engraved on the clothing of the Druidic Priests. There were three rays of light as from the heavens, engraved in gold on their head dress and robes. When Christians eventually came to the Island of Britain and preached Jesus (*Yeshua*) as God, they preached the most familiar name of their own deity to Celtic Druidism. So, in the ancient British tongue, Yeshua never assumed its strictly Greek, Latin, or Hebrew form, but remained the pure Druidic *Yeshu*. It would seem that the ancient Celtic Briton never changed the name of the God he worshipped.

The strangers from far away in the east said, "…and truly our fellowship is with the Father, and with His Son, Yeshu Christo." (See 1 John 1:3).

Stonehenge, England

All of us have heard of Stonehenge. Stonehenge, as we see it today, is the ruin showing three thousand plus years of exposure to the elements. Its first founder was Hu Gadarn, 1500 BC, a Celtic/Druidic priest. The temples of the Druids were circular and obelistic, like Stonehenge. They were open on every side and above, with the heavens as their roof. The monolithic stones were composed of immense, single stones on which metal was not allowed to attach. There were wide avenues leading to the temples, and national religious processions moved through these on the three great festivals of the year.

During the times of the third through the first centuries BC, there were also Druidic universities in every area of ancient Britain, where each land-owning family sent at least one child to become a priest. It took twenty years for a novice to complete all the curriculum of the priesthood and become a Druidic priest. He would go back to his tribal area to become one of the priests of the COR, or county, and sit as judge in judgment of disputes and to depart wisdom. Some Druidic priests became travelling ambassadors and travelled to the other islands or to the continent and even as far as Greece and Turkey.

Listening to more evidence that God purposely prepared the Cymric Celts to become Christian, we hear that the Druidic priests explained to their people that God was not only all pure light, but that he was the alpha and the omega, the beginning and the end. He also had divided the heavens and the earth. In their language, the heavenly realm was designated Gwynfyd and the earth was *Abred*. Abred had inhabitants called *Abredolians* (people), who lived in the current incarnation of their *rhith* (lifecycle). These humans were always hoping for re-incarnation upon death. Finally, there was Annyn, which was the underworld, where rebellious Abredolians went upon death.

However, through doing good before their death, Abredolians could go from the current rhith to the next and higher rhith (reincarnation). According to the faith, mankind was fallen from Gwynfyd and Du-w had assigned them to Annyn (hell) but that he had immediately made a way back to Gwynfyd through stages of existence in Abred (the world). Each man and woman could rise through the various cycles of Abred. If their soul willingly found the knowledge of the good, preferred good, and abided by its choice, then at the death of its body, it could re-enter Gwynfyd from which it fell.

Can we now begin to see the parallels and differences between Christianity and Celtic Druidism? First, a trinitarian god was the creator of all on earth. As Celi, he created the heavens, the earth, and the underworld, or hell. Second, he had a part of himself called Yeshu, who represented the people of the earth and ministered to them through their passages of reincarnation called rhiths and third, there was a Spirit of Truth that guided the elders in managing communication and morals between peoples.

Now, stay with me, even though I am speaking of the Druidic religion as believing in reincarnation. It will all become clear presently. Let's define the Druidic priest just a bit more. They preached that the collective lineage of the community was what gave it power. And, their lineage was from God through their ancestors who had originally come to the land of Brytagne from the continent.

"Ancient Druids considered the brotherhood and sisterhood as the root of community. The local community was also one equal of the State organization which provided double power for all."[8]

"In the ancient world, the Druids were the only priesthood of peace. Clad in his white canonicals, the Druidic Herald presented himself between two armies and every sword was instantly sheathed."[9]

Why would every sword instantly be sheathed? Because even if the clans had great arguments over land or over injustices, the Druidic priest represented the elders, who reported to God, who judged rightly those that were the rebellious and they would be condemned to Annyn. The tribes might war with themselves, but to hurt or kill a priest was to be immediately consigned to an eternity in Annyn (hell).

Druidic Priest

"The Druids were in a constant state of seeking 'the ultimate truth.' The Druidic elders sat at each Cor or county seat, and were the religious and civil mediators. They were called "The Ecclesiastics." The Druidic elders oft repeated that, "In 'the way' was 'the truth' and in the truth was 'eternal life'.[10]

Druidic Influence Far-reaching

> "All the streams of Greek philosophy are traced to the fountains of the West." —Plato

As evidence of this, as we look into ancient Hellenistic literature, we find that the pre-historic (before Homer) poet philosophers of Greece were Druidic: Musaeus, Orpheus, and Lineus. Scholars agree that these were the beginning of Hellenistic philosophy and literature. Of the attainments of the Druids in all the sciences, especially in the area of astronomy, the classic judges of eminence—Cicero and Caesar, Pliny and Tacitus, Diodorus Siculus and Strabo—speak in high terms.[11] In these and other's writings the Druids were known as statesmen, legislators, priests, physicians, lawyers, teachers, and poets. They taught the Greeks natural philosophy, astronomy, arithmetic, geometry, medicine, and oratory. Their sacred animal for sacrifice was the bull; the sacred tree, the oak, the sacred grain, wheat; the sacred herbs, the trefoil and hyssop. The canonical vestments of the

Druids were white linen robes with no metal but gold used in any part of the dress. The Druidic cross was wrought in gold down the length of the back of his robe. (This is interesting, since a "cross" was not used in public punishment in the islands prior to the Roman conquest.)

The Druidic name of their homeland was *Brytagne* meaning "the high stones of worship," and their Druidic Principle, adopted by the Greeks for a thousand years, was "*Y Gwir erbyn y Byd*," "The Truth against the World."[11] Take a look at the early Greek philosophers and you will find this to be at the core of their messages.

GETTING TO THE POINT

Here's where it all comes together. When the earliest Christians travelled to the islands and said that Yeshu-a was the **Way**, **Truth** and the **Life**, they immediately had the inhabitant's attention.

They told the story of Pilate asking Yeshua, "What is Truth?" and Yeshua replying, "For this I came into the world, to testify to the truth. Everyone on the side of truth listens to me" (John 18:37).

After this unmistakable introduction, the Christians also said that Yeshua had come to the world in their homeland of Israel and that he had died for all Abredolians in order that they would not have to go through many "rhiths" to attain Gwynfyd. And that through Yeshua, they could immediately go to heaven upon death, and there was no danger of ever going to Annyn or coming back to a pain-filled earth if they put their faith in Yeshua and his gospel, or story of good news, which was written down by the followers of Yeshua who had been allowed to live with him for several years before Celi took him back to Gwynfyd.

All this made perfect sense to the people and the leaders of Brytagne. Many of them became immediate Christians as they learned of the great news. Some did not come over to Christ Jesus, but fled to the island west, Hibernia, (Ireland) where they could continue for a time the "nature-based Druidic religion" without the gospel of Yeshua. It is from **these** Druids that we have come to know Druidism as the nature-worshipping, Christ-less people that they became upon rejection of the gospel.

(Later, we will learn that a certain British priest went to spread the gospel to these people, a man named Patrick.)

We can now realize why Christianity was able to sweep over the island country of Britain so swiftly within a generation of Christ's death and resurrection. But in upper Brytagne, there were also those tribes who had migrated from the north and east into Scotland and the coastal east who were not Cymric Celts and who would come against the Christian Celts. But exactly **who** brought Christianity to the Isles and when? Well, be patient, as we need to offer just a bit more background.

Our last clue to the ease of early Christian growth in Brytagne is the language. For now we are going to focus on the Welsh and southern English area Cymric Celts. They became God's corps of communication for the gospel. Listen to a recent comment from one of our pre-eminent English linguists:

"Celtic grammar is underneath all of those utterly ordinary utterances in Modern English…We can assume that Celts were speaking Celtified English starting with the first generation who grew up bilingual, as far back as the fifth century, and throughout the Old English period."[13]

Matter of fact, scholars agree that Old English had similar language case markers and three genders as had the Greek language. And, unlike any of the Germanic languages, English turns its verb-noun progressive into its only present tense. Also, like biblical Hebrew, Celtic (Welsh) puts its verbs first. Finally, like Hebrew and Aramaic, and unlike any other Western language, Old English/Celtic forms the past tense by changing the vowels inside the word.

"This means that, even without recordings of seventh-century Celts speaking 'Englisc' and peppering it with phrasings copying Celtic grammar, we can assume that this was the case, because it quite simply must have been… After a while, this was English."[14]

The Cymric Celtic language was understood by those foreigners who sailed from the Holy Land speaking Greek and Aramaic, which is closely related to Hebrew. The language of the Celts was nurtured by God into the English language that was, eventually, not only to bring the Good News of Jesus but that has united the modern world for the advancement of his kingdom down through two-thousand years—Great Britain to the U.S. to the world!

So, by religious base, culture and language, the people of the British Isle were prepared for certain strangers to land on their shore and spread the gospel of Jesus Christ.

Finally, we have a summation testimonial from Reverend R.W. Morgan, who, in the mid-1800s in Britain conducted historical research on Christians in his country. "Two cardinal reasons, we have seen, each of national weight and extent, inclined the British mind to accept Christianity—the first, its identity in many important points with Druidism; the second, its uncompromising antagonism to the whole system of the Roman state mythology. The Roman persecution of both religions identified them still further in the popular mind. Nowhere, then, in Asia, Africa, or Europe, could the apostles find richer or a better-prepared soil for the gospel."[15]

Enter The Romans and Their Empire

"The Druids teach that by no other way than the ransoming of a man's life by the life of man, is reconciliation with the divine justice of the immortal gods possible." —Julius Caesar [15]

The first Roman conqueror to come to Brytagne was Julius Caesar in 55 BC He wrote about the country and the Druids in some detail. He wrote some interesting facts about them:

"The Druids, in their civil transactions, use the Greek alphabet."[17]

This quote tells us that the Druids were not only the religious leaders, but also the civil leaders of the counties, or Cors, and that they had connections with the Greeks.

In acquainting himself with the leaders of Brytagne, Julius Caesar was the recipient of the religious thought of the Druids; namely, that reconciliation to God was obtained through the life of a man who sacrificed himself for others and for country. This also made them fierce warriors, according to Caesar. Satan had his hand on the Romans and Caesar, but like King Nebuchadnezzar of old, God was going to use them, in spite of themselves, to his glory. Satan thought that he had the upper hand and the assault could be carried forward to kill the Bible in the British Isles. But, poor Satan, he couldn't compete with God.

So, when and why did Caesar and the Romans come to Brytagne? As they say, "Follow the money!"—chapter two.

Sources

1 Robinson and House, *Lexicon of N.T. Greek*, (Holman, 2012), 101.

2 Craig Lampe, *The Forbidden Book*, 60.

3. F.W. Farrar, *Life & Work of St. Paul*, vol 1 p. 466.

4. Arthur Constance, *Noah's Three Sons*, Zondervon 84.

5. Gilbert, Adrian, *The Holy Kingdom*, Bantam Press, 1998, 65.

6. J. R. R. Tolkien, *On Fairy Stories* 72.

7. Lucan, i. 444 f. The opinions of writers who take this view are collected by Reinach, RC xviii.137.

8. Higgins, *Celtic Researches* 196.

9. Higgins, *Celtic Researches* 196.

10. Higgins, *Celtic Researches* 196 / Dr. Francis Nigel Lee, TBCPCI, I Version 16).

11. Artemidorus, quoted by Strabo, *the Orphic Hymns: Avienus de Britannia.*

12. Dr. Francis Nigel Lee, *TBCPCI*, I Version.

13. McWhorter, John, *Our Magnificent Bastard Tongue*, Penguin Publishing, 2008), 42, 62.

14. McWhorter, John, *Our Magnificent Bastard Tongue*, 15, 17, 38.

15. Morgan, R.W., *Saint Paul in Britain,* (1860; Artisan Publishers, 2006) 100.

16. Julius Caesar, *Gallic War*, Lib. V.

17. Julius Caesar, *Gallic War*, Lib. V.

Images

Morguefile.com, where photo reference lives. This morgue file contains free high resolution digital stock photographs and reference images for either corporate or public use.

CHAPTER TWO

HERE COME THE ROMANS

JULIUS CAESAR WAS NO PUSHOVER. Having conquered Egypt, North Africa, Spain, France, and western Germany, he desired next,— Britain. On the 5th of August, 55 BC, he crossed the English Channel with two divisions of Rome's finest troops. The campaign lasted fifty-five days. Caesar failed to advance seven miles inland from the beach. Historian Dion Cassius stated that Caesar's original intention was to carry the war into the interior, but finding his forces inadequate to defeat the British in the field, he retreated to the shores of Gaul (France) again.

Julius Caesar bronze statue in Rome Italy

On May 10, 54 BC, the next spring, Caesar tried again. This time he commanded an army of 30,000 men embarking on 1,000 ships. The campaign slogged through Britain's interior only seventy miles and was repelled at St. Albans. On September 10th, a peace treaty was concluded and a tribute of minerals was agreed upon. Roman Aulus Gellius wrote an account of Caesar's battle over Britain and speaks of a blood-curdling British war cry which shook the Romans again and again: "*Tori pen i Caesar*," "Off with Caesar's head."

Why would the great Julius Caesar risk his reputation and his army against so strong a foe? We had mentioned that the money should be followed, did we not? Well, it seems that the land of Britain, mostly Wales and the western coast, had valuable mines that had been fought over for several hundred years, and Caesar wanted them.

"Brittany had significant sources of tin which show evidence of being extensively exploited after the Roman conquest of Gaul during the first century BC and onward. Devon and Cornwall were important sources of tin for Europe and the Mediterranean throughout ancient times. Iberian tin was widely traded across the Mediterranean during the Bronze Age, and extensively exploited during Roman times. The Roman armies used tin in many ways: armour, utinsels, etc."[1]

"During the Roman period, massive gold veins exploitation took place in the Mendips and Dolaucothi. Further metallic lead pigs originating from Peak District in Derbyshire have been discovered, though the most acquainted site is the Dolaucothi Gold Mines near Pumpsaint in Wales. The gold mines were investigated by Jones and Lewis in 1969. The Roman presence in the area is dated from the beginning of their establishment in Great Britain and for a period of 300 years."[2]

"In mid-Wales, copper was the reason for their early exploitation. S. Timberlake and the Early Mines Research Group in 1986 explored them. Charcoal and stone hammers were found inside the tip of the mine. The Great Orme Mine exploitation, on the north Wales coast, began in the Bronze Age and continued until the nineteenth century. The dolomitised limestone deposits are rich in copper which early miners extracted mostly by malachite."[3]

Why is this information important to us as we consider Christianity's introduction to Britain?

- Joseph of Arimathea was a <u>merchant of mines</u> for the Roman Empire as well as a member of the Sanhedrin. According to the Gospels, Joseph believed in Jesus, buried Jesus in his own tomb, and (probably) witnessed his resurrection and ascendance along with the 500 witnesses mentioned in the Gospels. It is believed that Joseph had ships that regularly traveled to Britain.
- Another Christian traveler and an apostle, Simon Zelotes, also went to Britain.[4]

We can trace a timeline of Christianity in Great Britain via the ancient documents and scholarly commentary, from AD 37; just a few scant years after the resurrection of Christ and Pentecost. As a merchant and decurion of mines, Joseph was a very important man in Israel. As a decurion, he was one of ten men in Israel who were upper-class merchantmen. These ten were public servants appointed by the Senate to serve Roman cities in various capacities. They had to report to and go along with the rule of Rome. Joseph's ships would have sailed from Caesarea through the Roman Empire, as far as Britain, and brought manufactured wares and goods from the Mediterranean to trade. Then the ships would also be loaded with the ore of Britain, Gaul, and Spain, which was tribute to Rome. The merchantman (in this case, Joseph of Arimathea) would ferry the ore to the smelting plants of the Roman Empire for a fee, but also would profit from the other trades he had made along the way. Now, consider that this seafaring decurion of minerals for Rome became a follower of Yeshua during Jesus' life on earth.

The biblical evidence shadowed this when Joseph went to ask Governor Pilate for Jesus' body from the cross. Joseph was known and respected. This is why Pilate granted the request. Apparently, Joseph, also being a member of the Sanhedrin, had suspected that the Jewish leaders would kill Jesus and he, with Nicodemus, had already prepared for the burial by storing all the balm (pounds of it) and the strips of cloth for use as he and the disciples lowered the body on that terrible day of Jesus' execution. The

Bible narrative suggests that two members of the Sanhedrin had become undercover disciples of Jesus: Nicodemus and Joseph of Arimathea. Why else would Nicodemus speak up as he did in Jesus' behalf, if not. And, why in the world would Joseph risk his very lucrative shipping business, if he, too, was not a follower?

After the burial of Jesus, we suggest that Joseph stayed in Jerusalem until Pentecost and was a witness at the ascension of Jesus into heaven, present with at least 500 others. Getting back to work organizing his trading business, Joseph would have been excited at his chance to spread the gospel of Jesus Christ throughout the empire. He could use his ships and men, who would port in all ten of the Mediterranean harbors where he had been trading, to spread the good news of Yeshua and his sacrifice for mankind. Would he not have been particularly interested in telling the Druids of Brytagne that Celi had sent Yeshu to save them? And so, sails caught the wind that "blows as it will" by as early, we believe, as AD 37.

The Prince of Evil

However, the trading and the witnessing would get harder and harder as the years progressed. Christians were not welcome in the Empire. They were the brunt of many injustices by Roman rulers; one, in particular, started the ball rolling. In AD 37 Gaius Germanicus, otherwise known as Caligula was named caesar of the Roman Empire. His father had been Caesar Germanica, the general who subdued the western German tribes for Rome. The title of "Caligula" was actually a nickname given to Gaius when he was a boy traveling with his father's troops. It means, "little soldier's boot" because he wore a small pair of the regular hob-nailed boots that adult troops wore into battle. He also became a spoiled brat. The name Caligula was as much a taunt as anything else. (As in, "Here comes the little general again in his big man boots.") Later, as a young man, Gaius was kept away from his father's troops and in Rome by Emperor Tiberius because he was next in line for the throne, and Tiberius kept his friends close and his enemies closer.

Caligula

Caligula's father died in battle and almost immediately after aged Tiberius' death; a few years later, Caligula was appointed emperor. Soon thereafter, someone tried to poison the "little general." Caligula almost died. In the palace intrigue, people pointed the finger at family, friends, and strangers. Many were executed. Finally, in his paranoia, Caligula pointed his own finger,—at the sect of Christians. This was the first official persecution of Christians and Jews in Rome. We do not know exactly what events transpired during that time, but we believe that Joseph of Arimathea is next found making the center of his shipping concern the Isle of Iona on the western coast of Scotland, just north of all the mines in Britain and safely out of reach of Caesar Caligula. Apparently, he continued his business for a few years while avoiding Rome and using his money and influence to build churches in Britain and Scotland. By the locals, he was called a Ceile-De, a friend of God. Other historians have translated the term, "A Certain Stranger." This was not the actual translation but a descriptive for a foreigner. However, it was the same person. Iona island and the northern Welsh coast of Britain was the birthplace of the *Ceile-des, Culdees*, those who followed Celi, their name for the personage of God, the Father.

We have record of a native king of the Britains, named Bran, who ruled from AD 40. He was eventually called 'Bran, The Blessed' and was termed the first British King converted to Christianity. The actual story of this will be told later, but suffice it to say that the British had accepted Christianity within, at most, twenty years of Christ's death.

The ancient legends of Great Britain record that, during his last merchant sailing voyage, Joseph picked up an apostle in North Africa. This was none other than Simon Zelotes; Simon the Zealot—and ferried him to Iona in AD 42 to aid in the work in Britain.[5]

According to Glastonbury chroniclers, there was a gravestone for Joseph of Arimathea in Avalon in the year AD 67 which read:

"Joseph, Ceile-de."

Later, Latin scribes of the church added an epithet to the stone:

"Docui, Quievi"—I taught; I have entered my rest."[6]

This was a reference to what the Lord's servants said in Luke 17:10, "We have done what was our duty to do." Glastonbury could certainly have been where Joseph was laid to rest. However, Welsh histories show evidence that his first years were spent in Wales with the Cymry. British author, Adrian Gilbert gives an account from his own recent tour of Wales. "We were at a place called Llanilid, that is to say, the church or holy estate of St. Ilid ... one of the oldest ecclesiastical foundations in Britain. He informed me that St. Ilid is the Welsh name for Joseph of Arimathea. The name Ilid seems to have been derived from 'Gilead'—that is the Galilean, and it was used as a title of affection for him. He was the tutor of a king called Bran, the Blessed, and just down the road from where we were, not more than a mile or so distant, was Trefran or The Manor of Bran. This traditionally was where Bran lived, whilst Ilid lived nearby. In those days, Christians—British ones anyway—didn't worship in churches. Like the Druids before them, they held their gatherings in the open air under the eye of the sun. The Welsh Triads, and the equally neglected lists of the Lives of the Saints, contain clear and accurate accounts. They describe the arrival in Britain of Christian missionaries, led by St. Ilid (Joseph of Arimathea), and how they came at the behest of Caradoc's daughter, Eurgain, who is credited with being the first British convert to the new religion."[7]

The ancient British *Chronicles of Hardynge* also mention Joseph of Arimathea by name, and that he converted the British King Arviragus and baptised him.

One last thought about Joseph of Arimathea. He is not mentioned in the Bible after his heroic deed in obtaining and burying the body of Jesus in his own tomb. However, we can consider that someone of his caliber who was also devoted to Jesus would not have just gone on simply as a merchant of Rome. Our last clue to his discipleship is in his name. The land called Arimathea is in northwest Judea in the historic area of the tribe of Ephraim. Ephraim was the second son of Jacob's son Joseph, who became Egypt's great leader. The Hebrew tribal name Ephraim means "increase." From all we have discovered, it seems that <u>Joseph of Arimathea</u> was bound in his heart to live up to his name and provide an increase of the Lord's disciples. What better place to settle than the "rustic nation" of Brytagne, off the "radar" of the Roman Empire with their great civic distractions, and their pagan gods, including Caesar worship?

Chronological Summary of the Beginning of Christianity in Brytagne

AD 37–59 – Joseph of Arimathea settles. He was referred to as "Ceile-de," "Friend of God" (later spoken as "Culdee").

AD 42 – Joseph brings Simon Zelotes by ship to Britain.[8]

AD 57 – Joseph travels to the Continent, to the apostle Philip, to ask for brethren to help build churches and spread the gospel.

AD 58 – Philip sends twelve disciples to Britain with Joseph (his dear friend, returning) as leader.[9]

As time went on, other pre-Nicene fathers of the Christian Church also chronicled concerning the Christians in Britain from very early dates:

- Tertullian (AD 155–222) wrote in *Adversus Judaeos* that Britain had already received and accepted the gospel in his lifetime, writing; "All the limits of the Spains, and the diverse nations of the Gauls, and the haunts of the Britons–inaccessible to the Romans, but subjugated to Christ." [10]

- Hippolytus (AD 170–236), considered to have been one of the most learned Christian historians, puts names to the seventy disciples whom Jesus sent forth in Luke 10, includes Aristobulus of Romans 16:10 with Joseph, and states that he ended up becoming a pastor in Britain.

- Eusebius of Caesarea (AD 260–340), one of the earliest and most comprehensive of church historians, wrote of Christ's disciples in *Demonstratio Evangelica*, saying that "some have crossed the ocean and reached the Isles of Britain."

- Saint Hilary of Poitiers (AD 300–376) also wrote that the apostles had built churches in the second century and that the gospel had passed into Britain many years earlier.

SUMMARY OF THE CHURCH BEGINNING IN BRYTAGNE

So, we have established that there was a society of Christian churches in northern Britain during the first century, the first of whom were preaching Christ and building more churches around the same time that the Apostolic Council in Jerusalem took place in about AD 50. (This was the council that was an assembly of the apostles and elders whereby they released Gentile converts from the necessity of circumcision and other observances of the Mosaic ceremonial law.) It is interesting to note that this council was called during the first "controversy" of the Church; wherein "the church fathers" were trying to "protect" Christianity.

Do you see the beauty and irony of God's plan? The Jewish apostolic religious leaders were struggling within the mind-set of the Jews in their selfish turn of religion before Jesus was born. The Britons had none of this sectarian strife between Jewish Christians and Gentiles. They were told that the kingdom was a spiritual one until Jesus would come again and that his Church was to be one of coming together to encourage one another and then go out to preach a salvation by faith in his name; *Sola Fide*.

They were told that when he was ready to leave for heaven, Jesus had promised to send his disciples the "Spirit of Truth" who would lead them into all truth. The Britons were specifically told that Jesus said the coming of the Spirit of Truth was to be the prearranged sign that his followers should now go out from Jerusalem to "the uttermost parts of the earth." All of these teachings are evidences of the fact that this new church was to be a spiritual entity founded and directed by the third part of the trinity, the Holy Spirit. <u>Just as the the Cymric Druidic priests had prophesied.</u> So, there was little controversy in this "rustic land." The evidence suggests that Druids became converts to Christianity by the thousands and tens of thousands within the first century.

The Apostle Paul Enters the Scene

Most Christians know that the apostle Paul was a Roman citizen. Modern biblical scholarship believes that Paul had a Jewish father and mother who were wealthy citizens of Tarsus. The following is how it most probably developed from there. Paul's father was in the tent-making business and taught young Saul (his Jewish name) the lucrative family business. His mother saw to it that he was nurtured in the Jewish faith at home. Historians surmise that sometime in Paul's childhood his father died and his mother remarried a high-level Roman citizen and Gentile. Within that marriage, a half-brother to Paul was born. He was Rufus Pudens Pudentinus and was taught Roman ways. He became a powerful man in the area of Tarsus and was acquaintances with Roman royalty. Meanwhile, older brother Paul had already begun his journey on the Jewish Pharisee route while his mother and brother stayed among the Gentiles in the area we know today as southern Turkey.

When Paul had his Damascus Road experience, he turned to the way of Christ Jesus, and we have an excellent story of his conversion in the biblical book of Acts. What we don't see filled in from this account is the answer to what happened to Paul during the years that he disappeared from sight immediately after he met with Peter and James in Jerusalem. We do know that the Bible tells us that he went back to Tarsus. Here he is back home again. It would not stretch the imagination much to say that he employed his tent-making skills and taught all who were in his household about Jesus Christ and his miraculous conversion that had taken place. It may be that, during this time, his mother and Rufus were influenced by Paul toward Christianity. Now, let's park Paul's family there for a few pages.

Back to Ancient Brytagne

We turn to the conflict that was almost a continual state of war between the British and the Roman Empire during the first century. In the year AD 50, while Paul is beginning his third missionary journey and is called from Troas to Greece, the Romans are in a pitched battle with the king of the

Welsh Celts, Caractacus. Through ten years and many battles on British soil, the Romans lost tens of thousands of men. The conflict dragged on so much that no less than two Roman generals requested to be relieved of command. Historians tell us that Emperor Claudius even travelled to the embarkation point in France to oversee the troops. He was livid that a simple, pagan king and rabble-rouser could stymie the Roman Empire for years and endanger Rome's valuable mining operations.

Finally, after a decade of battles, the Romans routed the Celts and Caractacus was on the run in AD 51. He ran northeast to the adjoining kingdom of Isurium and sought asylum from Queen Cartismandua. The queen took him in and gave him a room in her castle. In the middle of the night, armed men entered his room, bound him, and turned him over to the Romans. It turns out that the Romans had bribed Cartismandua with a large loan of money and a treaty agreeing not to take over her territory if she would help capture Caractacus.

Caractacus was taken to Rome in chains, and his leaderless army dispersed into the mountains of Wales and Scotland. Within several months, Caractacus was brought before Emperor Claudius in Rome. Roman historians report that much of the royalty of Rome was watching as Claudius asked if Caractacus had anything to say before he was sentenced. Here was their account of the reply: "Your Imperial Majesty, I stand before you today as your enemy of ten years. Had I yielded sooner, my misfortune would have been less notorious and your conquest much less renowned. And now, Caesar, if you spare my life, I shall be an eternal monument to your clemency. My fame is clear, but on my fate your glory or shame await."[11]

What a brilliant argument to a caesar of the Roman Empire! Apparently Claudius also thought so and ordered Caractacus to be under house arrest in Rome for seven years and then released if he swore to go back to Britain and make no more war on and, also, be vassal to Rome. Claudius also ordered Caractacus' father, King Vran (or Bran), and his children to be under house arrest in Rome at the same time. The children were Gladys, renamed Claudia, and Linus.

The Pauline Connection

Here is where the story gets really interesting. When the extended family of Caractacus arrived in Rome and presented themselves to Claudius, he was so impressed with the daughter of Caractacus that he adopted her and renamed her Claudia Britannica. (He already had a son whom he had named Britannicus in honor of his triumph over Britain.) This Claudia soon married a young senator from Tarsus named Rufus Pudens Pudentinus. The young couple was given a home near the palace and the Romans called it the *Palatium Britannicum*. Living with them were Claudia's brother, Linus, the old British king Bran and Caractacus. The biblical mention of them begins in Romans 16:13. Paul is finalizing his letter to the Romans by greeting all the brothers and sisters of the church in Rome. He says, "Greet Rufus, chosen in the Lord, and his mother and mine"(NKJV). Perchance, Paul's own mother was living there too. Add to this greeting the greeting of Paul as he is finishing his second letter to Timothy in 2 Timothy 4:21: "Do your best to get here before winter. Eubulus greets you, and so do Pudens, Linus, Claudia and the brothers."

The third observation that we would make concerning this subject is a quote from Clemens Romanus, who is also mentioned by St. Paul in his epistles, who states in his writings (the genuineness of which has not been questioned by any church scholar) that Linus, the first bishop of Rome, was the brother of Claudia Britannica, "*Sanctissimus Linus, frater Claudiae.*" Clemens was the bishop of the Christians in Rome after Cletus, who was the preceding bishop for twelve years after Linus was martyred. That's right. The first Christian bishop of Rome was a Brit from Wales and was probably strengthened in Christ by Paul during his house arrest from AD 58–60. Even the great church historian Irenaeus, in AD 180 writes, "The apostles, having founded and built up the church at Rome, committed the ministry of its supervision to Linus. This is the Linus mentioned by Paul in his Epistle to Timothy."[12]

Other biblical evidence shows that Paul, in his Philippians salutation to the church says, "All the saints send you greetings, especially those who belong to Caesar's household" (Phil. 4:22 NIV). And another time, he says, "Greet [in Rome] Herodian, my relative" (Rom. 16:11 NIV).

So, to make a long story somewhat shorter, the Emperor Claudius, proud conqueror of Britain and adopter of British royalty, was poisoned the next year in October of AD 54, and his nephew Nero, a seventeen-year-old narcissist, was installed on the throne. For the first seven years of his reign, Nero was tutored and bridled, so to speak, by Seneca and other Roman elders. He was bent upon restoring the grandeur of Augustus' day. He was so intent on building monuments and leading a life of lechery that he ignored the apostle Paul, Rufus, Claudia, Bran, and Caractacus, who were Christians living right under his nose. (Claudius' son Britannicus was not so lucky. He was a threat to Nero. Nero's mother, Agrippina, had him poisoned.)

Bran is said to have been released to go back to Britain early in AD 57 and the story goes that he took with him one Aristobulous who was one of Christ's seventy sent out to evangelize by Jesus and who Paul also sent out. The record shows that three years later, in AD 60, Caractacus was released also to return to Britain and help quell the Boadicean War there against Rome. (Queen Boadicea was royal cousin to Claudia Britannica, but that is another story.) Just one year later, the year 61, Paul is released from house arrest in Rome and travels to Spain. Some also think that he eventually went to Britain, which was only about a three-week boat trip from Spain, in order to visit Aristobulous there and see the Christian work among the brethren. After all, Paul is next seen three years later in Greece, where he is captured and sent back to Rome under arrest. That is plenty of time to have gone to England and stayed for a year or more. We do have a letter written by church historian Theodoret in AD 435 which states, "Paul, liberated from his first captivity at Rome, preached the gospel to the Britons and others in the west. Our fishermen and publicans not only persuaded the Romans and their tributaries to acknowledge the Crucified and his laws, but the Britons also and the Cymri."[13]

Rome in Decline

During this time, Nero had so squandered the Roman coffers that he had no money. He fought expensive battles on several fronts of the empire. At the same time, he desperately wanted to build a new palace complex near the city center. However, the old Roman senatorial quarters were there. Historians agree that in July of AD 64. Nero hired arsonists to put a torch to this area and burn three of the seven boroughs of Rome to the ground, killing 30,000 and destroying precious history in order to rebuild it as his new palace, sprung from the ashes.

When the rumors began to fly and fingers began to point, Nero (who had played his guitar, not his fiddle, when the city was burning) needed a scapegoat. He thought, "Why not the odious, atheistic sect that most Roman citizens disliked anyway? That's it. The Christians did it!" Nero rounded them up and prosecuted them vigorously. Many died. However, many became the diaspora to Europe and the original home of the free and the brave, Britain.

During that same persecution, it is recorded that in AD 66 the apostle Paul was brought out of the Mammertine dungeon and murdered a mile or so down the Appian Way by the sword of the executioner. Rome was cursed from that day forward not to ever be the place of progression for the kingdom of God. His plan continued in the far north of the empire. Meanwhile, back in Britain, King Caractacus of the Silurian Celts in Wales and northern England, was solidifying the kingdom and building more Christian church communities than had ever been known in any country. By the time he died in AD 80, Britain was known as the first Christian nation on earth, Nero was dead, Jerusalem was destroyed by Emperor Titus, and Linus was the head of a growing church in Rome.

Only God could bring together a story like that!

The Fruit of the Gospel in Early Britain

We have already made a good case for the acceptance of the gospel based on the pattern of Druidic teachings, which God had set up for quick gospel acceptance when the first disciples settled on the island. Once the gospel of Jesus Christ reached their ears, peasant and king alike were smitten by the glorious truth of the advent of God on earth and his saving grace. Christian churches sprang up all over Britain during the last half of the first century. This growth presented its own issues of discipleship, and Christian King Lucius of the Britains needed to act. He sent dispatches to Rome, and Bishop Eleutherius sent the missionaries Phagan and Deruvian to the island of Britain to preach the gospel. Historian William of Malmesbury puts the time somewhere past the <u>middle of the second century AD</u> Coming from the continent, these missionaries would probably have landed somewhere in Kent, and must have worked their way toward the west and north, preaching as they went. On their journey, historian Malmesbury tells us that, "they came to Glastonbury, where they re-constructed a church."[14] Logic would dictate that a church must have already been there for many years, else they would not have needed to reconstruct it.

William also writes, in his voluminous work *The Antiquity of the Church*, this narrative:

> "After the glory of the Lord's resurrection, the triumph of his ascension and the mission of the Holy Ghost the Comforter, who filled the disciples' hearts which still trembled with dread of temporal punishment, and gave them the knowledge of all languages, all who believed were together, along with the women and Mary the mother of Jesus, as Luke the Evangelist narrates; and the Word of God was sown abroad and the number of them that believed increased daily, and they all had one heart and one soul. Kindled therefore with the torch of envy, the priests of the Jews together with the Pharisees and scribes stirred up persecution against the church, killing Stephen the first martyr and driving far away almost all the rest. So while the storm of persecution raged, the believers were dispersed and went forth into divers kingdoms of the earth, which the Lord assigned to them, offering the word of salvation to the Gentiles. Now St. Philip, as Freculfus declares in the fourth chapter of his second book, came to the country

of the Franks, [northern France] and by his gracious preaching turned many to the faith and baptized them. Then desiring that the word of Christ should be yet further spread abroad, he chose twelve of his disciples and sent them to Britain to proclaim the word of life and preach the Incarnation of Jesus Christ, and on each of them he devoutly laid his right hand; and over them he appointed, it is said, his dearest friend, Joseph of Arimathea who had buried the Lord. They arrived in Britain in the sixty-third year from the Incarnation of the Lord, and preached the faith of Christ with all confidence. The king gave them an island on the borders of his country, surrounded by woods, thickets, and marshes, called *Ynis Witrin*."[15]

We put the pieces of the puzzle together, thus. During the beginning of the twelfth century, William, the British historian, spent some months at the Monastery of Malmesbury, which was built years after Glastonbury, which in turn was built years after Avalon (Iona). There he is afforded access to the library containing ancient documents of the church. He tells us in his history of the church that these documents recorded:

AD 37–AD 465, "Kirk" (Church) bishops of Mediterranean/Gauliean/Roman lineage, beginning with Simon Zealotes and Joseph of Arimathaea. (Greek= *kuriakon* [adj.] "*Kirk*" "*Kuriakon-doma*" Gr. = "The Lord's House".)

It is recorded that, later, the first abbot/bishop of the English line was at Glastonbury in AD 465.

Then, the tenth abbot, Maidulph in AD 675, was the abbey's Saxon re-builder.

After that, nine more Abbots of Malmesbury Abbey were named until AD 940 when the recorded lineage stopped because the next several abbots were still remembered by monks up until William's day of AD 1128.

Not only William of Malmesbury, but other eminent historians have weighed in on the beginnings of the church in England:

- "The church of Avalon in Britain, no other hands than those of the disciples of the Lord themselves built." (Publius Discipulus)

- "The mother church of the British Isles is the church in Insula Avallonia, called by the Saxons, Glaston." (Usher)
- "If credit be given to ancient authors, this church of Glastonbury is the senior church of the world." (Fuller)
- "It is certain that Britain received the faith in the first age from the first sowers of the Word. Of all the churches whose origin I have investigated in Britain, the church of Glastonbury is the most ancient." (Sir Henry Spelman)

So, with the early, first-century church accepted by the "rustic people" of the British Isle, including southern Scotland, let's back up and see how the church was accepted and by whom. Of course there were thousands of believers in Christ, but most remain nameless. Rather, we have the names of the kings and queens, who, if they were following Jesus and his teachings, we are pretty sure that most of the populace were proselytes also. So, the kingdom is established in Britain during the first century. But we can't forget about Rome and her never-ending need for tin, gold, and copper from the mines on the western coast of the island, a land area later called Wales.

In the meantime, Rome...

Titus Flavius Vespasianus

Titus Flavius Caesar Vespasianus Augustus, AD 17—79 became Roman Emperor from AD 69 to AD 79. Vespasian was most reputed as a military commander; he led the Roman invasion of southern Britain in AD 43 and travelled back and forth to the island several times. Later, he subjugated Judaea during the Jewish Rebellion of 66. Matter of fact, Vespasian was called back to Rome because of the illness of the emperor and crowned caesar within a year. He had left a contingent of Roman soldiers in Britain in order to make sure that the mines were still operating for sending precious ore to Rome.

While the Romans were in Britain, they kept the mines running and made treaties with the local kings. They fortified the borders of Wales and made peace with the ruling class because they needed local labor to run the mining operations.

The Succession of Celtic British Christian Leaders

Remember that in AD 40 King Bran, The Blessed, was king of the Britons. But he became a captive in Rome, as we have discussed and, after a few years, was released to return to his homeland. In AD 57, his son, King Caractacus, was converted under the apostle Paul in Rome. He became king upon his father's death in AD 60. Caractacus, restored to power, consolidated the kingdom and fought the Picts (painted people who were non-Celtic in origin) in the extreme northeast of the island. These skirmishes were the first on record as being fought by the Christian Celts with Roman aid. Matter of fact, legend has it that the two armies became allies for many years because of common interests against vicious tribes in the east of Britain and Scotland. King Caractacus and his son Cyllinus fought side by side.

It is surmised that Caractacus, and his children, brought several copies of the gospels from Rome and copies of some of Paul's doctrinal writings. During subsequent years, one of the more prominent British brothers in Christ was one, Beatus, so named because of his steady following of the Beatitudes. He resided in the church at Underseven, England, and his tomb, inscribed in the year AD 96, can still be seen there. After forty years as king of Britain, Caractacus died, and his son, Cyllinus, continued the Christian kingdom of Britons for an additional thirty or so years.

In AD 120 Cyllinus passed the kingdom to his son, Coill who

continued the Christian faith in the royal household and throughout Britain. We will see later that King Coill (or Coel) will be revealed as the Great, Great Grandfather of Constantine the Great, who will be so important to Christianity during the fourth century.

By this time Christianity had been firmly planted in Britain for almost 100 years. There was no person on the western and central area of the Isle who could remember __not__ living in a Christian nation. The churches were even sending missionaries to the Continent. In AD 170 it was recorded that, "A missionary of the British Church, St. Cadval, founded the Church of Tarentum in France and went from there to Switzerland and Germany."[15]

As early as AD 192, Tertullian, theologian of the church, wrote, "The extremities of Spain, the various parts of Gaul, the regions of Britain, which have never been penetrated by the Roman arms, have received the religion of Christ."[17]

And in AD 230, historian Origen wrote, "The divine goodness of our Lord and Saviour is equally diffused among the Britons, the Africans, and other nations of the world."[18]

For the next 100 years, Britain continued to have a vibrant Christian Church. Coill's son Lucius was born next in line. If you remember, he is the king who sent back to Rome for missionaries. He and Queen Gladys were blessed with baby Princess Strada who eventually married King Coel of Glouchester. Their (Strada and Coel's) daughter grew up to be Princess Helena who was given in marriage to Constantius, the Roman general and co-emperor in charge of Gaul and Britain during that time. He was also next in line to become the emperor of the Roman Empire. Their son would grow up to be the Christian emperor Constantine, the Great. We will hear more about him in the next chapter.

British historian John Morris in *The Age of Arthur* wrote:

"The early tradition is that Coel ruled the whole of the north, south of the [Hadrian's] Wall, the territory that the Notitia assigned to the dux [Roman military leader]; but that in later generations it split into a number of independent kingdoms. It suggests that…he was the last Roman commander, who turned his command into a kingdom." He is credited with founding a number of kingly lines in the North and was regarded as an ancestor figure, suggesting that the territory he controlled must have been substantial."[19]

"Duke Coel of Colchester, say the old chronicles, by an insurrection became king. The Senate, rejoiced at the overthrow of an enemy, and sent Constantius to Britain. Coel, fearing, sent ambassadors to meet him and shortly died. Constantius was crowned, married Helena, daughter of Coel, the most beautiful, cultivated, and educated woman of her time. By her he had a son, Constantine, afterwards called the Great."[20]

Later writers such as Henry of Huntington and Geoffery of Monmouth associate Coel with Colchester and make him the father of Saint Helena of Constantinople, the mother of Constantine the Great. Geoffrey's *Historia Regum Britanniae* expands on the legend of Coel, including material about his rule as king of the Britons and his dealings with the Romans.[21]

Today, we have a song about him, which is sung by children.

> Old King Cole was a merry old soul
> And a merry old soul was he;
> He called for his pipe, and he called for his bowl
> And he called for his fiddlers three.
> Every fiddler he had a fiddle,
> And a very fine fiddle had he;
> Oh there's none so rare, as can compare
> With King Cole and his fiddlers three.

Old English Version

> Good King Coel,
> And he call'd for his Bowle,
> And he call'd for Fiddler's three;
> And there was Fiddle, Fiddle,
> And twice Fiddle, Fiddle,
> **For 'twas my Lady's Birthday,**
> **Therefore we keep Holyday**
> And come to be merry.

This song was sung in praise of the Christian King Coel. Legend has it that, on festive occasions, the king would celebrate with three fiddlers playing songs. The three players represented God in his three persons; Father, Son, and Holy Spirit; all playing the same tune (being of the same essence.)

The great early British historian, Bede, wrote about these activities during his time, only 375 years later. If this seems like a long time, remember that America's English beginning, which we know so well, was about 375 years ago. Here is Bede's mention of that time in Britain's history.

"There was on the east side of the city, (Canterbury) a church dedicated to the honour of St. Martin, built whilst the Romans were still in the island, wherein the queen, who, as has been said before, was a Christian, used to pray."[22]

Geoffrey of Monmouth expanded the story of Constantine in his *Historia Regum Britanniae*, an account of the kings of Britain from their Trojan origins. According to Geoffrey,

"Coel was king of the Britons when Constantius, here a senator, came to Britain. Afraid of the Romans, Coel submitted to Roman law so long as he retained his kingship. However, he died only a month later, and Constantius took the throne himself, marrying Cole's daughter Helena. They had their son Constantine, who succeeded his father as king of Britain before becoming Roman Emperor."[23]

It is interesting that this legendary father of Helena is supposed to be the same as "Old King Cole, the merry old soul," making Constantine thus the grandson of a King of Britain and a Mother Goose hero.[24]

Similarly, we have a mention by Christian historian and theologian, Eusebius. Eusebius was the Christian bishop most favored by Constantine the Great and had unfettered access to the king and his court.

"Helena Flavia Augusta, the heire and onely daughter of Coelus, sometime the most excellent king of Britaine, by reason of her singular beautie, faith, religion, goodnesse, and godly Majesty was famous in all the world."–Eusebius

Following is a chart of the family tree of Christian British royalty during the first through the third century and the connection with Paul, the apostle.

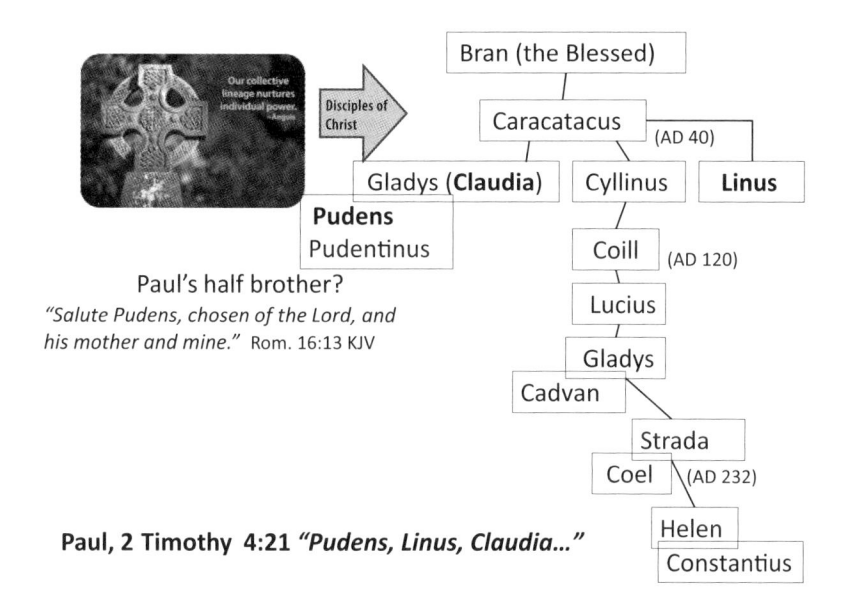

```
                              Bran (the Blessed)
                                    |
            Disciples of       Caracatacus
              Christ          /     |        (AD 40)
                             /      |             |
              Gladys (Claudia)   Cyllinus       Linus
              Pudens              /
              Pudentinus         Coill    (AD 120)
   Paul's half brother?          |
"Salute Pudens, chosen of the Lord, and    Lucius
 his mother and mine." Rom. 16:13 KJV       |
                                          Gladys
                             Cadvan      /
                                        /
                                      Strada
                                Coel  \  (AD 232)
                                        \
                                        Helen
Paul, 2 Timothy 4:21 "Pudens, Linus, Claudia…"
                                      Constantius
```

Summary

Some will say that we have painted a rosy picture of heaven on earth within Britain. We readily agree that no family and no nation is free of challenges. Neither were the Isles of Ancient Brytagne (Britain) so endowed. However, our point is that there was a Christian heritage in Britain from the first century AD onward.

Two of the most rigid Roman Catholics of their period, Polydore Vergil and Cardinal Pole affirmed in Parliament that, "Britain was the first of all countries to receive the Christian faith."

Historian Genebrard stated, "The glory of Britain consists not only in this, that she was the first country which in a national capacity publicly professed herself Christian, but that she made this confession when the Roman empire itself was Pagan and a cruel persecutor of Christianity."[25] And these ancient people produced one of the few truly Christian, world emperors that would aid the Christian cause. Was he perfect? Is anyone? But we think that you will be pleased and surprised by what you learn in the next chapter about Constantine the Great from the "rustic isle."

The apostle Paul, in his letter to the Colossians, says, "All over the world this gospel is bearing fruit and growing, just as it has been doing among you since the day you heard it and understood God's grace in all its truth." This was not hyperbole with Paul. He was living in Rome with Linus, Pudens, and Claudia, (under house arrest) in the Palace Brittanica when writing to the Collosians, and he knew that the gospel of Christ went to the end of the known land at that time beyond the reach of the Roman Empire!

God's plan has never been foiled by the Evil One and his devotees whether in Rome, the Middle East or from the Norse kingdoms, whose emperors, generals, and pirates spent great sums of money and human capital to derail the advance of his kingdom. Let's reveal God's rustic champion of the fourth century in the next chapter.

Sources

1. Gerrard, 2000, *Penhallurick* (1986), pp. 86–91.

2. Shepherd (1980), 219; *The Institute of Metals* (1991), 14; Tylecote 1964, 26.

3. O'Brien (1996), Timberlake 1990b; Timberlake 2003b.

4. McBirnie, *The Search for the Twelve Apostles*, 213.*

5. Adrian Gilbert, *The Holy Kingdom* (Bantam Press, 1998), 122–123.

6. Lars P. Qualben, *A History of the Christian Church* 48, Eusebius, 3rd Century, "Simon in N. Africa").

7. Hearnes, *Antiquities of Glastonbury*, Leland ibid, RW Morgan.

8. Lars P. Qualben, *A History of the Christian Church*, 48, Eusebius, 3rd Century, "Simon in N. Africa".

9. William of Malmesbury, (c. AD 1128).

10. Tertullian *Apol.* xxxvii., adv. Jud. 7: "The haunts of the Britons inaccessible to the Romans subjugated to Christ." About A.D. 150 the Church of Edessa counted the king among its members (see F. C. Burkitt, *Early Christianity outside the Roman Empire*, 11, Cambridge, 1899).

11. Tacitus, *The Annals of Tacitus*, Book 12, vs 37.

12. Illtigius, *Apostolici Patres*, lib. Vi, c. 47, circa 150 A.D., "Concerning those bishops who have been ordained in our lifetimes, we make known to you that they are these; of Antioch, Eudoius (Eubulus) of the church of Rome, Linus, the son of Claudia, (and) Clemens the second."

13. Theodoret, *De Civ. Graec. Off.*, lib. Xi (Niceph., lib. Ii, c. 40.

14. William of Malmesbury, (c. AD 1128) an historian regarded highly by modern scholars, was a guest of the Glastonbury Abbey for a period of time during the second decade of the twelfth century. He called this structure "the oldest Church in England," and, henceforth, it was known simply as the Old Church, serving as a symbol for the ancientness of Glastonbury's Christianity. "De Antiquitate Glastoniensis Ecclesiae" (Enquiry into the Antiquity of the Church of Glastonbury).

15. Hearnes *Antiquities of Glastonbury* Leland ibid, RW Morgan.

16. MS Vellum of the Church of Tarentum, Catalog of the Saints in the Vatican, 1641 A.D.

17. Tertullian, *Def. Fidei*, 179.

18. Origen, In Psalm CXLIX.

19. John Morris, *The Age of Arthur*, 54.

20. This is in substance the account of Geoffrey of Monmouth (5.6) and Pierre de Langloft (1, p. 66–7). The story is mentioned by Henry of Huntington (Bk. I. 37), who perhaps wrote before Geoffrey (in 1137 [?]), and Richard of Cirencester (2. 1. 33). Waurin (Vol. I. Bk. 2. 43) makes "Choel" Count of Leicester, but in general the mention is identical with Geoffrey. The famous Brut of Layamon (ed. Madden, 2 [1847] p. 35) is translated with amplifications from Wace's Brut, and this in turn from Geoffrey. This writing makes Coel Earl of Gloucester.

21. Henry of Huntingdon (c. 1129), *Historia Anglorum*, Book I, ch. 37,

Geoffrey of Monmouth, *Historia Regum Britanniae*, Book 5, ch. 6

22. Bede, H E i 26

23. The *Eulogium Hist.* calls Helena (1. 337) daughter of a British king. It is also mentioned by many others; e.g. Voragine's, *Golden Legend*.

24. Hayden, *Index to Eulogium*, p. 45, and Giles, note on Geoffrey, p. 162.

25. Cardinal Pole, Message to Parliament, 1555.

*Nicephorus (Patriarch) of Constantinople wrote: "Simon born in Cana of Galilee who was surnamed Zelotes, having received the Holy Ghost from above, traveled through Egypt and Africa, then Mauretania and Libya, preaching the gospel. And the same doctrine he taught to the Occidental Sea and the Isles called Britanniae." Nicephorus tables of universal history (*Chronographikon Syntomon*), were in great favor with the Byzantines, and were also circulated outside the empire in the Latin, and also in Slavonic translation. The chronography offered a universal Christian history from the time of Adam and Eve to his own time in AD 800).

IMAGES

Julius Caesar bronze statue in Rome Italy. © Luis2007 | Dreamstime.com

Caligula © Rangpl | Dreamstime.com

Titus Flavius Vespasianus. © Rangpl | Dreamstime.com

CHAPTER THREE

BY THIS SHALL YOU CONQUER

Before we get to Constantine and his history, we must get caught up on what was happening in Rome and with the Roman Church during the time of AD 100–300. As we now know, the Christians in Rome were the first to be routinely persecuted. Not only were they constantly in fear of imprisonment and death, but there were heretical theologians and movements that threatened the very existence of the church of Jesus Christ. It is not the object of this work to go too far into detail concerning the various challenges to the Orthodox Church. However, we can name several. Gnosticism, Docetism, Cultism, Stoicism, Epicureanism, and several other –isms, threatened to water down or take over the church that Paul, Peter, and the other disciples had worked hard, through the Spirit, to establish.

It was only natural, and essential, for the church in Rome and churches elsewhere to refute these false teachings. The apostle Paul refuted several of them in his letters. The Roman church was adamant that these heresies not take hold. And, the leaders were willing to do almost anything to make it so. In that regard, they went too far in several instances in order to "protect" the church of Jesus Christ. In doing so, they began to change true orthodoxy in the process. We will give one particular instance at this time as an example.

When the Docetist cult began to preach, their leaders said that Jesus was not really part of the triune God. They reckoned that God was God, but that he only worked through Jesus, who was just a man. Of course this was heresy. But, instead of going to the Scriptures solely for their refutation, the Roman Church came up with the idea of transubstantiation. Transubstantiation is the actual transforming of the Communion bread and wine into the body and blood of Jesus. The church began to teach that Jesus was SOOO much a part of God that when a true orthodox priest prays over the Communion, miraculously, the bread and wine change in substance, proving that Jesus was not only part of God when he walked the earth, but that he continues to be so, and shows it every time a priest of the church prays the communion. Magic! This also created a one-upmanship of the Roman priest over the Docetic priest in the eyes of the congregation. And, of course, Jesus only came during the mass at the bequest of the official and paid priest of the orthodox church. Very convenient.

This practice of transubstantiation is never mentioned until over 100 years after Christ's death and resurrection. It was not mentioned because it was not true. The bread and wine never changed into the body and blood of Christ, but it was a way for the established priesthood to say, in effect, "See Jesus was a part of God because he proves it every time we have Communion by coming from heaven to earth and being with us in the transformed bread and wine." Of course, the orthodox priest had to pray over the Communion in order for transubstantiation to take place. If he, the revered priest, pronounced that the exchange had taken place, no parishioner dared to deny it. It was sort of like the story of the emperor's new clothes. (The emperor could parade around naked and no one dared to say he had no clothes on, except a little "rustic" child.) We will discuss transubstantiation more at a later time, but you get the drift that it was a power play by the established leaders of the church to combat Docetism and protect Christianity. (Their attitude? "Thanks God for giving us the Scriptures, but we've got this with a made-up story that works with the sheeple.")

This and many other practices began to be implemented by the established church in order to fortify it. What they forgot was that, if Jesus was the head of the body of the church, it was his job to defend and fortify it, not theirs. And it brought on the cascade of lies of the Roman Church. As our mother's would say, "When you tell a lie, then you have to tell two more lies in order to cover up the first lie." So, during the decades and centuries following, the "Catholic" or Roman Church began to accept lie building upon lie, building upon lie, to consolidate its power and authority. When the proverbial pendulum swung one way toward a heretical sect, the established church swung it back—and almost always too far.

Below are some of the heretical sects that Rome was fighting against to keep the church pure. This fight, in itself, was not a bad thing. However, once the church was fully established, it went too far and became exactly what it fought against—heretical.

Gnosticism—taught that Christ never dwelt on earth in human form. The term *Gnostic* derives from the Greek word *gnosis*, which means "knowledge." The Gnostics believed that they were selected to be the ones knowing a secret knowledge about the divine, and Christ, as part of God, could never have allowed himself to be "earthly and impure." (Of course, that was exactly the Scriptural point, so he could live as a man and as true God/man die for our sins.) Paul wrote against this best in his letter to the Colossians.

Another of their heretical stances was that angels "eminated" from God because he couldn't touch earthly matter, and the angels were mediators to God and to be worshipped. What does the Roman Church have today, but a whole list of angels to pray to. The Bible says, "No." Christ is the only mediator between God and man.

Montanism—taught that Montanus (second century) had received a series of direct revelations from the Holy Spirit, independent from Holy Scriptures. The sect placed themselves above other Christians who believed in the Bible alone. Montanus was rejected because he tried to preach and write thoughts that were "extra-biblical." In time, and to protect Christianity, the popes had to one-up Montanus and the other heretics, so the pope became the only one who could speak for God as his vice-regent. So what happened? The popes wrote their own traditions that were "extra-biblical."

Arianism—taught that the Father God and Jesus were not co-eternal but that Jesus was created by God and inferior to him. The Catholic Church "one-upped" the Arians by saying that not only were Jesus and God co-eternal, but that the pope was superior and speaker for God on the earth, so nobody on their side was a speaker for God like the pope.

Because of these heretical assaults on the Christian church, in the year AD 230 a Syrian text, the *Didascalia*, was written by an anonymous author, and it states for the first time anywhere: "The bishop (as the highest priest in an area) rules over the soul and the body and loosens a heavenly power on earth."

And the church membership was directed, "You (parishioners) are commanded to give, and it is for him to dispense (money)."

It was from this small, almost inconspicuous, beginning that the orthodox, Roman Church began to go awry. Within 300 years, tradition (including a lot of fear-mongering, made-up stuff) of the church was held as equal to Scripture, with the clergy, conveniently promoted by themselves, over all other Christians.

Chronology of Customs and Traditions (rules) of the "Protective" Roman Church

AD 230—The *Didascalia Apostolorum*

A treatise that told parishioners how, when, and where they must obey the bishop and the priests because they, with Peter as the first pope (another lie to increase the prestige of the priesthood), were given authority over the church by God. To go against them was to go against God.

AD 280—The Apostolic Tradition

Mostly hyperbolic facts about what the apostles did and what the popes were doing that were God's will and that the tradition was approved and orchestrated by God.

AD 380—The Apostolic Constitutions

Extrapolation of the Apostolic Tradition, giving a list of rules and church regimen that was accepted by the "true church."

AD 530—The Catholic Canon

The rule-book-become encyclopedia (seven volumes) of the traditions of the church and the decrees/pronouncements of the popes.

The church had defended itself right into the very heresies that the early Christian Fathers had once tried to defend against! We will see many more examples of this as we continue in this work. Sad, but true. Out of the church's struggle with the heresies of Gnosticism and Montanism, etc. came the organization of the episcopal form of church government. At first, all the elders had the same rank but, over time, certain presbyters would take the lead and become "overseers" of the elders; in Greek, *episcopos*, from which we get the word *bishop*. By the middle of the second century, practically all church cities had bishops. These bishops, then, formulated the Imperial Church in Rome.

Meanwhile, the numerous opposing heretical gatherings had formed churches of their own in the area of the Mediterranean, so the authentic church, in order to distinguish itself from the heretical churches, called itself the catholic (universal) church. Our rustic point is that there was great struggle in the Christian religion of the contiguous Roman Empire, but very little struggle in the "uttermost part" of the world called Brytagne or Britain. There was no need for an episcopal form of church government to keep the heretics out. The British Church remained, more or less, a pure Jesus movement under the watch-care of the disciples in each *cor*, or county.

A study of British history reveals that by AD 100 the majority of Welsh and Britons were Christians. Again, British author Adrian Gilbert comments on this "The fourteenth legion was withdrawn from Britain to Germany in AD 69, leaving a total of only some 15,000 troops to establish garrisons to guard the borders and defend the remaining Roman settlements. Outside these, which were essentially trading stations, the rest of Britain, with a population running into millions, was still governed by its traditional hierarchy of kings, dukes, clan chieftains, and so on... British histories show that by that time the majority of Britons, including the leading families, were all Christians."[1]

How Does Constantine Figure Into Church and Bible History?

As we have established, Constantine's father was Constantius, the Roman General and one of the tetrarchy of Roman Emperors in charge of the empire under Diocletian.[2] When he came to Britain, he was feared. So, to firm a pact, King Coel offered his daughter, Helen, to be Constantius' wife. The marriage was consummated, and Helen began the life of a military wife, —she travelled to wherever her husband was stationed. The first stop after Britain was Moesia (Serbia). (This is why historian Geoffery of Monmouth said that the kings of Britain were of "Trojan origin".) Since the empire's king during the coming of age of Britain was Constantine, and he was born relatively near the home of the ancient Trojans, these were connected.

Statue of Colossus of Constantine the Great in Rome, Italy

Constantine spent his childhood in Moesia (Serbia). Helen and Flavius Constantius were a faithful couple, and Constantius was a good father to the young prince. Constantine attended the lectures of Lactantius, a Christian scholar in the city of his youth. He was sent to Rome early in life to learn Roman ways and culture. Since Helena remained with Constantius, she sent Lactantius with Constantine as his tutor and companion. When he was of age to join the Roman army, Emperor Aurelian (co-regent with Constantius and Maxentius) placed him in his Imperial Guard. He fought in Spain and across the Mediterranean. His Christian tutor, Lactantius continued to accompany Constantine as an employee of Helena, and he taught Constantine Christian principles.

After Constantine came to power as emperor, Lactantius wrote about the times and the calling.

"All our adversaries have now been crushed, peace has been restored to the universe, and the church. God has aroused princes who have done away with the criminal and bloodthirsty empire of the tyrants."[3]

God's Warrior to the Rescue of His Church

In the late spring or early summer of AD 305, Constantius recruited his son to help him campaign in Britain against the Picts beyond Hadrian's Wall on the border between Scotland and Britain. Pagan Pict warriors had been threatening all of Christian Britain. Constantine spent a year in northern Britain at his father's side, campaigning against the Picts. Suddenly, Constantius died on the 25th of July, AD 306 in Eboracum (York). Before dying, he declared his support for raising son Constantine to the rank of full Augustus.

The Alamannic (German) King Chrocus, in service under Constantius in Gaul, then proclaimed Constantine as Augustus. The troops loyal to Constantius' memory followed him in acclamation. Gaul and Britain quickly accepted his rule. Because of his fame and his being proclaimed emperor first in the territory of Roman Britain, later Britons regarded Constantine as a king of their own people. In the twelfth century, Henry of Huntingdon included a passage in his *Historia Anglorum* that Constantine's mother Helena was a Briton, the daughter of King Cole of Colchester.

Bronze statue of Constantine the First in York, England, the spot where he was proclaimed Augustus in AD 306

Look at Constantine's eyes in the statue. He "holds the world" at the hilt of the sword, but gazes under it at the cross. Most statues have monarchs and soldiers looking out and have their swords raised in their hand. A sculptor's rendition, yes, but could it have been a sign of his heart that the artist reveals? Consider the following true story of Constantine's rise to power.

OFF TO ROME

With his Roman troops and Chrocus' divisions at his back, Constantine marched through Gaul and northern Italy to take his rightful place as emperor. Along the way, he had a vision that he should put a symbol of his heritage on the shields of his warriors. It was the *Chi-Rho* (Greek) that was the symbol of Christianity in Britain and Rome. Notice the alpha and omega, too, on this stone cross of the era.

THE BATTLE

"Constantine's mind was prepared. He was alert and ready to act. He gathered all the forces, German, Gallic, and British, that he could muster, entered Italy by way of the Alps, and marched to meet the much more numerous forces of Maxentius—but now there were no enemies in the rear, and he was free to push on to Rome. On his way whither, if not earlier, he had his famous vision of the cross. He reached the Tiber October 26th."[4]

"Maxentius crossed the Tiber, and joined battle. His apparently unwise action in staking so much on a pitched battle has its explanation. His object was, it is said, by a feigned retreat to tempt Constantine across the bridge of boats which he had built in such a way that it could be broken, and the enemy let into the river.

"The dissipated soldiers of Maxentius gave way before the hardy followers of Constantine, fired by his own energy and the sight of the cross. The defeat was a rout. The bridge broke. Maxentius, caught in the jam, was cast headlong into the river, and after a vain attempt to climb out on the steep bank opposite, was swept away by the stream."[5]

Constantine soon marched into Rome, the undisputed and victorious emperor of the Roman Empire.

Think of the eternal implications. In less than 300 years, Jesus Christ had gone from a little-known rabbi who had been crucified in Jerusalem to the accepted Savior of the British Roman Emperor now marching through the capital city, and his (Christ's) "initials" were being brandished by every soldier! By the year AD 313, Emperor Constantine sat in Constantinople (Istanbul, Turkey) unchallenged from east or west.

"His first act was to issue a proclamation in favor of the Christians. This was followed by many other acts in their favor—building of churches, et cetera. From this time on he was much identified with Christian affairs, and the main events are given in extenso by Eusebius."[6]

It is interesting that approximately only 10–12 percent of the empire's populace were known to be Christians at that time. It could have been no higher than 20 percent. Why would the new emperor have made it his first act to legalize Christianity if he wasn't bound to do it by heritage and conviction? Our position is that he did it precisely because of these. Some have questioned whether Constantine was really a Christian. Why not give those on the scene a say in the discussion?

The account in Eusebius of the thoughts by which he (Constantine) inclined toward Christianity has the greatest plausibility. He says that "considering the matter of Divine assistance, it occurred to him that those who had relied on idols had been deceived and destroyed, while his father… had honored the one Supreme God, had found him Saviour, …he judged it folly to join in the idle worship of those who were no gods…and felt it incumbent on him to honor no other than the God of his father."

In Constantine's personal letters to the bishops after the council at Arles—he wrote expressions like "Christ the Saviour," "brethren beloved," "I who myself await the judgment of Christ," "our Savior." These quotes from letters show that Constantine was well advanced in his commitment in AD 314. The facts of his Christian advisers, of his laws in behalf of Christians, various substantial favors to them, and his recognition of their God as his one God, makes it almost idle to discuss the question. Was Constantine a Christian in 314? He seems to have been.

"[After securing his empire] the emperor diligently attended divine worship and is portrayed upon medals in the posture of prayer. He kept the Easter vigils with great devotion. He would stand during the longest sermons of his bishops… And he even himself composed and delivered discourses to his court in the Latin language, from which they were translated into Greek by interpreters appointed for the purpose. He dwelt mainly on the truth of Christianity, the folly of idolatry, the unity and providence of God, the coming of Christ, and the judgment."[7]

"If the fruit proves the motive, he consistently used his power for what he thought public good. This he did in Gaul, after his victories, in his legislation, and in his internal improvements."

In disposition for his burial, "anticipating with extraordinary fervor of faith that his body would share with the apostles themselves…He accordingly caused twelve coffins to be set up in this church, like sacred pillars, in honor and memory of the apostolic number, in the centre of which his own was placed, having six of theirs on either side of it."[8]

Finally, here is a direct quote by Constantine the Great: "A great godlessness was pressing down on men, and the state was threatened with total ruin, as though by a plague. There was an urgent need to find an effective remedy for these evils. What, then, was the remedy found by the Deity? God called on me to serve and swore that I was capable of carrying out his decision. So it was that I left the sea of Brittany and the country where the sun sets and, commanded by a higher power, agreed to drive out and disperse the terror that was reigning everywhere, so that the human race, informed by intervention, might return to the service of the holy law and the blessed faith might become widespread under the power of the Most High."[9]

We should also notice that, when Constantine convened the Council of Arles:

- Three bishops from Britain attended the Council of Arles called by Emperor Constantine in AD 314. The emperor paid for their passage and provided room and board.

- We have a record of the retirement of Christian bishops, Theon and Tediac, retiring from their "sees" in London and York in AD 586.[10]

They supplied a list of Diocletian persecution of the British Church. (Diocletian reigned from AD 286, and ruled over the "great persecution" in AD 303.) This list had senior British bishops on it and over ten thousand Christians in Britain. This list was probably provided first to Constantine in Arles in 314 at the council called by him or, at least, the history of British Christians was discussed at length with the other bishops in order to connect the churches by heritage.

So, it remains for those who question whether Constantine, the Great was a Christian to bring their proof texts. If we might be so bold as to venture a rebuttal of the "usual suspects," it is said that Constantine waited until the month of his death to be baptized. Our understanding of the times in Christianity is that one was expected to become notably humble and to pledge at baptism that they would follow ALL the teachings of Jesus, including renouncing all violence. This would have caused the emperor to, in effect, abdicate his rule. He chose the compromise. He would postpone baptism until his rule was almost over. Thus, keeping discipline in the empire so that Christianity could grow among the people.

There is also the matter of Constantine executing a few of his family members because of treachery and conspiracy. We refer the reader to King David who made war against his own son because of treachery and to keep the kingdom for God intact. God has said that David was a man after his own heart. Was David perfect? No. Was Constantine perfect? No. Were they both men after God's own heart and commissioned by him to carry out "The Plan?" We say the evidence convinces us to say "yes."

Finally, some say that Constantine "made Christianity the state religion." History shows that he did not. He <u>legalized</u> Christianity and allowed it to flourish with each bishop speaking for his own congregation and able to nurture them from a point of living with his people daily. Just as Constantine would not allow the old Roman religions to dominate Christianity, he did not allow Christianity to dominate them. This is reminiscent of our Lord Jesus' attitude. He refused to work miracles for the Pharisees to prove that he was God's sent One; keeping intact their freedom of choice. Religious freedom was also Constantine's position. We see proof of this in the fact that he had councils and convocations of the Christian world's accepted bishops and elders and provided a place for them to work and come to a consensus on Christian living and doctrine.

For the record, the emperor that actually made Christianity the state religion was Theodosius the first, who reigned fifty years after Constantine's death. However, the fact is that because of the legalizing of the Christian Church, many heathen-influenced people joined up and some of their practices were transferred in. Many church leaders were so happy and grateful just to be able to have <u>any</u> services without the threat of persecution and death, that they tried to make peace with influential heathens who wanted to be comfortable in religious services that incorporated some of their former practices. Some of these superstitions surrounded having relics of great religious leaders of the past who had great powers. So, many churches of the empire began to worship the relics—bones of the apostles and saints, fragments of the cross, fragments of clothing, etc.

Having a relic held in one's church building was a drawing card for others who valued being "closer" to God because of these things, so, pagans were able to bring them there. There was prestige and growth involved. So, this was tolerated. Someone once said, and rightly so, "It's not just what you preach, it's also what you tolerate." They began to tolerate what was not in Holy Scripture because it "worked" to make them feel better. The end justifying the means, so to speak. Do we see vestiges of this sort of practice in our churches today? This practice was unheard of in rustic Britain before AD 500.

More Evidence of the "Protective" Church

During this time, Arianism was also beginning to infiltrate the new, Imperial Church government. This so-called Christian sect held the view of Arius, a Christian priest who lived and taught in Alexandria, Egypt. Arius taught that God the Father and the Son were not co-eternal, seeing the pre-incarnate Jesus as a divine being <u>but created</u> by and inferior to the Father who created him. The other main church cities under Constantine's rule took great exception to this heresy, but Constantine himself was not exactly sure that the Arians were wrong. (He had a bit of an "Emperor-God the Father" complex and could not logically see how Jesus could totally co-exist with God.) So, Constantine called for a Council in AD 325 that we now call the Council of Nicea, to debate the doctrine of the Trinity.

Can we begin to see that the Britons were <u>way</u> ahead of the mainstream Catholic Church? They understood from their heritage that a Trinity was possible and had no problem dismissing heretics like Arius. That thought process didn't stand a chance in "unsophisticated" rustic Britain. But, Emperor Constantine now had a sophisticated and polluted Roman Empire to negotiate through.

The Council of Nicea, attended by about 300 bishops, dealt with the Arian heresy. The bishops agreed that Jesus was the same substance as the Father; *Homoousion*, "of the same substance," in the Greek, <u>not</u> *Homoiousion*, "of like substance." The difference in the Greek is "one iota." (Brings a historic connotation to the saying, "I don't care one iota, for that.") The council brought up the Gospel of John verse 1:12, wherein the apostle wrote that, "All who did receive him, [Jesus] to those who believed in his name, he gave the right to become children of God…" They pointed out that John used the Greek word, *gignooskoo* for the word "name" and that meant "the complete revelation of" God. That settled it for the majority. And so it was,- and is.

The Nicene Creed came out of this council, followed by the Constantinoplitan Creed in AD 381.

"I believe in one God, the Father Almighty, Maker of heaven and earth, and of all things visible and invisible. And in one Lord Jesus Christ, the only begotten Son of God, begotten of the Father before all worlds; God of God, Light of Light, very God of very God; begotten, not made, being of one substance with the Father, by whom all things were made.

"Who, for us men for our salvation, came down from heaven, and was incarnate by the Holy Spirit of the virgin Mary, and was made man; and was crucified also for us under Pontius Pilate; he suffered and was buried; and the third day he rose again, according to the Scriptures; and ascended into heaven, and sits on the right hand of the Father; and shall come again, with glory, to judge the quick and the dead; whose kingdom shall have no end.

"And I believe in the Holy Ghost, the Lord and Giver of Life; who proceeds from the Father and the Son; who with the Father and the Son together is worshipped and glorified; who spoke by the prophets.

"And I believe in the holy catholic [universal] and apostolic church. I acknowledge one baptism for the remission of sins; and I look for the resurrection of the dead, and the life of the world to come. Amen."

The average British Christian would have said, "But, of course. Why did it take you guys so long to get to that conclusion?" So, once again, the rustic, unsophisticated Britons were ahead of the game. This was because the sophisticated and civilized peoples kept butting heads from their own diverse backgrounds and polluted traditions. There needed to be a collection of the tenants of Christianity that ALL could look to for the Christian faith. So, how did they come to it?

Constantine's Bibles

It is interesting to note that most scholars agree in AD 330 Constantine commissioned a council of Christian leaders to make fifty copies of the Christian Scriptures and commanded that these copies should be circulated throughout the empire as the religious guidebook for the populace. Incredibly, we still have today what are believed to be two of these copies and one immediate subsequent copy of the originals. One of the originals is called the Codex Sinaiticus, the other is Codex Vaticanus, and the one generation later copy is the Codex Alexandrinus.

"Among his many other donations (to the church) were fifty monumental copies of the Bible commissioned from Bishop Eusebius's specialist scriptorium in Caesarea: an extraordinary expenditure on creating deluxe written texts, for which the parchment alone would have required the death of around five thousand cows. It is possible that two splendidly written Bibles of very early date, now called respectively the Codex Vaticanus and the Codex Sinaiticus after their historic homes, are survivors from this gift." [11]

What is the Codex Sinaiticus?

Codex Sinaiticus, a manuscript of the Christian Bible, written in the middle of the fourth century, contains the earliest complete copy of the Christian Bible. The hand-written text is in Greek. The New Testament appears in the original vernacular language (*koine*) and the Old Testament in the version, known as the Septuagint, which was adopted by early Greek-speaking Christians. In the codex, the text of both the Septuagint and the New Testament has been heavily annotated by a series of early commentators.

The significance of Codex Sinaiticus for the reconstruction of the Christian Bible's original text, the history of the Bible, and the history of Western book-making is immense.

By the middle of the fourth century there was wide but not complete agreement on which books should be considered authoritative for Christian communities. Codex Sinaiticus, one of the two earliest collections of such Bible books, is essential for an understanding of the content and the arrangement of the Bible, as well as the uses made of it.

Within the New Testament of the codex, the Letter to the Hebrews is placed after Paul's second letter to the Thessalonians, and the Acts of the Apostles between the Pastoral and Catholic Epistles. The content and arrangement of the books in Codex Sinaiticus sheds light on the history of the construction of the Christian Bible.

The ability to place these "canonical books" in a single codex itself influenced the way Christians thought about their books, and this is directly dependent upon the technological advances seen in Codex Sinaiticus. The quality of its parchment and the advanced binding structure that would have been needed to support over 730 large-format leaves, which make Codex Sinaiticus such an outstanding example of book manufacture, also made possible the concept of a "Bible" as we know it.

Codex Sinaiticus is one of the most important witnesses to the Greek text of the Septuagint (the Old Testament in the version that was adopted by early Greek-speaking Christians) and the Christian New Testament. Christian history tells us that Constantine called a symposium in the year 339 in order to gather together all the bishops of the church in order to "authorize" the Bibles he had sponsored. The notes of the convention record that the only bishops who took Constantine up on his offer to pay for travel expenses were the three bishops from the Isle of Britain.

It is entirely possible, and probable, that these bishops took an original copy of the Greek Bible back to Glastonbury on their return trip to Britain, Constantine's maternal homeland. Perhaps it is still there, in some dusty library basement.

Codex Alexandrinus

Alexandrinus Leaf, British Museum

Codex Alexandrinus received its name from the circumstance that its earliest known location was the Egyptian city of Alexandria. It is dated to about AD 375. It contains the entire Greek Bible, minus Matthew 1:1

through 25:6, John 6:50 through 8:52, and 2 Corinthians 4:13 through 12:6. At the end are added some early Christian writings commonly used in teaching: the first epistle of Clement, and the second epistle of Clement up to 12:4.

The codex was sent as a gift to King James I of England (the same James who commissioned the King James Version) by Cyril Lucar, who at the time was the Eastern Orthodox bishop of Alexandria. It reached England in 1627.

The British Museum and the British Library split in 1973, and the codex is now kept in the latter.

In the New Testament of the Alexandrinus manuscript the order is Gospels, Acts, Universal Epistles, (catholic epistles) Pauline Epistles, with Hebrews placed before the Pastoral Epistles and Apocalypse. The leaves, of thin vellum, 12 3/4 inches high by 10 inches broad, number at present 773, but were originally 822, according to the ordinary reckoning. Each page has two columns of forty-nine to fifty-one lines.

These documents from the fourth century are very important to our Christian heritage and connect the "rustic church" in Britain to us today. These were available to our next "character" who, by his reactionary writings, began to kill the Bible in the hearts of the religious. The foremost theological writer from the era immediately after Constantine was Augustine of Hippo.

Augustine's Ill-fated Theorizing

Augustine was a Latin-speaking theologian in North Africa. He was brought up in the AD 350s and 360s in the small town of Hippo. According to history, his father was a non-Christian, but his mother was very pious and saw to it that he went to the School of Carthage to learn Christian theology, philosophy, and the literature of Rome. After college, Augustine settled down with a mistress and had a son named Adeodatus. Mama was not happy! He decided to leave Hippo and pursue academic success in Rome and Milan; all the while, tormented with doubts as to his status in eternity. (This might have something to do with the fact that his pious mother followed him and lived near him in Milan.) Finally, at his mother's urging, in AD 385, he sent his mistress back to Carthage after fifteen years living with her. She left their teen-aged son with Augustine's mother in Milan.

Augustine made his living by teaching rhetoric to those who would run for office or teach in the academy. He was a student of Plato's writings and was very good at what he did. However, he was continually plagued by thoughts of God's punishment. He wrote about those times:

"My two wills, one old, one new, one carnal, one spiritual, were in conflict, and in their conflict wasted my soul. Thus, with myself as object of the experiment, I came to understand what I had read, how the flesh lusts against the spirit and the spirit against the flesh. I, indeed, was in both camps, but more in that which I approved in myself than in that which I disapproved…

"It is therefore no monstrousness, partly to will, partly not to will, but a sickness of the soul to be so weighted down by custom that it cannot wholly rise even with the support of truth. Thus there are two wills in us, because neither of them is entire: and what is lacking to the one is present in the other."[12]

His mental pendulum swung too far as he justified his sins of the flesh to quiet his troubled mind. In his day, the religious elite, who had already begun the take-over of the Christian Church, were very influenced by the Greek philosophers Plato and Aristotle. They had "refined" their philosophy into a belief in Dualism: soul versus body. The soul was where the spirit of a person lived, and the body was the "transport" of the soul. They believed furthermore that the physical was the lower part of a person, which he or she held in common with all other animals. Aristotle stated that the goal of a person should be to move upward to develop the spirit which made him or her all that they were meant to be. (Of course, the Bible had rejected this from the beginning. The Bible says that the individual is a unity-body, soul, and spirit.) However, Augustine could not ease his mind about his past without separating his spirit from his physical deeds.

Listen carefully to Augustine's convoluted logic in fine Platonic tradition. This is the quote from his *Confessions* that was often used to justify the sins of future popes and priests:

"And it became clear to me that corruptible things are good: if they were supremely good they could not be corrupted, but also if they were not good at all they could not be corrupted: if they were supremely good they would be incorruptible, if they were in no way good there would be nothing in them that might corrupt…But if they were deprived of all goodness, they would be totally without being. For if they might still be and yet could no longer be corrupted, they would be better than in their first state, because they would abide henceforth incorruptibly…If they were deprived of all goodness, they would be altogether nothing: therefore as long as they are, they are good. Thus, whatsoever things are, are good; and that evil whose origin I sought is not a substance, because if it were a substance it would be good."[12]

He seems to have justified his actions by coming to believe that one can live in both "camps" at the same time—the flesh and the spirit. And, he believed that evil was not a substance and did not exist in reality. He could live in sexual misconduct and still be okay with God because his spirituality could overcome it when he finally got back to it. This faulty thinking proved crucial to the official church departing from the Bible within a few generations of its time. Augustine took another mistress after the first decided to leave him because he would not marry her. But, after a while, he grew tired of her, too. Mama was still haunting him and convinced him to stop having sex out of wedlock.

Having renounced cohabitation but still lecturing on the Bible as philosophy, Augustine began preparing to lecture on the Apostle Paul and the Book of Romans. He was challenged by Romans, chapter 13, verses 13–14, "Put on the Lord Jesus Christ, and make no provisions for the flesh, to gratify its desires…" Mama was proud. Augustine began to correlate the sexual act with original sin, even though there was no biblical precedent for it. (The Catholic Church would later use Augustine's writings and example, as a church father, to justify celibacy for all clergy.) He went back to his home town to create a community of celibate monks, which is where his major literary work was done.

One far-reaching tenant of Augustine's view of faith was an interpretation of Jesus' parable of the wedding banquet (interesting choice) found in Luke 14:23, wherein the host filled up places at the table with an order,

"Compel them to come in." Augustine's commentary on this parable was that Christian government had the duty to support the Church by punishing heresy or schism and compel people to join in lock-step with the church. Over the next thousand years, Roman Church tradition identified with Augustine's interpretations in order to make itself the supreme power on earth. Never mind that the inflection in the Greek for the word *compel* means, "to convince for their own good." Convincing and coercing are two very different things. Too bad Augustine was rusty in his Greek.

The Greek word the New Testament uses is *anankazo*, meaning "to constrain by persuasion." This is not to be misconstrued to be *angaruo* in the Greek, "forced physically." We see such force and the correct word for it in Matthew, chapter 5, where a man is forced to go a mile carrying a Roman soldier's pack and in Matthew, chapter 27 where Simon of Cyrene was forced (*angaruo*) to carry Jesus' cross. However, where we find a totally different word, *anankazo* is in Matthew, chapter 14 and Acts 28, when the word is used as Jesus "compelled" the disciples to get into their boat and when Paul says he was "constrained" to appeal to Caesar. The Greek word used in these last two passages of Scripture plainly are the same that Jesus used in the parable about the wedding banquet in Luke, to convince by persuasion NOT "to force into."[14] Augustine was right in many things that he subsequently wrote concerning religion. He was very wrong about this. The Roman Church committed many atrocities during the Dark Ages and the Renaissance while quoting him in this regard. May God forgive us as we climb from the darkness into the light of truth about this.

The well-documented story is told that a British monk named Pelagius was teaching in Rome at the same time as Augustine was teaching (about AD 400). He was very popular with upper-class Romans. Pelagius challenged them, and all classes, to work within society to show their Christian morals. This was hard for Romans in their culture to accomplish. He called them out from their culture of Latin lust and Greek "stinkin-thinkin" by telling them that the New Testament teaches a mysterious unity within people of the spiritual, mental, and physical; that these three could not be separated morally, with the morality of lust compartmentalized away from the spiritual man, which Augustine originated.

Though Pelagius was incorrect in his overall theology, his teaching sounded very much like the later Puritans from England, whose teaching placed responsibility on the shoulders of all Christians to act according to the highest moral standards demanded by God within society.

The trouble was this: Augustine had sided with the established church that said God was spiritual and not physical, and "the flesh" was no good, so one could be spiritual and could also indulge in the flesh as long as he said that the spiritual was most important and the flesh was sinful and secondary. They agreed that it was sometimes necessary to indulge in sex and then get back to heavenly thoughts (just like Augustine did). They rationalized that both sexual lust and spiritual purity could co-exist if needed; lust as a necessary evil, don't you know?

Pelagius said that this sort of thinking was used to provide a false excuse for Christians to avoid making any real moral effort within society and culture. Augustine got the existing church leaders, who wanted to indulge in sexual sin and be justified by confession, to ban Pelagius. That took care of that. He was never heard from again. This action, perpetrated by the Imperial Church, allowed sinful men in charge of the church to justify celibacy for church leaders while gratifying their sexual desires with prostitutes and mistresses. This, while supposedly leading the people toward the truth of God. It was, and is, appalling! We shall see the far-reaching effects of this theological fallacy as we proceed through this book. Keep it in mind.

For modern-day application, we can now see that the "three strikes and you're out" reality began during this time. When we combine the facts that:

1. Augustine and the Roman Church hierarchy accepted the non-biblical view that spiritual and physical could be separated in mankind, justifying sexual sin,

2. The Roman Church later wanted to keep all their property and wealth rather than it being "stolen" by legal heirs to priests and bishops (so they forbade marriage, but okayed prostitutes and mistresses for the same),

3. When prostitution and venereal disease became rampant, priests turned to men and boys for their sex, and also, those lusting for women, retained monogamous mistresses.

And, all of this endorsed by the "Christian" Church!!

The effects of this come all the way to the nineteenth- and twentieth-century scandals wherein devout Catholic families sent their sons to be altar boys and priests only to have sent them into the homosexual community of priests which debased and shamed them,- and their families. Then, when the homosexual community communicated secretly that the best and safest place for those who were sodomites to practice their lust was in the Catholic seminaries, they flocked there.

Sadly, it continues to this day. And all in the name of God! It is no small matter! The Roman Church continues to try and put out the flame that they started with Augustine by moving the chess players around the board and damning any twenty-first-century Pelagius-protestor who simply agrees with the Bible. Justifying lust, greed, and pride, while producing the effect of sloth, gluttony, wrath, and envy makes the Roman hierarchy guilty of committing <u>all seven</u> of the deadly sins, while preaching against them to their parishioners. Jesus had something to say about hypocrites in his day, did he not?

Augustine

Pelagius

One of the most interesting asides about this religious contest is that the Roman Church has always said they brought Christianity to the Irish in AD 432 and the British in AD 597. If so, what was a Christian British missionary doing in Rome in the AD 390s. arguing with Augustine and getting banned by Roman Pope Innocent I? And this, two hundred years before Pope Gregory "first" sent missionaries to Britain!

Speaking of Christian Britain

About this Pope Gregory mission, the sixth-century Welsh Christian monk named Gildas, who wrote in approximately AD 550 said that "there was a fiery invasion of impious men." He quoted a fifth-century (AD 400's) document, The Groan of the British, telling of a Britain lacking Roman protection: "The barbarians drive us to the sea and the sea throws us back on the barbarians." And, by the years of AD 450–550, Wales was seeing a fervently Christian "Age of Saints." Dozens of Welsh churches date from the sixth and even fifth centuries, and the oldest cathedral in Britain proper was begun by Denoil in Bangor in AD 525. At much the same time, the Britonic priest, St. Petroc, was preaching in Cornwall, and St. Columba was travelling from Ireland to the Scottish island of Iona, founding a monastery there in 563.[15]

One More Example from History

In the National Trust of England, there is documentation, originally written by the historian Bede, that in the year of 615 Pagan King Ethelfrith, from the eastern side of the island, mounted a military campaign to subdue the Celtic Welsh. Along the way, he encountered 1,200 Welsh Christian monks near the old town of Chester, and slaughtered them "for opposing him with their prayers."

Are we to believe that this late sixth-century Roman priest named Augustine (not Augustine of Hippo) who was sent by the pope in AD 597 either brought or created 1,200 Christian monks in northern Wales in a scant eighteen years? Of course not. Nor, is there any documentation that Irish Christians thought there was any need to convert the Welsh. There is one existing record that Pope Gregory's Augustine actually reached the Welsh Christians in 598. He had a meeting with the Welsh clergy who refused association with the pope in Rome and his form of Christianity. The Celtic (Welsh) representatives said, "We have nothing to do with Rome; we know nothing of the bishop of Rome in his new character of the pope; we are the British Church, the archbishop of which is accountable to God alone, having no superior on earth."[16] "An angry Augustine allegedly threatened the British that, 'If you will not have peace with your friends, you shall have war from your foes.' He returned to Kent, in Southern England, empty handed."[17] This very documentation proves that the Christian religion had been in the Isles of Britain for many years at that time. It also tells us something about the religion of the popes and their "Christian attitude."

British historian R. W. Morgan helps us with an ancient quote from The Venerable Bede (Roman Priest) about this time and the conflict: "Britons, declared Bede, are contrary to the whole Roman world and enemies to the Roman customs, not only their mass, but in their tonsure. The Britons refused to recognise Augustine, or to acquiesce in one of his demands. 'We cannot,' said the bishops, 'depart from our ancient customs without the consent and leave of our people.' Laurentius, the successor of Augustine, speaks yet more bitterly of the antagonism of the Scottish Church: 'We have found the Scotch bishops worse even than the British.

Dagon, who lately came here, being a bishop of the Scots, refused so much as to eat at the same table, or sleep one night under the same roof with us."[18]

We will talk about the increasing polarization between the rising behemoth of the Roman Church and the "rustic church," which was growing through trials and victories in Ireland and Britain in chapter four.

Sources

1. Adrian Gilbert, *The Holy Kingdom*, (Bantam Press, 1998), 103–104.
2. Dairmaid MacCullough, *Christianity, The First Three-thousand Years* (Penguin, 2009) 189.
3. Lactantius, *Christianity, The First Three-thousand Years* (Penquin, 2009) 189
Lactantius, On the Death of Persecutors I, 2-3

4. Zosimus (2. 15), Eusebius V. C. 1. 38, Praxagoras, Anon. Val. p. 473; Lact. c. 44;

5. Chron. Pasch. p. 521, &c., Paneg. [313] c. 17, bold mine.

6. Soz. 1. 8), (Soz. l.c.; V. C. 2. 24, and 48

7. Phillip Schaff, *History of the Christian Church*, vol 3. Eerdmans, 34

8. Soz. I C; V. C. 4. 60

9. Eusebius, *Vita Constantini*, II 28 (The Life of Constantine.

10. Gee and Hardy, *English Church History*, 1

11. *Christianity, The First Three Thousand Years* (Penguin, 2009), 1

12. Sheed, *The Confessions of St. Augustine, Book 8*, (Sheed & Ward Publishing), 164–165, 173

13. Sheed, *The Confessions of St. Augustine, Book 7*, (Sheed & Ward Publishing), 146

14. *Englishman's Greek Concordance of the New Testament* (Baker Books, 1979), 41

15. Simon Jenkins, *A Short History of England* (Profile Books, 2011), 14

16. Blackstone, vol. IV, 105 and shift number 16 to number 17

17. Simon Jenkins, *A Short History of England* (Profile Books, 2011), 21

18. Bede hist. frag., quoted by Usher, "Ancient Irish Church," c. 4, Hist., lib. ii c. 2/ Laurentii Epist. ad Papam; Bede, Eccles. Hist., ii. c. 4

Images

Statue of Colossus of Constantine the Great in Rome, Italy © Neurobite | Dreamstime.com

Bronze statue of Constantine I in York, England | Dreamstime.com

Alexandrinus Leaf, British Museum

CHAPTER FOUR

Never the Twain Shall Meet

IT SHOULD BE CLEAR THAT WHAT WE ARE DOING in this study is contrasting the Christian Church in Britain with the Roman Church which became predominant throughout the Mediterranean region. It is our treatise that the true church was planted by the apostles and disciples of Christ during the first century AD. In this chapter, we will see the widening contrast between the two and how Rome tried to kill the Bible except where it could be of use to its powerbase. We have cited many ancient resources in the first three chapters. We will add many more during this one in order for those who champion the Roman Church to see that we are not being derogatory but simply stating the distasteful facts. We begin with historical statements about the continuing state of the British Church during the early centuries AD and a short review of some facts we have already shown. Years before the Roman Church landed on its shores, the growing British Church was accosted by the Devil in the form of Saxon raiding parties.

"The early British church held from the first a very isolated position, and was driven back by the invasion of the pagan Saxons, about the middle of the fifth century (AD 450), into the mountains of Wales, Cornwallis, Cumberland, and the still more secluded islands. Not till the conversion of the Anglo-Saxons under Gregory the Great did a regular connection begin between England and Rome."[1]

"Adding to the mythical lore of Glastonbury Abbey is speculation that it was founded by Joseph of Arimathaea. In his work *De Antiquitate*, William of Malmesbury (tenth-century) writes: 'There are documents of no small credit, which have been discovered in certain places to the following effect: "No other hands than those of the disciples of Christ erected the church of Glastonbury. Nor is it dissonant from probability; for if Philip, the Apostle, preached to the Gauls, as Freculphus relates in the fourth chapter of his second book, it may be believed that he planted the Word on this side of the Channel also."

William speculates on the possibility of the validity of an earlier tradition that there had been a first-century apostolic mission to Gaul led by the apostle Philip.

Freculphus, an early ninth-century Continental chronicler, repeated a claim made in the 630s by Isidore of Seville about Philip's mission to Gaul.[2]

The Ruins of Glastonbury

The reader will remember that we have recorded in this book mention of tens of thousands of Christians within an organized set of churches by the time of Constantine in the early fourth-century. We have a record of the retirement of Christian bishops, Theon and Tediac, from their "sees" in London and York in AD 586. They supplied a list of Diocletian persecution of the British Church. (Diocletian reigned over the empire from Rome in AD 286 and instigated the "great persecution" in AD 303). This list had senior bishops on it and mention of over ten thousand Christians in Britain.

Other Proof Texts of the Early Brithonic/Tutonic Church

Not only had the gospel of Jesus Christ penetrated the British Isles by the fifth-century, but there was considerable influence in pockets of civilization on the shores of Scandinavia. The Gothic Bishop Wulfila or Wolflein (Little Wolf) in the fifth century translated nearly the whole Bible from the Greek into the Gothic dialect. It is the earliest example of Teutonic literature, and the basis of comparative Teutonic philology. We still have a vellum copy that we can see and touch.

MSS Upsala, Codex Argenteus, (fragments)188 pages exist on permanent display at the Caroliina Rediviva library in Upsalla, Sweden.

The manuscript is written in an uncial script in the Gothic alphabet, reportedly created by Ulfilas (AD 311–383).

This manuscript shows that the Gospels were held in esteem not only in Britain, but in Jutland and lower Scandinavia as well. Our modern dramatists group all of this area's history under the heading of The Vikings. And, to be sure, there was considerable raiding of and settling in the British Isles. However, there was, as we have seen in chapter two, also an influence of Christianity in substantial pockets of civilization. One of the stellar examples is seen in the true story of St. Patrick of England and Ireland. Notice that England is mentioned first and Ireland second. St. Patrick was born and raised a Welshman! In his commentaries, he spoke of "the sons and daughters of Scottic chieftains were seen to become monks and virgins of Christ." And this, <u>before</u> so-called official, Catholic Christianity reached the island in AD 597.

St. Patrick was Welsh and lived in AD 389–461

The story from historians has it that Patrick, age sixteen, was captured by an Irish chieftain named Niall Noigiallach during a raid in Wales and carried back to Ireland's county Antrim. During his captivity, he cried out to the God of his father's for deliverance. After more than six years of slavery, he was miraculously delivered and allowed to go back to his home in Britain. He decided to become a monk and made his way to Gaul where he studied at the monastery of Tours. He was so exemplary of Christ that he was made a bishop in AD 432. However, after seeing the terrible plight of the peasants in Ireland, he chose to go back to Ireland as a free man and minister to the people there. He spent the rest of his life building Christian communities in the island. Because of this, moderns mistakenly think that he was Irish.

Padraig (Patrick) himself tells us that his father, Calpurn, in Wales, was a deacon, then a priest; Padraig says Dad Calpurn was also a Decurion—alias a minor local magistrate or headman over ten families. (Cf. the "rulers of tens" in Exodus 18:21.) His grandfather Pottitt was a Presbyter in Briton. An eleventh-century chronicler gives Padraig a great-grandfather Odiss, who also was a Deacon.

Summary of St. Patrick's Heritage

- Patrick lived in the years 389–461. So, Potitus lived in approximately AD 300, and Odiss before that.
- Patrick's writings are a multitude. Many mentions of Scripture and of baptism. His grandfather was a *presbyteri*. His father was a *decurio* (leader of ten) and a *diaconum* (Gr. = *Diakonos*), a deacon.

- In his numerous extant writings there is no mention of Romish veneration of Mary, the Eucharist only through a priest, veneration of holy relics, or prayers to saints, prominent in Rome.[3]
- In his writings, Patrick quotes from: Exodus, Psalms and Malachi, The Gospels, Acts, 1 John, Paul's Letters, and Revelation.[3]

Patrick obviously held copies, at least in Latin, of all of these documents, indicating he used an entire Bible as we know it today. However, his calling was to Ireland, and there is no documentation that he ever again visited or sent disciples to the Isle of Britain. There was, apparently, no need. He was a Celtic Welsh missionary to Ireland.

His strict adherence to Holy Scripture and Christ-centered post-millennialism—help establish that Padraig (St. Patrick) and his ancestors were all Proto-Protestants, alias Primitive Presbyterians. Not Catholics. [4]

Patrick's Creed:

"Because there is no God, nor was there ever any in times past, nor shall there be hereafter, except God the Father unbegotten, without beginning, from whom all things take their beginning, holding all things, as we say, and his Son Jesus Christ, whom we affirm verily to have always existed with the Father before the creation of the world, with the Father after the manner of a spiritual existence, begotten ineffably, before the beginning of anything. And by him were made things visible and invisible. He was made man; and, having overcome death, he was received up into heaven to the Father.

"And he gave to him all power above every name of things in heaven and things in earth and things under the earth; and let every tongue confess to him that Jesus Christ is Lord and God in whom we believe. And we look for his coming soon to be; he the Judge of the quick and the dead, who will render to every man according to his deeds. And he shed on us abundantly the Holy Spirit, the gift and earnest of immortality, who makes those who believe and obey to become children of God the Father and joint heirs with Christ, whom we confess and adore as one God in the Trinity of the Holy Name." –Patrick's Confessions, c IV

This is a fantastic creed! It shows us that, before the Imperial Roman

Church, by its own admission, first sent official emissaries to Britain, both the Irish and the British Church had: a creed, the Gospels from the early Latin and/or the Greek, AND they possessed all of the New Testament through Revelation, while preaching those beliefs to the people.

Another famed British Church Father of this time was the renowned Gildas. There are numerous statues of him in the north of Britain and in Scotland. He is often pictured holding a "Celtic Bell" of church authority.

Gildas

In *De Excidio et Conquestu Britanniae*, Gildas mentions that the year of his birth was the same year as the Battle of Mons Badonicus, in AD 482 Gildas' rhetorical writing style indicates a classical Latin education that could hardly have been available to any Britons after the fifth-century. His work *De Excidio et Conquestu Britanniae*, which contains narratives of the post-Roman history of Britain, is the only substantial source for history of this period written by a near-contemporary. The scholar David Dumville suggests that Gildas was the teacher of Finnian of Moville, who in turn was the teacher of St. Columba of Iona. The *Historia Ecclesiastica* was copied often in the Middle Ages, and 160 manuscripts containing it survive. There are two parts:

Part one has much minutiae about Roman and Saxon invaders plus other harsh happenings to the British people and her church:

- subjection and rebellion, about her second subjection and harsh servitude,
- concerning religion, of persecution, the holy martyrs, many heresies, of tyrants,

- of two plundering races, concerning the defense and a further devastation, of a second vengeance and a third devastation,

- concerning hunger, of victory, of crimes, of enemies suddenly announced, a memorable plague, a council, an enemy more savage than the first, the subversion of cities, of life's hardships and concerning those whose survived,

- concerning the final victory of our country that has been granted to our time by the will of God. (This last point is most interesting. Gildas writes about the meaning of and the heritage of the British as God's chosen people. Don't forget, there is a PLAN.),

- most importantly, Gildas writes; "We certainly know that Christ the true son, afforded His light and the knowledge of His precepts to our island in the last year of Tiberius." <u>This was written by AD 550 about the coming of Christianity in the year AD 36.</u>

Meanwhile, Back in Rome During the Same Centuries

In the year AD 366, there was a dispute between Christian groups in Rome. Bishop Damasus and Bishop Ursicinus rivaled for the newly vacated papacy. Damasus was a political figure, a nobleman from Portugal. Damasus has been described as "the first society pope," and was apparently a member of a group of Iberian (Spanish/Portuguese) Christians, largely related to each other, who were close to the Iberian Caesar, Theodosius the First.

Hundreds of the Italian followers of Ursicinus, who had been picked for the papacy by the previous pope, Liberius, protested the power grab by the followers of Damasus. They gathered in the large cathedral of Rome to pray for God's intervention. Followers of Damasus surrounded them, locked them in and burned the building down around them, thus reducing the opposition to a few powerless Romans and securing the papacy for Damasus. He graciously accepted the papacy from his murderous followers.[5]

The prefects banished Ursicinus to Gaul. There was further violence when he returned, which continued after Ursicinus was exiled again. Because the people considered that they had the right to choose their own bishops, something had to be done. It was not possible to accomplish this quickly but, eventually, the Imperials got their way. A decree of AD 502 by Pope Symmachus ruled that laymen should no longer vote for the popes and that only higher clergy should be considered eligible.[6] This was the beginning of the official Imperial Clergy, which continues until this day.

The Sophistication of Roman Christianity

Damasus began immediately to promote Rome as the Christian pilgrimage city of the empire. He began building monuments to saints for those on pilgrimage to visit. He promoted the dubious fact that Peter was the first pope in Rome. Also, in the year 382, he persuaded his personal secretary, Jerome, to begin a new translation of the Bible from Hebrew and Greek into Latin Vulgate. Jerome was introduced to certain pious, Latin ladies who would not only financially support him but travel with him as his service corps when he went to Palestine to do his work. Pope Damasus died the following year, leaving Jerome to fend for himself, but his support corps remained.[7] British historian Dairmaid McCollough speaks of the Vulgate translation in his monumental work, *Christianity, The First Three Thousand Years*:

"Undeniably, Jerome's Vulgate was a work of Latin literature, but there was nothing much like it in Latin literature which predated the arrival of Christianity. That was the problem for Damasus and his new breed of establishment Christians. They wanted to annex the glories of ancient Rome, but they had no time for the gods who were central to it."[8]

Jerome's Bible

Jerome worked on the Latin version of the Bible for many years, all the while being sponsored by the elite families of Rome. He put Rome's best spin on the biblical text, very much hoping that his scholarly work would vault him into the papal chair. He was wrong. His text was used for over a thousand years to boost Rome into prominence through the Latin language as the established theocratic language, but he, having proved his usefulness, languished and died in Palestine, a recluse scholar.

Jerome mistranslated the Old Testament and the New. Some of his Old Testament translations were comical.

"One of the most curious was at Exodus 34, where the Hebrew describes Moses' face as shining when he came down from Mount Sinai with the tablets of the Ten Commandments. Jerome, mistaking particles of Hebrew, had turned this into a description of Moses wearing a pair of horns—and so the lawgiver is frequently depicted this way in Roman Christian art."9

Jerome

Michelangelo's Moses with horns

How Did We Get
The State Roman Religion We Got?

THEODOSIUS.

In the latter part of of the fourth century, Emperor Theodosius I made Christianity the official religion of the state and began to converge the Christian Church with the Roman Church and, ominously, the Church with the State.

Theodosius wanted to resurrect the glory of ancient Rome and attempted to rule from the western part of the empire. Since his decrees of the State (empire) made Christianity the official State religion, the bishop of Rome gained a de facto leadership position over all the other bishops. It was during this time that another council was called—the Council of Carthage—also in the western part of the empire.

The scant historical background we have on Theodosius has he and his Father, Theodosius the Senior, living in the Spain of their birth when the current emperor asked the newly retired Senior to put on his uniform again and save Roman Britannia from losing its mining operations due to large-scale raids of Saxons and Franks who took over the garrisons of Rome there. Theodosius Senior came to the rescue with his son, Junior, as one of the commanders. Most of Britain's Christianity welcomed this, as the heathen raiders were a great threat. (This is a perfect case of God using a "crooked stick to make a straight lick," as some might say, and save his chosen, rustic people.).

"In the Spring of AD 368, the Romans landed in Britain. Theodosius marched his troops to Londinium which he made a base of operations. There he began to deal with the invaders. He divided his troops into many parts and attacked the predatory bands of the enemy, which were ranging about and were laden with heavy packs; quickly routing those who were driving along prisoners and cattle. He wrested from them the booty which the wretched tribute-paying people had lost. And when all this had been restored to them, except for a small part which was allotted to the wearied soldiers, he entered the city, which had previously been plunged into the greatest difficulties, but had been restored more quickly than could have been expected, rejoicing and celebrating. By the end of the year, the barbarians had been driven back to their homelands, Hadrian's Wall was retaken, and order returned to the diocese."[10]

"Upon returning to Rome, Theodosius the father and the son were hailed as heroes. Theodosius, the First (the son) eventually became emperor in Rome and favored Rome over Constantinople. He sent one of his sons, Honorus, to rule the eastern part of the empire and became the friend of the adoring Christian leadership in Rome. This began the split between the church, west and east."[11]

Theodosius Out-Romans the Romans

As emperor, between AD 389–392, Theodosius promulgated the "Theodosian decrees" (instituting a major change in religious policies), which removed non-Nicene Christians from church office and abolished the last remaining expressions of the old Roman religion by making its holidays into workdays, banned blood sacrifices, closed Roman temples, and disbanded the vestal virgins. Theodosius refused to restore the Altar of Victory in the Senate House, as asked by non-Christian senators. The emperor, for the first time, became a crusader for Roman Christianity.

In AD 392, he became sole emperor (the last one to claim sole and effective rule over an empire including the western provinces). From this moment till the end of his reign in 395, while non-Christians continued to request toleration, he ordered, authorized, or at least failed to punish those responsible for the closure or destruction of many temples, holy sites, images, and objects of old Roman pagan piety throughout the empire.

In AD 394, he ordered the Council of Carthage to convene, where the concepts of purgatory and prayers for the dead (already allowed in the churches of Rome) were debated and upheld to be performed church-wide. Non-Roman bishops argued that no mention in Holy Writ, nor practice of these had been traditional in any other churches of the empire previous to those in Rome, but to no avail. These were, then, made tradition AND law. Theodosius died the following year.

The Latin Bible Canon

Three years later this same good-old-bishop group was called together again. The Council of Carthage, on the 28th of August, AD 397, issued a canon of the Bible. In the Canonum Ecclesiae Africanae, which presents a compilation of ordinances enacted by various church councils, and authorized by the Carthage Council, the following paragraph appears:

It was also determined that besides the canonical Scriptures, nothing be read in the church under the title of divine scriptures. To quote the agreement:

"The canonical Scriptures are these: Genesis, Exodus, Leviticus, Numbers, Deuteronomy, Joshua the son of Nun, Judges, Ruth, the four books of Kings, two books of Paraleipomena, Job, the Psalter, five books of Solomon, the books of the twelve prophets, Isaiah, Jeremiah, Exechiel, Daniel, Tobit, Judith, Esther, two books of Esdras, and two books of the Maccabees.

Of the New Testament: four books of the Gospels, one book of the Acts of the Apostles, thirteen epistles of the apostle Paul, one epistle of the same writer to the Hebrews, two epistles of the apostle Peter, three of John, one of James, one of Jude, and one book of the Apocalypse of John."

There was considerable debate on whether the Deuterocanonicals were on a par with the previously accepted cannonical books. Eastern members argued that those books were used only as history by the Jews. The venerated Jerome, who translated the Bible into the Latin Vulgate even argued such. Subsequent councils did approve them to be read in the churches, but only under the heading of history books and not inspired Word of God. Subsequent councils also argued the canon inclusions and exclusions for centuries within the empire.

However, in Britain, the original Hebrew and Greek canon, which we have today in the Protestant Bible, were accepted as the only inspired Word of God until the Roman Catholic Church subjugated the island in AD 664.

Emblem of Leo I

ROMAN SUPREMACY BECOMES THE DEVIL'S NEW ATTACK-DOG AGAINST MANKIND

In the year of 460, while the British Church was growing and sending missionaries to Gaul, Ireland, Germania, and Spain, a perfidious movement continued to take shape in Rome. A new rising bishop of the Roman Church proclaimed himself pope and began to concentrate church civil power under the emblem of the "keys of the kingdom." This pope claimed the mantle of Roman leadership of the Church of Jesus Christ by cementing the connection of the papacy with the apostle Peter. The emblem that he constructed, indeed, in our opinion, concocted, has the "keys" to the kingdom of Christ with the three leveled crown above representing God, the Father, the Son and the Holy Spirit. And so, to claim the right to rule the church in the world from Rome. How did the bureaucrats in Rome come up with this justification? They did what so many do, even today, in order to justify their selfish viewpoint. They took one passage of Scripture and used it for their purposes. This always leads to error. Jesus and the church fathers taught us for over 400 years to take every passage of Scripture and interpret it via the whole book of the Bible. This attachment to Peter was improper practice based on Matthew 16:17–19. It was, secondarily, faulty history, since there is no historical verification that Peter even entered Rome during his lifetime.

Matthew 16:13–19 is the passage wherein Jesus asks his disciples, the Twelve, who they think he is. After some speculation, Peter says that Jesus is the Son of God. Jesus remarks on this with the comment that Peter was right and that this belief (in Jesus as the Son of God, sent by God) causes followers to hold the keys to the kingdom. So, the pope took A, the passage; connected it to B, Peter leading the church in Rome from the first century and wielding the keys to enter God's kingdom, and made the equation equal C, the Roman Church and its leader, the Pope, is sanctioned by God to rule the world until Jesus comes again. Let's see what church arch-historian Phillip Schaff says in his commentary about this:

"It is an undeniable historical fact, that the greatest dogmatic and legislative authorities of the ancient church bear as decidedly against the specific papal claims of the Roman bishopric, as in favor of its patriarchal rights and an honorary primacy in the patriarchal oligarchy." [12]

Dr. Schaff goes on to say that there was an oligarchy of seven bishop led churches who led the different areas of the world and their churches. That Rome, calling herself the head, was historically and Scripturally in error. The ante-Nicene and post-Nicene church fathers, without exception, for 400 years, saw apostolic equals in the churches at: Rome, Ephesus, Thessalonica, Corinth, Antioch, Jerusalem and, from AD 323, Constantinople. Rome was counted as only one of seven, but honorably, because of the sacrifices of the church in Rome under persecution. The apostle Peter himself, in his first letter says: "Finally, all of you, be like-minded; be sympathetic, love one another, be compassionate and humble" (1 Peter 3:8).

However, Pope Leo decided that only Rome, with him in the lead, could correctly aid and protect the church of the empire. It is interesting that the idea of Peter as Rome's first bishop was first proposed in a letter written by a North African bishop who was attempting to score points against his local Donatist opponents by stressing the North African's links to Rome. It was this foreign bishop's linkage on the basis of Matthew 16:17–19 which became the foundation of Roman Catholic hierarchical rule over Christendom. This letter found its way to Rome and became the basis of Peter's papacy legend. Fiction became greater than truth.

Historian Dairmaid McCollough gives us the account: "Ironically, it was actually a North African bishop point-scoring against his local Donatist opponents by stressing the North African Catholics' links to Rome, who is the first person known to have asserted on the basis of Mathew 16:17–19 that, 'Peter was superior to the other apostles and alone received the keys of the kingdom, which were distributed by him to the rest;' yet significantly it was in the time of Damasus that this thought occurred to the North African, sometime around 370." [13]

Leo I

"The whole world acknowledges the Roman see as director and governor; that neither Gallican nor other bishops should, contrary to the ancient customs, do anything without the authority of the venerable pope of the Eternal City; and that all decrees of the pope have the force of law." –Decree, AD 460, Leo I

This statement is the first bald-faced lie of the early papacy. There was no such thing in the ancient customs. When other bishops of the various leading churches learned of this and protested, Leo went on to declare:

"Whoso disputes the primacy of the apostle Peter, [i.e., myself] can in no way lessen the apostle's dignity, but, puffed up by the spirit of his own pride, he destroys himself in hell." –Leo I, Epistle 10, al 89 (brackets mine)

Leo was using an old trick of the evil one. Try to redirect opposition by calling others prideful, when it is really you who are prideful. Then, the opposition spends so much time endeavoring to humbly vindicate themselves from the accusation, that you have time to consolidate power.

Very cagey.

The Rebuttal

Let's look at some other writings that speak of primacy in the church that Jesus Christ founded.

Cyprian of Carthage (died in AD 258), who was the first African bishop to be martyred, wrote that bishops were the spiritual successors of the apostles in the church. No bishop, in his opinion, had the right to impose his authority upon the others. He said that the church in Rome was primary over all others and implied that it was <u>because of her sufferings</u>. However, he refused to assent to the primacy of "Peter's successors." He reminded the bishop of Rome about the chastisement of Peter by Paul and said, "We (bishops) should not obstinately love our own opinions" (Epistle 70).

Cyprian also is quoted to say, "The bishop should be chosen in the presence of the people, who are thoroughly familiar with the life of each one, and who has looked into the doings of each one in respect to his habitual conduct" (Epistle 67). This is corroborated by Hippolytus of Rome (c. 170–236), who preceded Leo by almost 200 years. He wrote, "Let the bishop be ordained after he has been chosen by all the people" (Apostolic Tradition 2). Do we remember what the Celtic and Scottish bishops said to Roman Catholic Bishop Laurentius, "We cannot depart from our ancient customs without the consent and leave of our people?"

Nevertheless, by AD 500, a pope in Rome was firmly ensconced as leader of a hierarchy bent on preserving the church, as they perceived it, at all costs. The Imperial Church was created and nurtured in Rome.

"The idea of a seated bishop presiding over the liturgy but also pronouncing on matters of belief and adjudicating everyday disputes, became so basic to Western Christian ideas of what a bishop represented that the

Church annexed a second word for 'chair,' *cathedra*, previously associated with teachers in higher education, and used it for the city church in which the bishop's principal chair could be found: his cathedral. The buildings which the Church now put up for the worship of their great congregations reflected the bishop's role as politicians and statesmen."

"Smaller pastoral units served by a single priest [was] the parochial or parish. That was what the Pastoral Epistles had described when they considered how a bishop should lead his people, but now the situation had radically changed. Willy-nilly, but mostly without much protest, bishops were becoming more like official magistrates, because their Church was being embraced by the power of the empire."[14] It was during this time that priests and bishops began to universally encourage the congregants to refer to them as Father.

This is in direct contradiction to Jesus' command also in Matthew:

"And do not call anyone on earth 'father' for you have one Father, and he is in heaven" (Mt. 23:9).

Not only were the papists defying this Scripture, but they were claiming that the kingdom of Christ had already come and that the pope was in charge of what should happen during this time of the Gentiles and anyone who questioned him was worthy of condemnation. Opponents claimed that The Book of Revelation taught that the true kingdom was not a worldly one but in the hearts of true followers of Jesus Christ. They noted Scripture passages in Revelation: so the pope, in return, said that Revelation should not be in the Bible. He proceeded to delete it. That took care of that. Eastern bishops and priests reiterated:

"The true kingdom could only be set up within the Jewish nation as covenanted. To spiritualize those covenants as some do is to make the oath of God of little value. If the covenants teach any truth clearly, it is this: that the Jewish nation and the kingdom are inseparably connected, that during this time of the Gentiles, imposed on account of sinfulness, the kingdom cannot be in existence." [15]

It was only after the year AD 230 when Origen, under the patronage of the proposed pope in Rome, insisted on the "dignity and perpetuation" of Roman power and insisted the "kingdom" was now in place. Once the state-church was declared by Theodosius in AD 380, the "kingdom of Christ" under the supervision of the popes became possible and popular.

All this was enacted, notwithstanding the pervasive and repetitive teaching of the apostles in the New Testament. The Apostle Peter, he who was named as the first pope by the Imperial Church, said in his first sermons, (Acts 2:14–36 and 3:12–26) that Jesus was the resurrected Christ who would make his enemies his footstool.

Peter insisted that; Christ must remain in heaven until the time comes for God to restore everything as he promised long ago through his holy prophets. This second advent would be "the kingdom restored," not a concentrated papal hierarchy on earth.

In his writings, the apostle Paul fully corresponds with Peter, locating the fulfillment of the promises held by the Jews to the future coming of this Jesus, the Christ.

The Apostle James, in his epistle, records that instead of a kingdom now established, believers are "heirs of a kingdom" and exhorts them to a patient waiting for "the coming of the Lord" when the kingdom will be realized.

In the epistles of the Apostle John, instead of proclaiming a kingdom now established, he encourages readers to look for the coming of Jesus. In the Apocalypse, he shows the trials and tribulations of the church in the future and positively asserts that only at a certain time the dominion or kingdom of Christ would be manifested.[16]

"The gospel of the kingdom as given by the Great Church Fathers—the apostles, Papias, Barnabas, Irenaeus and Justin (AD 50–AD 230–for almost 200 years)—was widely different from 'the gospel of the kingdom' as presented by Augustine, Jerome or Eusebius."[17] All the latter were supported by bishops in Rome or the statelike-church in Constantinople.

The papacy continued with their narcissistic notions throughout the fall of Rome to the invading Huns, Ostrogoths, and Visigoths. The popes in Rome made deals and treaties with the leaders of the invaders that if they would leave the Vatican un-touched, the popes and the episcopate would lead the people, under the power of Christ, to obey their new masters. Thus, the Vatican remained un-touched by the "vandalism" that scourged the rest of Rome.

Why does this matter to us as modern-day Christians?

"This [Roman Church] 'worldview' negates the idea of justification by faith [in Christ] making the pleasing of the pope the cause of righteousness of a Christian. It debases the Christian religion to the level of all other works religions. So long as men think they see and hear Christ in the pope and believe that they are worshipping and honoring Christ by serving and obeying hierarchies as 'pure divino,' we need never expect them to believe that Christ will ever reign here in person."[18]

Most importantly, this worldview opens the Pandora's Box of an earthly king, the pope, who can, in the name of God, legislate, judge, and coerce anyone not obeying the hierarchy, to the point of injury, death, and damnation in order to get his way.

"It is a sad truth that if we once admit that the visible church, in any one of its forms, is the kingdom of Christ on earth, we close the doors to the exclusion of private judgment, elevating said church into the position of arbiter of God's word in the form it may possess. Consistency then demands an outward unity, and, in the efforts to secure such unity, force may be employed, and as a result, violence is done both to religion and man; the canons and work of fallible man are elevated to tests of allegiance, resulting in crimination, excommunication, and anathema. The fountain itself being impure, the stream flowing from it, whatever pure and refreshing springs alongside of it may commingle with it, will carry on this impurity."[19]

"It is not surprising that the papacy should so tenaciously hold to the doctrine that the church is the kingdom, since everything so distinctively Popish, as Bellarmine (quoted by Bowers, in preface to *History of the Popes*) assures us, depends on it. For out of it proceeds the pope's supremacy, the vice-regent rule, the entire papal governmental machinery. It is the foundation upon which the superstructural pretensions are built. If this is removed, the whole falls."[20]

The Papacy Takes Complete Control

At this time the pope that came onto the scene ratcheted-up the control of the Imperial papacy and directed it, through his appointed bishops, from the sophisticated cities of the empire,- toward church and state rule over the rustic world.

Gregory, the Great

Pope Gregory, the Great was from a wealthy family in Rome. Before he was appointed pope, he was the prefect (lawyer) of the city. He was a Roman aristocrat, combining wealth and spiritual rule. Gregory was obsessive about the "last days" of the world. He had seen war, death, and decay of his world in Rome and had a sense of urgency about delivering the world for Christ before it was too late. He was determined that his writings be preached, along with the Latin Vulgate Gospels, throughout the world.

"To forever have the 'episcopal fountain' flow and to keep the faith pure," Pope Gregory (AD 590) claimed the "throne of St. Peter" in Rome and centralized his power toward complete autocracy. Gregory did not call himself the "pope." He insisted that he was just the bishop of Rome. Why would he do that? Was it a sense of great humility? That's the way it looked. Well, it was political. He had observed how previous popes had endeavored to reunite Christendom under the popes in Rome. But, the continuing problem for Rome was the bishopric of Constantinople backed by the emperors of the East. They continued to call themselves Patriarchs of the Universal Church (i.e., popes of the "official" Christian Church). Gregory adopted a stance of passive aggression.

"It may have been in order to highlight the pride embodied in the Oecumenical patriarch's title that Gregory adopted one of aggressive self-deprecation, which his successors have used ever since: 'Servant of the servants of God.'"[21]

However, Gregory's independent actions of appointing governors to cities, providing munitions of war, giving instructions to generals, sending ambassadors to the Lombard king, and even negotiating a peace without consulting the emperor were decisive acts that revealed the papacy as an independent civil power. This paved the way for future kings to become heads of the church as well as popes to become kings of countries. There goes the neighborhood!

In a real sense, Gregory decided that if he couldn't beat the popes of the East, those pesky patriarchs in Constantinople, he would consolidate the rest of the Western world under the pope in Rome. So he went west and north to conquer under the banner of the Universal "Servants" in Rome. This was an egotistical misuse of Jesus' saying, "The last shall be first and the first shall be last," found in Matthew, Mark, and Luke, and Matthew 20:26 where Jesus told his followers, "Whoever wants to become great among you must be your servant, and whoever wants to be first must become your slave." Gregory would admit to being the servant while taking every opportunity to be first and the greatest centrist ruler since Caesar Augustus.

In AD 597, Gregory sent Bishop Augustine (of Rome, not Hippo) to Britannia, and, with the aid of heavily bribed King Ethelbert of Kent, insisted on the loyalty, of tenth-generation Celtic Christians, to the Pope in Rome. This is when the <u>dark ages began and the war between chosen Christianity, centered in Britain, and Romanism of the popes, is sparked. Undaunted, the reign of the papacy and its hierarchy dominated and insisted on priesthood ruling the laity in all the Western world.</u>

The Doctrine of the Laity Assures Control

Witness a valued Catholic Church historian, Alexandre Faviere, and his judgments concerning the separation of priesthood and laity:

"The Christian who goes back to the origins soon discovers that there is no question of 'lay' [laity] in the New Testament. There is no trace of the term! There is not even a trace of any reality that could be transposed and put in parallel with our contemporary phenomenon of the 'laity.' On the contrary, most of the elements that we use to help us to define the laity today as a specific category are quite absent from the New Testament."

"What must strike and even shock modern man most of all, however, is the early Christians' habit of calling themselves 'saints' without any trace of nuance or of degree in this 'holiness.' There are countless examples of the use of this term both in Acts and in the letters of Paul.

"In the New Testament, then, the term *kleros* is applied not simply to the ministers, but to the whole of the believing people. What, however, are we to understand by the word that we traditionally used in Judaism and the pagan world to denote priests–*hiereus*? Here the facts are even clearer. This word is never applied to ministers. It is only used either for Christ himself or for the whole of the believing people. The priestly function–the true priesthood—is peculiar to Christ, who has enabled all Christians to share in it. In the Christian communities of the first century, there was no independent priestly function that was exercised by a special caste or minister." [22]

However, the pope began to cement the control of his clergy by forcing doctrines on the people in the West.

The eight "Doctrines" that entered the Roman Church from about AD 400 until modern times, culminated in the Roman horrors of torturing and burning Christians in the fourteenth, fifteenth, and sixteenth centuries.

1. **N.T. Church Authority of the Scriptures**–*Sola Scriptura*, "only the Scriptures," was the by-word of the church of Jesus Christ for the first 200 plus years of Christianity.

   ⬇

   Tradition and Authority of "The Church"–The "Tradition" became the addition to the Scriptures that the Holy Spirit through the Apostle John warned about in Revelation, chapter 22. And, the pope's writings or decrees became supposed holy writ.

2. **Body of Christ**–Until about AD 400, church bodies under the leadership of elders, the Pauline model, could be anywhere with the believers, no matter their background, if they professed belief in Jesus Christ and leadership of the Bible.

   ⬇

   Church Members–The Roman Church and the Eastern Orthodox Church insisted that "membership" on the rolls of a particular church sanctioned by the pope or archbishop was the door to everything Christian.

3. **Saving Grace**–For the first 400 years of church history, salvation was by grace, and works were works of love because of salvation.

   ⬇

   Sacramental Grace–Taking of the sacraments, exactly as the pope required, by a Roman priest, in a Roman church, became the avenue of salvation.

4. **Faith**–Faith alone in Jesus Christ and his salvific work was seen as sufficient for salvation for the first 400 years of Christianity.

Works–Faith plus works in the name of Jesus through the official Roman church, and given to the officials of that church, became the constant open door to heaven.

5. **Christ as Mediator**–Christ was the head of the church in the eyes of church leaders for the first 400 years in the majority of the assemblies of Christians. Only belief in Jesus as Savior was needed, for he sat at the right hand of the Father and he had sent the Holy Spirit to be within every believer, so there was a "priesthood of the believer" and no priest, bishop, or pope was needed to mediate between man and God.

Priests, Virgin Mary, and "Saints" as Mediators–Almost 500 years after Christ, and contrary to the New Testament, the Roman Church said that Mary and dozens, then hundreds, of "saints," whom the Roman Church recognized, could mediate for sinners with God, as long as one paid the price to the priest for a token that would introduce the sinner to the mediator.

6. **Worship of God Freely**–Every act of worship was a free gift, and offerings were not to pay for buildings, priests, church hierarchy, etc., in the first- through third-century church.

Payment to Worship and Worship of Relics–Around AD 400 is when the Roman Church began to collect relics (so-called parts of apostles and saints bodies and items they touched) and place them in cathedrals so believers could come and pray while adoring them, all of which had a price.

7. **Focus on the Kingdom of God**–The potential of the kingdom of God was within each believer, and the kingdom of God was also in the future, when Jesus would come again for his people. Justin Martyr and Clement of Alexandria (c. AD 150) spoke of the church as a gathering of the saints to receive instructions through the Scriptures, not a central place (a cathedral) but each gathering.

Focus on the Kingdom on Earth–The kingdom was said to be established on earth under the command of the substitute king, the pope, when Jesus was resurrected and Peter was given the keys to the kingdom. The popes, then, reign on earth for Jesus until he returns.

8. **Great Commission**–For the first 200–300 years of the church, going out to the world and teaching disciples was the focus.

The Monasteries and the Cathedrals–After AD 300–400, the church built monasteries and cathedrals and the church dwelt within. The focus was interior and inbred. But, of course, outsiders were "compelled" to come in.

These eight changes were seismic for the church. With their implementation empire wide, the split between the true church of Jesus Christ through the teaching of the apostles in the Bible versus the Roman Imperial Church began in earnest. This formative period of church history in the Roman Empire was one where new Christians viewed themselves as on an earthly pilgrimage. They were taught that they were unworthy of salvation, and its obtainment would come to them by an infusion of God's grace through the church and its sacraments; which was only realized through priestly pronouncement. Even then, continuous work was required for them through life, death, and purgatory. And, if they loved their families, the righteous were required to purchase their souls, too, throughout the progression of life and death.

Since time and space prevent us from recording the entire record of the papacy from 600 forward, we will give just a short outline of the progress of the church now called "Catholic."

AD 607—Pope Boniface, the first bishop of Rome to be called "pope" and "Universal Bishop" by decree of Emperor Phocas. (The saints of the church, the people, had nothing to do with it.)

AD 800—Charlemagne of the Franks is crowned first holy Roman emperor of the West by Pope Leo III, thereby instituting the pope as ruler of emperors.

AD 1046—Three popes hold office concurrently. At the council of Sutri, Pope Silvester III was exiled, Pope Gregory VI admitted to buying the papacy and, eventually, resigned, and Pope Benedict IX resigned. The council appointed Pope Clement II to replace the three disgraced popes. (Which one held the keys to the kingdom, the one who bought the papacy?)

AD 1054—The Roman Church is divided into East and West. The Eastern was Greek and called the Eastern Orthodox and the Latin Roman Church was the West. Pope Leo IX excommunicated Bishop Cerularius, patriarch of Constantinople, who in turn, excommunicated Leo.

AD 1139—The Lateran Council made all clerical marriages not only unlawful but illegitimate. (Clergy could keep concubines and have bastards, but the church kept the property.)

AD 1075—Gregory VII (pope) claims the title officially as vicar of Christ. (As such, he could wield the sword of holy justice to rule the church, all Christians, and "make the world holy.")

AD 1073–1291—The era of the Crusades. The Muslims broke out of Palestine, Arabia and North Africa that they had held since Muhammad's raiders had their initial growth spurt. From western Africa, they swept with great speed through Spain and into the heart of France. They were beaten back into Spain by French and German warriors. In the east, the Islamic Turks had taken from the Arabs Palestine and Syria, had invaded Asia Minor, and were seriously threatening Constantinople itself. Europe felt that it was only a matter of time until all were subjects of the Islamic terror, which faith demanded conversion to Islam, slavery, or death. The fear was that this would, eventually, wipe Christianity from the face of the earth.

During the Crusades, Constantinople was the home of thousands of Greek-language documents, biblical treasures held there since Constantine's reign. Christians had already lost Jerusalem, but the historical books of Christianity might be lost forever if Constantinople was taken by the Islamists. During almost 200 years and eight crusades, concerned Christians from all of the Holy Roman Empire fought the alien Islamic killers. We must keep in mind that the Christians were willing to die to defend Christendom. The Turk Muslims were willing to kill trying to destroy Christians and Christianity. There is a difference! Were there some crusaders that were totally UNChristian? Of course. But, nevertheless, God had a plan and that plan did not include losing Constantinople, as long as she held sacred, holy, and historical documents there.

Even King Richard of Britain got involved in the Crusades. The Briton Christians went to war not so much to save Rome or Constantinople, but to save Christianity. Richard could see Islam sweeping to the doorstep of Britain within another generation. His fleet of ships were instrumental in supplying the crusaders with needed aid and, more than once, rescuing them when the Islamists had them backed up to the beaches or ports.

But, we get ahead of ourselves by this digest about the intervention of the Islamists. That will be exposed in chapter seven. Let's return to describe the contrast of the church in rustic Britain and its development during these same 500 years of Roman State rule just outlined.

In chapter five…

Sources

1. Phillip Schaff, *History of the Christian Church*, (Erdmanns, 299).

2. Britannia.com/Britannia History.

3. Dr. Francis Nigel Lee, Nordskog Publishing.

4. Light in the Dark Ages, Edman, p. 101.

5. Henry Wace, "Ammianus Marcellinus," *Dictionary of Christian Biography*.

6. Ambrose (Epistle iv, underline mine).

7. Alan Cameron, "The Date and the Owners of the Esquiline Treasure," *American Journal of Archaeology*, 1, Centennial Issue (Jan., 1985): 135–145,Cameron, 136, Cameron, 142-143.

8. Diarmaid MacCollough, *Christianity, The First Three Thousand Years,* (Penguin, 2009) 197.

9. Diarmaid MacCollough, *Christianity, The First Three Thousand Years,* (Penguin, 2009) 197.

10. Ian Hughes, *Imperial Brothers: Valentinian, Valens and the Disaster at Adrianople* Pen & Sword, 2013.

11. The Barbarian Conspiracy, British History.

12. Philip Schaff, *The History of the Christian Church* 1866.

13. MacCollough, Diarmaid, Christianity, The First Three Thousand Years, (Penguin, 2009), 294.

14. MacCollough, Diarmaid, Christianity, The First Three Thousand Years, (Penguin, 2009), 197.

15. G.N.H Peters, *The Theocratic kingdom of Jesus, The Christ*, vol. 1 (Kregel, 1952), 422.

16. G.N.H Peters, *The Theocratic kingdom of Jesus, The Christ*, vol. 1 (Kregel, 1952), 438-440.

17. G.N.H. Peters, *The Theocratic kingdom of Jesus, The Christ*, (Kregel), 1952 vol. 1, p. 505.

18. G.N.H Peters, *The Theocratic kingdom of Jesus, The Christ*, vol. 1 (Kregel, 1952), 514.

19. G.N.H Peters, *The Theocratic kingdom of Jesus, The Christ*, vol. 1 (Kregel, 1952), 653.

20. G.N.H Peters, *The Theocratic kingdom of Jesus, The Christ*, vol. 1 (Kregel, 1952), 662.

21. MacCollough, Diarmaid, *Christianity, The First Three Thousand Years (*Penguin, 2009), 328.

22. Alexandre Faviere, *The Emergence of the Laity in the Early Church* (Paulist Press, 1984), 3–7. Bold and italics mine.

Images

The Ruins of Glastonbury © Guenter Baumann | Dreamstime.com

Michelangelo's Moses with horns I© Nonmim | Dreamstime.com

Theodosius

Leo I | Dreamstime.com

Gregory, the Great | Dreamstime.com

CHAPTER FIVE

AND SO, THE CONTRAST BECOMES MANIFEST

MEANWHILE LET'S ONCE AGAIN RETURN to the "rustic" islands called Brytagne (Britain) during the preceding 500 years from AD 600–1100.

"In the meantime, King Oswy, in the north of England and in Scotland, strengthened Christianity in all parts of Briton except Kent."[1] Kent was ruled by pagan English King Aethilfrith, who desired to be the ruler of the entire island. His clan of immigrant Angles had overrun the southeastern tip of England a generation earlier.

There is a great stone monument in Glamorgan, Wales, dated to AD 550, called The Sampson Stone. The vertical shaft of stone is really the main body of a great cross which stood at a crossroads leading to the center of the Cymric Celtic kingdom. It reads, "In the name of God most high, here begins the cross (kingdom road juncture) of the Savior, which Sampson the Abbot prepared for his own soul and the soul of Ithael and

Arthur, the Ruler.[2] It seems that God had succeeded in setting-up a kingdom of Christianity in southwestern Britain and Wales that was solid and growing. However, the Evil One would not go quietly. The New Romans came back with a vengence.

As we have mentioned, in the year of AD 597, Pope Gregory sent missionaries to Britain in order to set up the "official" (i.e., Roman) Church in the British Islands. Of course, we have seen that there was truer Christianity in Britain hundreds of years before that time, indeed back to the first apostles in the first century. However, the pope and the Roman hierarchy did not recognize this church as official, because it did not worship God through the Imperial Church system that had been set-up for the last several hundred years in Italy.

The missionaries from the pope were met with graciousness by church leaders, until they began saying that their system was the true church of Jesus Christ and no other body could be recognized by God, nor should it be recognized by the local kings. They insisted on supremacy over the church of Britain. We have a written record of the British Christian's response to that:

"We have nothing to do with this Rome; we know nothing of the bishop of Rome in his new character of the pope. We are the British Church, the archbishop of which is accountable to God alone, having no superior on earth. Be it known and declared that we all, individually and collectively, are in all humility prepared to defer to the Church of God, and to the bishop of Rome, and to every sincere and godly Christian, so far as to love every one according to his degree, in perfect charity, and to assist them all by word and deed in becoming the children of God. But as for any other obedience, we know of none that he whom you term the pope, or bishop of bishops, can demand. The deference we have mentioned we are ready to pay to him, as to every other Christian, but in all other respects our obedience is due to the jurisdiction of the bishop of Caerleon, who is alone, under God, our ruler to keep us right in the way of salvation."[3]

The British arch-historian of antiquity, The Venerable Bede (c. AD 695) chronicles what happened next. His comments are penned by modern scholar Henry Marsh in his book, *Dark Age Britain*. (Note that when Marsh speaks of Britons, he includes the Welsh in the term.) Continuing his narrative of events in Britain, Bede prints a vivid picture of the bitter controversy between Augustine and the Christian Britons. When Augustine came on his mission, Pope Gregory gave him full authority over all the bishops on the island. The Britons were very naturally resentful. Why should Rome, which had for so long neglected them, now presume to set over them a stranger, who had moreover cast his lot with their enemies? He dwelt among them and was building churches in the land of the hated English (Angles), who had so recently and so savagely bludgeoned the Britons from their province.

"Augustine invited the Britons to a conference in AD 603, (five years into his arrival) but the meeting was fruitless and Augustine made matters no better by warning them that if they refused union with the church, which he led, they would be attacked by their enemies… The Britons were not merely content, but proud, to continue their ancient practices. Over the previous hundred years, Rome had redefined and modified certain aspects of belief. The Britons, isolated by distance and (from) the fog of war which enveloped the Continent during the fifth and sixth centuries, had heard nothing of this and continued their old ways. So did the Scots in the north, who had earlier been converted by the Britons."[4]

Then came New Rome's first attempt, since the Caesars, to kill the Bible by eradicating its teachers. There was no more effective technique in a society of mostly oral learners. The story is documented by Bede and also found in *The Welsh Annals* recorded near the same time under the heading of the "Cair Legion." Near the modern town of Chester, England, Aethilfrith massed an army during late AD 603. This was, coincidentally, only less than a year after Augustine had threatened the Britons and Welsh to join in lock-step with Rome or face the consequences. Welsh Prince Solon, son of King Cunain, met him with an army half the strength of the enemy. Accompanying the Welsh/Briton army were 1,250 monks from all of western England. They lined an adjacent hilltop to watch and pray. The English pagan army, with mercenaries hired by the pope, overwhelmed the

Welsh and defeat became a rout. As Welsh soldiers retreated into the hills, King Aethilfrith turned on the Christian monks. He grimly remarked that if they were attempting to use the force of prayer on him they were also soldiers, and fair game. He ordered his troops to slaughter them all. Which they did. It would take three hundred years for the Welsh to build a new rustic Christian priesthood. By that time, the papacy had an overwhelming presence on the island which would last for over 700 years. The only good news was that Augustine died the following year in 604.

It took a long period of time, wherein these Roman, Imperial missionaries built their British power base and brought fresh relics from Jerusalem, writings of the pope and bribes for the king, for their system to be understood and tolerated. These "regal" missionaries, sent from the kingdom of the pope, asked for a synod to meet together and discuss real Christianity. During this meeting, the Synod of Whitby in AD 664, King Oswy was convinced that Rome had the true answers and that Romanism would be the accepted religion of his kingdom. However, the leaders of the traditional British church for over 600 years rejected this and withdrew to their home of Wales, northern England, and Scotland.

In Wales, Iona, Glastonbury, Scotland at large, and in the hearts of the true Christians of the clans, the pope and his regency was not recognized. They regarded the Scriptures as supreme and dedicated themselves to Bible study in the ancient Greek and ancient (before popes) Latin languages. Their primary holiday was Easter on Sunday each spring following the full moon in March. They met together as fellow believers and aided one another as needed. They had a free community of saints who were equals.

This church still remembered the apostles' teaching about Jesus as the only mediator between man and God. They had copies of the Gospels and the Book of Acts in the original language, wherein they could read about Jesus' way of life and his example for us. They had the teachings of Paul, the doctrines of the church for the first 500 years of the assemblies of the saints of God. They had a closed book of Holy Scripture, the Bible, wherein John had written, under the inspiration of the Holy Spirit of Christ, that no words should be added to these on pain of the curses held within. (There were no pope's decrees for the churches in Wales and Scotland.)

This was the church that Constantius, Helena, and Emperor Constantine believed in. This was the faith of their fathers. The Roman system was totally foreign to their faith. It was imposed as a system of power from a person who sat on the throne of the earth in Rome. But, this Roman faith and power base was insidious. Through the years it began to erode the church in Britain and Ireland through artful persuasion, bribery and, finally, force.

During the time of artful persuasion, Pope Gregory sent writings that were well formed. Gregory was an Italian nobleman, with no knowledge of Hebrew or Greek, but in an age where 90 percent of Britons were illiterate, writings were held in high esteem. Gregory was a good teacher. He wrote *Dialogues* (four volumes), which recounted the lives of the saints in Italy, the miracles that happened in early Christianity, and made a great treatise about the eternity of men's souls. He also wrote *Pastoral Rule*, a book which was his attempt to dictate the responsibilities of the clergy to have watch-care over the flock. This was impressive. If it was so impressive, thought the people and the kings of Britain, perhaps it was also true.

"Gregory also wrote a commentary on the four Gospels. On page 125 he states that the central idea of Matthew's Gospel is to correct false Jewish notions concerning the kingdom of the Messiah. With this as his premise, he goes on to say: 'He (Matthew) accordingly exhibits the kingdom not as a temporal one, like the Roman Empire, but as theocratic, or as a spiritual reign of God himself, in the person of the Messiah, in the hearts of men.'

"In point of fact, The Gospel of Matthew speaks of the preparation for the Messiah's kingdom to come, not a kingdom whose time has come."[5]

Gregory assumed from the Gospels that Christ had set-up his kingdom from the right hand of the Father and had appointed the pope to run the kingdom until his Second Coming. Like the serpent's words to Adam and Eve in the Garden, these words had the ring of truth to fallen men. They depended on selected passages of Holy Scripture, but the passages were only used as a set-up to a false premise.

This is a BIG deal! Why? Because it sets up spiritual regard for all succeeding writings of the popes and bishops. It begins the "tradition" of pope as vice-regent of the kingdom of God on earth! As the "traditional teachings" of the church then become equal to or superior to Holy Scripture, the pope becomes the de facto religious ruler of the world and THE KEEPER of the gateway to heaven or hell! It sets–up believers as earthly subjects of the pope first and Christ second. It sets-up the decrees and teachings of the pope as authority for the "rules" of sanctification first and the Bible, through the eyes of the Holy Spirit, second.

Venerated Christian Writer Watchman Nee is quoted to say, "Authority has its foundation in sanctification." He was relating to the biblical principle that submission to authority is commanded because God, our ultimate authority, has allowed earthly authority. However, obedience to authorities who are not under God's authority of sanctification is NOT commanded by the Bible because they are not delegates of God, but of man. Christians, in their faith, are to only obey God's delegated biblical authorities who reveal in their actions a clear process of the work of sanctification, such as the apostles and Paul.

The early Roman declaration that the pope was the "Vicar of Christ" and that his words (the pope's) were equal to those of the Holy Scriptures; that the pope was the "infallible interpreter of the Word" was terminal for the Romans, and they began to teach that the Bible was both literal and "spiritual" (which meant "mystical" to them), and that the mystical was most important. Then, as the infallible interpreter, the pope interpreted the literal as allegory and, by inference, implied that those who just look at what the Bible plainly said were ignorant of the true will of God. They must also accept the allegorical as truth. Here is an example of the logic.

The Bible talks about bread in stories.

A. The Old Testament story of manna from heaven in the wilderness was true.

B. The bread and wine of Melchizedek in refreshing Abraham was true and real bread.

C. The Passover meal was a true story with real bread for the body.

D. SO, (here comes the allegorical twist) the Eucharist bread becomes the REAL BODY of Christ when the ROMAN priest blesses it and you partake of it because you paid for the privilege of membership in the Roman Church. (Follow the money.)

This magical change in bread and wine was termed *transubstantiation*. The churches in Wales and Scotland saw this for what it was, a way to control the people of God. Because one could only take the Eucharist, which was commanded by the pope as a sacrament, if he took it from the Roman priest. All other Eucharist ceremonies were invalid. Northern England, Wales, and Scotland rejected it.

In fact, they said that the Scripture passages of Matthew 18 and 20, Mark 9 and 10, Luke 9 and 22, and John, chapters 13–17 all explained that this was not the biblical principle at all. The pope also claimed the "seat of Peter" in Rome as his authority to rule. This, from the verse in Matthew 16:18: "And I tell you that you are Peter and on this rock I will build my church."

Scottish, Welsh, and northern British church leaders replied to the pope's emissaries what they had learned during the days immediately after Constantine, the Great:

"Local traditions and Scripture do not include Peter among the first bishops in Rome; rather they tell of Linus, Anacletus, and Clement. The earliest allusion to Peter's founding of the church in Rome is in the writings of Dionysius, bishop of Corinth in AD 170,—and this is a quote attributed by Eusebius, 150 years later, and ends thus, 'The churches of Corinth and Rome were founded by Peter and Paul.'"[6]

Thus, the elders implied only what was surely known to the history of the church. Peter made it to Corinth and Paul to Rome, where they were martyred.

The Welsh elders also referred to Holy Writ in the Book of Romans, which is repeated by the Rev. Dr. Gaussen at a later date:

"Behold then, the apostle of the Gentiles, who, twenty years after his conversion, writes to them (the Romans) with greetings addressed to as many as twenty-eight persons living in the midst of them, by their proper names, and many others besides, and who has not a word to send them for the "Prince of the Apostles," as he is called, for the "Vicar of Christ,"—for his superior, -for the bishop of the universal church, -for the founder of the Roman church!!"[7]

They argued that in AD 56, the year that Peter was said to be pope in Rome, and the year that Paul was writing to the Roman Church, Peter would have been the <u>first</u> person that Paul would have recognized in that list of greetings to Roman Christians,—IF he was there.

Of course, this infuriated the Roman priests and further divided the two religious groups. As an aside that we will take a look at in-depth later, William Tyndale once made this quote about that:

"God's Word should rule only; and not bishops decrees, or the pope's pleasure. They have robbed all realms, not of God's Word only but… have set up that great idol, the whore of Babylon, antichrist of Rome, whom they call pope."

And this quote comes from one of the godliest men on earth, at the time, according to history, as we shall see later.

Back to Pope Gregory and his influence on the Western Church. He was the father of the episcopal/sacerdotal system of the Roman Church.

- Gregory made Sacerdotalism a sacrament.

  Sacerdotalism—the Communion ordinance takes effect only through the priest as celebrant. (i.e., No priest of Rome, no effective Communion. And, even the death of a loved one commanded a tithe from the family in order for the Roman priest to properly mediate for the dead to get to heaven.)

- Gregory officially adopted the veneration of Mary and named her "mother of God."

  Once again, Gregory used allegory to make his reasoning. He said that in Luke 1:46, Mary showed that she was "supernaturally endowed to be submissive and obedient to God." Then, with allegorical reading-in to Scripture, since God was the Father and Jesus was the Son, and the Son was one with God and the Son of Mary, then Mary was the mother of God. Gregory said that when Mary stated, "The Mighty One has done great things for me…" that meant that he had lifted her up so that she could be a mediator between God and man.

This "infallible interpretation" of the Pope caused others, then, to venerate her even more (with the enthusiastic encouragement of a Roman Church that needed money during later centuries).

For instance: "In 1439, The Synod of Basel, while there were THREE popes at the same time, issued a decree on the Immaculate Conception, by which Mary was declared to have always been free from original and actual sin. This was 1,400 years after her life and never mentioned by any church fathers for over 400 years before Gregory. But, now, Catholics could pray to her and give an offering to the priest who brought the 'good news' that she would hear the sinful penitent and intercede with Christ."[8]

They said it this way: "Mary is the Mother of God, the queen of the world, the queen of angels, the mother of the eternal emperor."[9] Catholic schoolman, Albertus Magnus, gives no less than forty reasons why she should be worshipped.

In a remarkable passage, Bishop Bernard represents her in the celestial places "drawing attention by her form so that she attracted the king (God) himself to desire her."[10]

This author (McCormack) has a candle, bought for one dollar at our big box store in 2014, which has Mary wearing a crown, holding the baby Jesus and sitting on a golden throne in heaven. The reverse of the candleholder has a prayer in both English and Spanish:

"Oh, most beautiful Flower of Mt. Carmel, fruitful vine, splendor of heaven, Blessed Mother of the Son of God, Immaculate Virgin, assist me in this my necessity. Oh Star of the Sea, help me and show me herein that you are my Mother. O holy Mary, Mother of God, Queen of Heaven and earth, I humbly beseech you from the bottom of my heart, to succor me in this my necessity. There are none that can withstand your power. Oh show me herein that you are my mother."

We are of the opinion that Mary would roll over in her grave should she hear the gross hyperbole, and, indeed, heresy of these biblically ignorant candle-makers. Jesus said he was the vine and we (Christians) are the branches. The titles of Flower of Mt. Carmel, Immaculate Virgin, Star of the Sea, and Queen of Heaven are all of Roman Church invention to boost her divinity of which the Bible never speaks!

Mary, Queen of Heaven pictorial

ᑉ Gregory instituted the prayers to saints for needs of the penitent.

Of course, for over a thousand years, the Roman Church has insisted that saints could intercede for sinners. They must be "certified" by the church hierarchy as really hitting the high mark of being a saint within the kingdom of Christ on earth, and one had to pay money to access this saint through the priest of the church. This was a great boon to the coffers of the church. And still is today!

The Welsh and Scottish church fathers said that the pivotal question for true church members was, "Are you a sinner trying to act like a saint or a saint of God who occasionally sins?" They answered that the second claim is the biblical claim and that the first, "sinners trying to act as saints" was not possible through works or prayers. They claimed that all Christians were saints, so there was no need for intercession by someone who was, while on earth, a sinner trying to act like a saint and work their way to heaven through the "kingdom of God on earth" in Rome.

Rome said that Christians must serve God to gain his acceptance. The descendants of the Cymric Celts said that Christians are accepted, and so serve God. Rome said that we follow him through the rituals to be loved. The Celtic Fathers said that his people are loved, so they follow. That it is not what we do that determines who we are; it is who we are that determines what we do. In modern theological terms, this means that we, Christians, have positional sanctification through Christ and are striving toward glorification through the process of progressive sanctification. The Roman Church not only left out positional sanctification, but made progressive sanctification come through Rome and via the pontiff, church saints, angels, and bishops. There is nothing in Scripture to base these heresies on.

Let's look closer at what Gregory, the lawyer and subsequent pope, declared.

- Gregory instituted "tradition" of the decrees of the papacy equal with Scripture as holy.

   We have already written of this within this book, but it is worth noting again that many of the traditional writings of the popes and bishops were steeped in allegorical interpretation, whereby an idea that is of God is "hidden" in the text of Holy Scripture and only the pope and other holy men are able to bring out the hidden meaning for the poor masses.

- Though it was practiced in Rome before his rule, Gregory officially instituted the concept of "purgatory" into the entire church and the paying of indulgences in order to exit purgatory.

   All of "scripture" that the pope required for this sacramental injunction was one obscure verse in an apocryphal book and the subsequent interpretive writing, in order to create a fantastic boon to the church treasury and to cement the "sheeple" to the Roman Church.

   Here's that reference: In 2 Maccabees 12:42–45, Judas Maccabeus is said to have taken up a collection to send to

Jerusalem, wherein, "He made atonement for the dead…" This is the only verse that the Roman Church calls on to justify the idea of purgatory, and it is not even in the canon of inspired Scripture! The passage is in the time period of the "silent or hidden" years that even St. Jerome said that God did not officially speak to the Jews. This is why he called these history books "The Apocrypha." That did not stop the church from invoking it.

Someone once asked, after Gregory's time, if Mary had to go to purgatory. This was a problem for the church, so the hierarchy had to cover one lie with another and "interpret" that Mary was "*theotokos,*" a part of the Trinity, and was borne straight to heaven by angels. See how this works? The pope can make <u>anything</u> justified.

Should the city of Rome be threatened by hostile forces, the pope could grant thousands of years off of the sentence in purgatory if the faithful would fight the foe. If another cathedral needed to be built, the pope could pronounce anathemas on an entire village or region and confiscate their property and possessions. If someone, even another bishop, threatened to expose the lies, he was pronounced a heretic and excommunicated or burned at the stake, and, of course, the property and assets were immediately forfeited to the pope. It was a sweet system, if you were part of the Imperial Church hierarchy.

Flash-forward About Mary

In 1962, Pope Paul VI made his closing speech at the close of Vatican II wherein he proclaimed Mary as Mother of the Church, the Mediatrix. The Roman Church is quasi-ruled by a woman who is "made-up" to be part of God because of her work of birthing Jesus. And, to this day, she is worshipped by the Roman Church masses.

It was through Gregory that ritual became dominant in the church. He introduced Gregorian chants by the monks. He stressed miracles and stories of angelic agents that stretched the limits of reason. The eminent church historian, Justo Gonzalez, summarizes Gregory's effect on the church of that day and the episcopal politics that controlled it:

"Gregory is an indication of the manner in which, in the midst of a period of political and intellectual decline, Augustine's theology was accommodated to popular faith in two main ways: by mitigating the most extreme (pure) aspects of the doctrines of grace and predestination, and by making room for superstitious beliefs and practices."[11]

As a natural progression of the unholy elevation of Mary to God status, the Catholic Church had to eventually also make her a perpetual virgin. Once again, a lie to cover a lie. And, the Gospel reading had to be stiffled and changed in new Latin Vulgate Roman Bibles. Again, British historian and author Adrian Gilbert helps us to understand:

"The Church, in promulgating the doctrine that Mary was ever-virgin had to draw a veil over Jesus' kindred by pretending that the word '*brother*' is being used in a wider sense to mean friends. This is simply not true. The Greek word used in the original Gospel of Matthew is '*adelphoi,*' which means 'brothers.' The Greek for 'friends' is '*philoi*' and surely this is the word the Gospel writer would have used if that is what he meant."[12]

The Imperial Church and State Collude for Evil

Perhaps the greatest ignoble act of all was Gregory's institution of giving a license for committing sins, called an indulgence. Indulgences were written permission papers that were the Roman Church's version of a "get out of jail free card." In the Dark Ages, the church was in collusion with the state, so that the state could not override the church if it said someone committed a crime. If that person possessed a paper indulgence signed by a valid churchman, they got off scot-free.

Indulgences were regularly given for forgiveness of ALL crimes against others. The church even had lists with prices for the priests to collect for sins. One of these was actually printed as such:

Robbery	$3.00
Burning a house	$2.75
Killing a layman	$1.75
Procuring abortion	$1.50
Ravishing a virgin	$2.00
Priest keeping a concubine	$2.25
Murder of father, mother, brother, sister, or wife	$2.50
Striking a priest	$2.75
Nun, for fornication	$5.00
Adultery by a priest	$10.00
Simony	$2.25
All crimes together	$12.00 [13]

Boy, it was great to be a good Catholic during the Dark Ages! Even today, if you have a candle…

Of course the idea of indulgences was based on a verse of Scripture. The pope said that Luke 13:5 read, "I tell you no! But unless you repent, you too will all perish," and, Luke 17:3 read, "If your brother sins, rebuke him and if he repents, forgive him."

Indeed these verses are correct for Jesus' words. However, Pope Gregory (who could not read or write Greek) conveniently interpreted the word *repent* in both of these verses to mean "penance."

But this was a gross and purposeful error. The word repent in Greek that is found in all of the first- and second-century manuscripts is the word *metanoia*, which is "repentance" fifty-eight times in the New Testament: repentance: *meta*=after; *noeo*=to think. Put the two together and the effect of metanoia was "after the fact" or "afterwards to think." In essence it meant to think about something later on and have a reversal of opinion about it.

In the pope-revised Latin Vulgate, '*metanoia*' was MIStranslated as *paenitentia* which came to mean penance or acts of penance that had to be done if one hoped to obtain grace.

The "System" Complete goes like this:

Penance was in three steps:

1. Contrition of the heart,

2. Auricular confession to a Roman-authorized priest,

3. Satisfaction—alms, fasts, pilgrimages, and fines (indulgences, determined by Rome).

Of course, penance only protected one while in this temporal state. If one was to be protected in the hereafter, there was always the money that could be paid to get out of purgatory also. This was a complete cycle of a system. From the cradle past the grave, one had to pay money and agree with the Roman Church in order to live in the present and go to heaven. Getting out of purgatory (hell's waiting room), after death, had its own price and systematic requirements.

The priests had their own sayings about these practices:

"When the coin hits the bottom of the offering plate, the sin is forgiven."

"As soon as money in the coffer rings, the soul from purgatory's fire springs."

During the Reformation, British and German rebellious priests William Tyndale and Martin Luther challenged this practice with these words:

Martin Luther—"*Metanoia* signifies a changing of the mind and heart, because it seemed to indicate not only a change of heart, but also a manner of changing it, i.e., the grace of God. For that 'passing over of the mind,' which is true repentance, is of very frequent mention in the Scriptures."

Tyndale—"*Penance* is a word of their [the papists] own forging, to deceive us withal, as many others are. Of repentance they have made penance, to blind the people, and to make them think that they must take pains, and do some holy deeds, to make satisfaction for their sins."

<u>Penance was found to be a non-scriptural, bald-faced lie—if one could possess the Greek Scriptures and could read Greek!</u>

<u>The pope's solution was perfectly simple: no person in the Holy Roman Empire was allowed to see or read Greek, only to do what the priest told them to do; under penalty of temporal and eternal doom. Church-endorsed slavery became *fait acompli*.</u>

As an aside, early in the sixteenth century, in Europe, Bishop Tetzel, the special envoy to Popes Julius and Leo, extracted enormous sums of money from the parishes for the construction of St. Peter's Basilica by granting pardon for penances in purgatory.

This same duo, Julius and the new Leo, declared Holy War on Jews to justify the mass slaughter of the race in order to steal their possessions to finance the building of the Vatican.

Leo is quoted as saying, *"How profitable the fable of Christ has been to us."*

By the year AD 1300, the papal system and its minions dominated Europe.

- ཟ It was illegal and punishable to own or read the Scriptures in any form without permission.

- ཟ Simony, the sale of positions in the church hierarchy, had become the rule, starting with the pope.

- ཟ The "Annates" or "First Fruits" (The first year of income in office was to be remitted to the pope in Rome. The bigger you wanted your salary later, the bigger the Annates.)

- ཟ Indulgences were rampant in all parts of the Romish dominion. (In order to pay the papacy)

The popes also instituted:

- "Reservations"—any ruler who wanted credibility from Rome (and not to be excommunicated) was to reserve the richest parts of his country for the use of the pope and the cardinals.
- "Expectancies"—the pope was allowed first right to sell the successorship to the highest bidder if a ruler or bishop died.
- "Commendations"—indefinite, provisional appointments on condition of payment of an annual tax (to be named by the pope).
- "Vuspoliorum"—the pope was the rightful heir to all church property acquired in perpetuity.
- "Tithing"—all church property and goods could be taxed up to 20 percent immediately for urgent wants of the papacy.[14]

For the masses of those who would follow Christ during this time, the papacy was a systemic slavery, even for those who were in the episcopate like priests and friars. It was "trickle-down economics" in Medieval times; and precious little good trickled down to the people of the church.

More Problems Arise for the Religious Mafia and Its System

During the 1200s, more separatist groups gathered in reaction to the popes and their systematic ruination of the church of Jesus Christ. They said that: in the Eucharist, the bread and wine did not change into the body and blood of Christ.

"Since the elements appeared not to change into anything but what they were, the pope ruled that the people would not actually take the bread and wine except once a year at Easter. All other times, only the consecrated priest would partake and then hold up the elements; certifying that they had indeed, in his (the priest's) holy observance, changed."[15]

Even Augustine, whom the Roman Church venerates, interpreted the Eucharist as an outward symbol of bread and wine that possessed a spiritual meaning. He said that the Lord's Table was a non-meritorious, spiritually real experience of receiving the gift of life. Per Augustine, "Jesus answered and said to them, 'This is the work of God, that you believe on him whom he has sent.' This is for them to eat the meat, not that which perishes, but that which endures unto eternal life. To what purpose to you make ready teeth and stomach? Believe, and you have eaten already."[16]

To console doubters in the Roman Church, the pope created and sanctioned the Festival of Corpus Christi (the body of Christ). To wit, after the church service, the "certified" body was put into an ornate box and paraded about the town.

"The festival then moved into the streets. A procession of clergy, town officials, members of guilds and confraternities (lay religious societies), and others followed the consecrated host. Believers knelt as the host, to them the body of the Lord of the universe, passed."[17]

Of course, the town officials, guild members, and confraternities were all paid to do this either by indulgences, relief from tithing, expectancies, or other remunerations.

Soon, statues of Mary were added to the procession, and the people began to kneel to "the box" AND Mary, the mother of God.

And, of course, new gifts could be raked in by allowing the people to pray to the Mother of God to get their prayers answered. Later, especially in the new world, saints of the church were also given their own festivals in order to raise even more funds for the building of the "church" and to get out of purgatory.

But the rustic rebels at the end of the earth continued to resist the "mother church." In the year 1302 the pope had had it with doubters and troublemakers. He came out with a new decree:

Unum Sanctum Bull (decree), November, 1302:

"We declare, define, and affirm that every man must obey the pope or forfeit his salvation." –The Roman Catholic Church

- Successive popes also decreed that the Bible was only to be written in Latin (the language of the popes and bishops).
- Only the priesthood could own a copy. (Even most local priests and friars were denied, lest they yield and give some Scripture to their congregants.)
- Anyone else would be prosecuted at all costs. (The Bible must not get into the hands of the "sheeple.")
- "We therefore decree and ordain, that from henceforth no unauthorized person shall translate any part of the Holy Scripture into English or any other language under any form of book or treatise."

—The Pope, 1408

All of these decrees should have settled things once and for all. Except for those pesky Scots and those annoying Brits and Welsh from their "rustic" island! They maintained that God requires nothing. He creates, elects, and sanctifies without need. We approach him with nothing to give and he gives to us out of Love.

In order to get an appreciation for the times, we must go back to where Pope Gregory was writing decrees of tradition and his emissaries were trying to get Britain to accept Rome as the "religious boss" and see what was happening in the British Isles. The set-up was being completed for an immovable object—the rustic, British Church—to be met with an irresistible force—the Roman Catholic Church. (And all the money, taken from their sheeple, that could buy-off kings and commoners alike.)

Meanwhile, Back in Briton and Its Isles AD 600–650

The sons of Æthelfrith (pagan king of the Anglo-Britons) were converted to Christianity, and raised as Christians. In Oswy's case, he became an exile at the age of four, and cannot have returned to Northumbria until age twenty-one, spending childhood and adolescence in a Gaelic milieu. Bede writes that "Oswy was fluent in the Old Irish Language and Irish in his faith.

"Oswy thought that nothing could be better than the Irish teaching, having been instructed and baptized by the Irish, and having a complete grasp of their language."[18]

However, with the help of an enormous bribe, at the Synod of Whitby in AD 664, Oswy gave in to Romanism and his kingdom became Roman, —again. Wales, northwestern England and Scotland remained as the only bastions of Celtic Christianity.

One place that it is noted that the early Gospel writings were held was in Streonaeshalch, now called Whitby Abbey. They were there during the late AD 500s. This also mitigates the Roman Church's historical view that Christianity was brought to the island in AD 597.

Streonaeshalch (Whitby Abbey), double abbey built in AD 500s

Bede gives no specific date in his history; however, Cædmon is said to have taken holy orders at an advanced age, and it is implied that he lived at Streonæshalch at least in part during Hilda's abbacy (AD 657–680).[19]

As we mentioned before, at the Synod of Whitby in AD 664, Oswy gave in to Romanism and his kingdom became Roman-lite. Iona, the Welsh uplands and Scotland remained as the only bastions of Celtic Christianity. This was the turning point of the spread of Roman Christianity into the south of England. King Oswy summoned the Romans of Canterbury to a synod at Whitby, where (verbal) battle was joined between Colman of Northumbria and Wilfrid of Ripon. Wilfrid, who had visited Rome and strongly supported its cause, represented Canterbury because he spoke Anglo-Saxon. To him, the authority of the pope, and the expansive Roman liturgy outshone the backwardness (rustic-ness) of the Celts. He swayed the synod and, more important, Oswy, as he preached with great gusto that St. Peter was "the rock of the church" and holder of the keys to life hereafter.

The "purely objective" Wilfrid became bishop of York. Rome quickly began to exploit its triumph. He was one of the first Britons to begin killing the Bible in England. Any holy books but Latin documents were seized and destroyed or sent to Rome under guard.

"The kings of Kent and Wessex were encouraged to write new legal codes based on those throughout the papal domains, exempting the church from civil duties and laying down the new Roman Catholic rules for social and marital conduct."[20]

Celtic Documents that Survived the First British Purge of the Imperial Church

The Book of Kells is the reflection of the theology of the great Bible College at Iona, tracing its heritage back to disciples who were followers of Jesus under the teaching of the apostle Simon Zelotes and Joseph of Arimathea. After Simon was martyred, British history has it that Joseph brought the writings of early Christendom to the British Isles. Including, perhaps, a copy of the Gospel of Matthew in Hebrew.

The Book of Kells, (cover) Trinity College Library, Dublin

Some scholars suggest the Iona Island monastery, founded by St. Columba, was the birthplace of the Book of Kells. It is thought to have been the work of several individual scribes over many years, likely before AD 806. The manuscript was held at Kells until 1661 when it was moved to Dublin where it remains as the chief treasure of Trinity College Library.

The Book of Kells is a copy of the four Gospels in Latin. It is known for the extraordinary array of pictures, and interlaced shapes. It is these details which give us picture-story communication from the Greek with the insight of the Hebrew mind-set that the monks—Hebrew, Greek, and Latin scholars—knew so well and, then, schooled the illustrators as they employed their craft.

At the time the manuscript was produced, Celtic monks were renowned throughout the rest of Europe for their work as scribes and illustrators.

The Book of Kells contains 680 pages (or 340 folios). Only two of the pages are not illustrated, while about thirty folios, including some major decorated pages, have been lost. The Book of Kells is the most famous manuscript in the Library of Trinity College, Dublin, where it is permanently on display.

"The Work Not of Men but of Angels…"

Giraldus Cambrensis, c.AD 1150

The Chi Rho page is probably the best known of all the pages of Kells. It gets it name from the shortened Greek form of the name of Christ—XPI —and introduces St Matthew's account of the nativity. The three letters form the main image and just two words appear on the page—*autem* meaning "now," and *generatio* meaning "the birth."

Tiny drops of a pure red lead were used to form backgrounds, outlines, and patterns, a style of ornament common in early Celtic manuscripts. The Book of Kells eventually became a primary source for the development of the English language. Modern scholarship has undeniably discovered that English gets its alphabet from the evolution of ancient Hebrew with Greek symbols and "voice" connectors.

Most of the world was without a picture language for over 1200 years. The Roman Church did not allow the original picture language, Hebrew, to be studied. Nor did it allow Greek to be read, except by its hierarchy under strict control. The story of English and our English Bible is one of the great battles that Satan waged to try and destroy us. The English language brings back the pictures of Hebrew and connects with the middle voice of Greek. English was literally constructed in its infancy as a modern language by Christians who combined Hebrew picture language and the best of Greek precision and "voice" to design the most perfect picture language for the world to adopt as the *lingua Franca* for the next 700 years—English.

The Book of Kells, (leaf) Trinity College Library, Dublin

None other than one of the greatest linguists and Greek scholars of all time, Westcott, speaking of Tyndale, observed:

"William Tyndale felt, by a happy instinct, the potential affinity between Hebrew and English idioms, and he enriched our language and thought forever with the characteristics of the Semitic mind."

Here's the Point

While the papists tried to cut off the Bible from the people, the Celtic Christian clergy made "picture-Bibles" that told the stories so that average people could understand Jesus' teachings directly from Scripture.

Book of Kells introduction page to the Gospel of John

The Book of Durrow (Dublin, Trinity College Library, MS A. 4. 5. (57)) is a seventh-century illuminated manuscript Gospel book. It was probably created between 650 and 700, in either Durrow or Northumbria in northern England, or on the Island of Iona in the Scottish Inner Hebrides.

And So, the Contrast Becomes Manifest

The first page of the Gospel of Mark from the *Book of Durrow*, England. Now in Dublin Trinity College Library

So, to summarize: southern England and Ireland were subjugated in the AD 600s and 700s to the pope in Rome, but the northern Irish, Welsh, Scots and northern Brits stubbornly held to their ancient Latin and Greek texts, making picture book Bibles and staying true to the apostolic-given faith. During this time period, the venerable Bede and his fellow clergy were writing about the Church in the Isles on the edge of the world and against the actions of the priests of the Imperial State Church.

The Church and the Bible in England and France of The Middle Ages

The "Venerable Bede" AD 673–735

Bede is well known as a British author and scholar, and his most famous work, Historia Ecclesiastica Gentis Anglorum (The Ecclesiastical History of the English People) gained him the title "The Father of English History."

His teacher was the nobleman turned monk, Benedict Biscop, who went to Rome and the Holy Land five times. Each time, he brought back Greek and Latin texts for the library of the monastery of St. Paul in Wearmouth, where he and Bede lived. In the winter of 735 he translated into Old English the Gospel of John and other favorite Scriptures from Psalms, etc.[21]

Bede wrote expository notes and commentaries on most of the Bible. He frequently made notes wherein he corrected the Latin Vulgate from the copies of the original Greek and from Old Latin. In his sixteen epistles, he writes of many transgressions of the Catholic clergy that was imported from Rome.

"There is great avarice in the bishops and disorder in the religious houses….

"If I had treated the drunkenness, gluttony, luxury, and other contagious diseases of the body politic my letter would be immoderately long."

Letter addressed to the Archbishop of York in AD 734.[22]

Bede also records that there was a great schism between the English old church traditionalists and the new Roman rulers of Kent County sent by Pope Gregory. The Synod of Whitby in AD 664 said that the Gregorian Calendar should be observed for the day and date of Easter. This changed the traditional observance of the Britons that had stood for hundreds of years. King Oswy, (bought by the Romans) decided that:

"The Roman method will be favored over the Celtic because Peter was the guardian of the gates of heaven and Columba (a Briton and traditional church leader) was not."[23]

Bede's Greatest Effort

Because most converts were illiterate, the images of the Celtic Church were hugely significant for their understanding of what was taught. Bede, the eighth-century Northumbrian monk, writes that religious imagery was for the "intent that all who entered the church, even if ignorant of letters, might be able to contemplate…the ever-gracious countenance of Christ and his saints." The decoration of the text itself portrayed for the illiterate converts the mysticism and glory of the literal "Word of God."

In the decade of the 670s, because so many of the British Church were reading the Bible in Greek, Pope Vitalian sent a scholar of Greek, Theodore, to England. The pope had found Theodore to be disruptive in Rome because he knew and read the Bible from the Greek. Almost as soon as Theodore landed in the Island, the pope sent a North African priest and Greek scholar Hadrian to Briton, to spy on Theodore. These two set up shop in Canterbury with Theodore as Archbishop and Hadrian as rector of St. Augustine Abbey.

These two maintained an outward loyalty to Italy, but boosted the "precocious belief among the English in their special destiny among their neighbours, both in the same islands and among the people of Europe. Thanks to Bede and to the leadership of Archbishop Theodore, they could see themselves as a covenanted people like ancient Israel, a beacon for the Christian world."

"Saxon and Celtic Christians between them made the Atlantic isles in the seventh and eighth centuries a prodigious powerhouse of Christian activity. Their energies flowed together in the islands themselves, in the founding of a network of new churches and monasteries, but they also followed the sea routes which Columbanus had pioneered into mainland Europe, conscious that they had received Christianity by mission and were determined to do the same for others."[24]

The New Testament of the Britons and Hibernia

The Durham Gospels (late seventh-century), were kept in the Durham Cathedral library.

The book was produced at Lindisfarne and brought to Durham when the monks of Lindisfarne removed to Durham because of Viking attacks. The Durham Gospels were written by the same scribe that wrote the Echternach Gospels.

Durham Gospels, Introduction page to the Gospel of John

Echternach Gospels, Introduction page to the Gospel of Mark, the Lion, being the symbol of the Gospel. (*Bibliothèque Nationale, lat. 9389, fol. 75v)

The Echternach Gospels were taken by the English Saxon Priest Willibrord to Luxembourg when he founded the Echternach monastery in the year 698. Willibrord, like many early medieval missionaries, traveled throughout Europe and used manuscripts to convert locals to Christianity. The Echternach Gospels are an example of many illuminated manuscripts that served as teaching tools as well as liturgical books. It is argued that the brilliant colors and stories-in-design of Hiberno-Saxon manuscripts, in particular, captured the core of Christianity for non-Christians.

The Anglo-Saxon Invasions

There is insufficient time in this treatise to do justice to the subject of the Viking invasions of the British Isles. Suffice it to say that most of them were raiding bands of cutthroats from Norway and from Denmark. For over 150 years, they harassed the coastlines and slaughtered the citizens there in order to take their possessions and children as slaves back to the semi-desolate regions of their homes.

But, God has his way in all things and, ironically, as some of the warring tribes of Vikings began to settle England and Ireland, their children began to be converted to Christianity. Within a century of their settling, the Saxons began to defend their Britain against attacks and fought with the original islanders against their cousins, the continuously raiding, barbaric Vikings.

Why the English Will Not Eat a Danish…

In the eighth century, the Danish Vikings, a roving onslaught of barbarians, landed in different parts of Britain, both in England and Scotland. After raiding the isles off of Scotland and rounding England, the sailing buccaneers moved to the coasts of Wales. "Yet the records of the raids are scarce and there is no coherent history of Viking Wales, the reason being that this is the Celtic country that most successfully withstood the attack of the Northmen in the early colonizing period, yielding less to them than did Scotland or Ireland, and showing to the invader a fiercer and a firmer front. Thus upon the first appearance of the Vikings in AD 795, when after ravages in England they came to Glamorganshire to lay that country waste with fire and sword, manfully rose the Cymry against them, routed them in battle, and, driving them back to the sea with heavy loss, saw them sail off to Ireland in search of an easier prey.

"That the foreigners made no permanent settlements of historical impact in the south at this period when the Irish colonies were founded must be due to the stalwart Cymry."[25]

In England, there was indeed easier prey. At first the Danes were repulsed, but in AD 857, a party of them landed somewhere near Southampton, and not only robbed the people but burned down the churches, and murdered the clergy of the official church.

Danish Warrior

In AD 868, these barbarians penetrated into the center of England, and took up their quarters at Nottingham; but the English, under their king, Ethelred, drove them from their posts, and obligated them to retire to Northumberland.

"In 870, another body of these barbarians landed at Norfolk and engaged in battle with the English at Hertford. Victory declared in favor of the pagans, who took Edmund, king of the East Angles, prisoner, and after treating him with a thousand indignities, transfixed his body with arrows, and then beheaded him.

"In Fifeshire, Scotland, they burned many of the churches, and, among them, that belonging to the Culdees, at St. Andrews. The piety of these men made them objects of abhorrence to the Danes, who, wherever they went singled out the Christian priests for destruction, of whom no less than two hundred were massacred in Scotland."[26] Through the ninth, tenth, and eleventh centuries, the Saxons made and broke numerous treaties with the popes for the land of the Britons.

However, many of the Saxons, including kings, were converted to Christianity by the Culdees, the Welsh, and the Scottish priests. This, to the point that Christianity became the state religion even far to the east in Norway by the eleventh-century. God will not be mocked. And, by this, he protected the flank of his chosen people in the Isles of Britain.

In the twelfth and thirteenth centuries, the "kirk" (church) of Jesus Christ grew within an Anglo-Saxon culture, - and the Bible, in the form of copies of the Codex Gigas, the Book of Kells, and copies of Paul's letters, was their influence.

During these tumultuous centuries, a king arrived to bring unity and peace. He is singled out because of his Christian rule, his resuscitation of the English Scriptures, and his routing out of those who would kill the Bible. We will see this explicitly in chapter six.

Sources

1. H. E. Eusebius, *Light from the Dark Ages* (Edman), Chapter 6.
2. Adrian Gilbert, *The Holy Kingdom*, (Bantam Press, 1998), 65.
3. Hengwrt MSS, Humphry Llwyd, Sebright MSS, Cottonian Library, British Museum.
4. Henry Marsh, *Dark Age Britain*, (Dorset Press, 1970), 115-116.
5. G.N.H. Peters, *The Theocratic Kingdom of Jesus, The Christ* (Kregel, 1952), 352, (bold mine).
6. H.E. Eusebius, ii 25 8, *Light in the Dark Ages* (Edman).
7. Gaussen, *The Plenary Inspiration of the Holy Scriptures*, 320, BICA, (underline mine).
8. Philip Schaff, *History of the Christian Church*, VI, 173.
9. Albertus Magnus, *Writings, Catholic schoolman*.
10. Philip Schaff, *History of the Christian Church*, V, 832-833 / Migne 145, 188, 62, 566.
11. Justo L Gonzalez, *A History of Christian Thought*, vol. 2 Abington Press, 1971), 72.
12. Adrian Gilbert, *The Holy Kingdom*, (Bantam Press, 1998), 303.
13. Craig Lampe, *The Forbidden Book*, 29, used with permission.
14. Schaff, *History of the Christian Church*, vol. V, pp. 786–789, 797.
15. Philip Schaff, *History of the Christian Church*, vol. V, p. 724.
16. Augustine, Commentary on John 25:12.
17. Joseph Lynch, *The Medieval Church: A Brief History*, Longman.
18. Bede, *Ecclesiastical History*, Book III, Chapter 5.
19. Book IV Chapter 25 of the *Historia Ecclesiastica*.
20. Simon Jenkins, *A Short History of England*, Profile Books, 2011, 23–24.
21. *Bede's Expository Works*, Tom. XCIII, Browne, l.c., 172–179.
22. Philip Schaff, *History of the Christian Church*, vol. 4, 675.
23. S. Their, *Patristische Texte and Studies*, 322.
24. Diarmaid MacCollough, *Christianity, The First Three Thousand Years*, (Penguin, 2009), 341, (bold mine).
25. Thomas Dowling, *A History of the Vikings* (1930, Fall River Press, 2013), 286.
26. *Foxe's Book of Martyrs*

Images

Mary, Queen of Heaven pictorial IMG_1730.JPG Morguefile.com

Danish Warrior © Krisgun01 | Dreamstime.com

Photos – Dreamstime.com

CHAPTER SIX

Standing in the Gap

Alfred the Great

Ælfrēd, Ælfræd, ("elf counsel") was king of Wessex from AD 871 to 899.

Alfred successfully defended his kingdom against the Viking attempt at conquest, and by the time of his death had become the dominant ruler in England. He is the only English monarch to be accorded the epithet "the Great." Details of Alfred's life are described in a work by the tenth-century Welsh scholar and bishop, Asser. A few details: Alfred fortified England, built a navy to take the battle to the Norsemen, and cleaned-up the cities with organized efforts.

Once he had defeated the Vikings, Alfred proposed that primary education for all children be taught in English, with those wishing to advance to holy orders continuing their studies in Latin. A problem, however, was that there were few "books of wisdom" written in English. Alfred sought to remedy this through an ambitious court-centered program of translating into English the books he deemed "most necessary for all men to know." It is unknown when Alfred launched this program, but it may have been during the 880s when Wessex was enjoying a respite from Viking attacks.

The earliest work to be translated was the *Dialogues of Gregory the Great*, a book popular in the Middle Ages. Remarkably, Alfred, undoubtedly with the advice and aid of his court scholars, translated into English eight works himself:

- Gregory the Great's *Pastoral Care*,
- Boethius's *Consolation of Philosophy*, (Originally written in AD 524),
- St Augustine's *Soliloquies*, the first fifty psalms of the Psalter,
- Excerpts from the Vulgate Book of Exodus,
- Orosius' *Histories against the Pagans*,
- Bede's *Ecclesiastical History of the English People* and
- Old English Martyrology.

King Alfred in a cathedral window holding a book

King Alfred during apex of his reign

Alfred's first personal translation was of Pope Gregory the Great's *Pastoral Rule*, which he gave the new title *Pastoral Care*. He prefaced it with an introduction explaining why he thought it necessary to translate works such as this one from Latin into English.

"Although he described his method as translating 'sometimes word for word, sometimes sense for sense,' Alfred's translation actually kept very close to Gregory's original, although through his choice of language he blurred throughout the distinction between spiritual and secular authority. Alfred meant his translation to be used by the British people and circulated it to all his bishops for reading in the churches."[1]

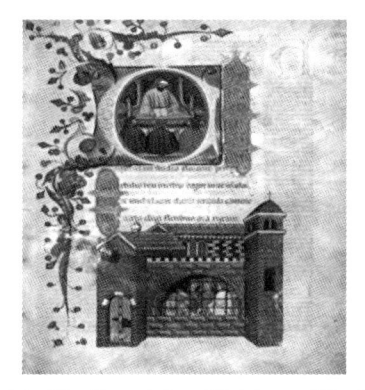

From a 1385 Italian manuscript of the Consolation: Miniatures of Boethius Teaching and in Prison. Reflects on how evil can exist in a world governed by God (the problem of theodicy), and how happiness can be attainable amidst fickle fortune, while also considering the nature of happiness and God.

King Alfred the Great pictured in a stained-glass window in the west window of the south transept of Bristol Cathedral. Notice the "Anglia" (English) scroll in his left hand, the free reading of which was enforced by the sword in his right.

Alfred, the Great

Here is Alfred, the Great in a Winchester cathedral window. He is shown to be the father of English education.

More History of English Men of "The Word"

Carolingian Manuscript, c. 831,
Alcuin (middle), dedicating his work to Archbishop Otgar of Mainz (right).
Born c. 735 York, Northumbria, Briton

At the invitation of King Charlemagne, Alcuin, a Brit, became a leading scholar and teacher at the Carolingian court, France, where he remained a figure in the 780s and 790s. He wrote many theological and dogmatic treatises, as well as a few grammatical works and a number of poems. He was made abbot of Tours in AD 796, where he remained until his death. History records that he was, "the most learned man anywhere to be found," according to Einhard's, Life of Charlemagne.

"Alcuin revised the Latin Vulgate in the year AD 802, by order of King Charlemagne, using old and correct manuscripts brought from the Holy Land. Charlemagne preserved a 'good Latin text' for some time until, at his death, the Italian pope forbade its circulation. Alcuin was zealous for the revival of preaching and for study of the Bible. On the other hand, he placed a low estimate upon religious pilgrimages and wrote that he preferred the money so spent should be given to the poor. He wrote many religious works, including *The Life of St. Willibrord, Bishop of Utrecht*, his own ancestor."[2]

A page from the Vetus Latina, the Old Latin, before Jerome translated the Vulgate Bible.

Probably the most well-known difference between the Old Latin and the Vulgate (Jerome's version sponsored by the pope) is in the *Pater Noster*, where the phrase from the *Vetus Latina, quotidianum panem*, "daily bread," becomes *supersubstantialem panem*, "supersubstantial bread," in the Vulgate. This was a purposeful mis-translation in order to keep and promote traditions of the Roman Church, which were used to manipulate the people.

Meanwhile, the Holy Spirit was not resting in the area of the "utmost part of the world" called Scandinavia.

Codex Gigas

The Codex Gigas from the thirteenth century is held at the Royal Library in Sweden.

About half of the codex consists of the entire Latin Bible in the Vulgate version, except for the books of Acts and Revelation, which are from the Old Latin, proving that Old Latin had once held primacy, but Rome had re-translated it badly for their own purposes.

Between the Testaments in the codex are Josephus' *Antiquities of the Jews and the Jewish Wars*, as well as Isidore of Seville's encyclopedia *Etymologiae* and medical works of Hippocrates, Theophilus, Philaretus, and Constantinus (in Greek). Following a blank page, the New Testament commences with Matthew–Acts, James–Revelation, and Romans–Hebrews. In addition, it contains Hebrew, Greek, and Slavic alphabets. This proves that there were Christian scholars in northern European areas that were interested in promulgating the truth of the Holy Scriptures and their true history, while the Imperial Church was trying to kill the Bible. However, as always, there were evil forces ready, willing, and able to wreck havoc.

THE VIKINGS AND THE POPES MAKE A PACT

The middle of the tenth century saw the pagan Vikings of Denmark and Norway marauding south into Francia (France and Holland) under the leadership of the Viking slaughterer Rollo. They sailed the Seine as far as Paris and laid siege to the city. The Parisians appealed to the pope and to Emperor Charles the Simple, who was in league with him, i.e., church and state. Aid was sent, but the stalemate and treaty produced the effect of the pope and emperor giving Normandy to the Vikings.

By the year 1066, Viking king, William the Conqueror, was strong enough to sail north and conquer the easier prey of England. He knew that the powerful and religious of Europe would let him take the British Isles as long as he left them alone. William was no Frenchman but the descendant of the Norse warrior Rollo. Pope Alexander the Second gave his blessing to the Vikings of Normandy as they sailed the channel. The Battle of Hastings was lost by the British in the autumn of the year, and William was crowned King of England in Westminster Abbey on Christmas day, 1066.

William returned immediately to Normandy leaving his brother-in-law, Odo, to run England. Odo was proclaimed bishop and king by the pope and ruled with an iron hand. The result? Four thousand Saxons lost their land to 200 Norman barons, bishops, and abbots. Two hundred thousand Viking Normans were imported to take over the land while about the same number of English died of slaughter and starvation, about a fifth of the population.

After William's death in AD 1086, his equally bloody son Henry I, began his reign. Through much intrigue and bloodshed in both France and England, Henry and his son, Henry II, strengthened their stranglehold on Britain. The pope's Roman Church was now more powerful in Normandy and England than in any place in Europe. It employed an estimated one in six of the population.

Subsequently, the sons of Henry II, Richard the Lionhearted and John, squabbled over the kingdom. Richard was the eldest and, yet, cared only for campaigning in the Crusades of the pope for booty in the Holy Land. He once said, "I would sell London if I could find a buyer." He spoke not a word of English and only spent a total of two years in the country during his lifetime. (So much for the Hollywood fairytale of Richard the Lionhearted.) Brother John was, by all accounts, as ruthless to the English as the Robin Hood narratives divulge. He was a Viking/French sobriquet. However, God would still not be mocked. John was weak and selfish. He lost the support of the barons and the bishops of England. In the year 1215, the barons insisted on some "rights" and drew up the first list of such, called the Magna Carta, which stated that every person would obtain justice. Harking back to the days of Alfred, the Great, they swore before heaven that the fear of God and eternal judgment is the foundation of every man's rights and no king or hierarchy could breach any clause of the charter. John signed it in the presence of the barons. He swore an oath before God that he would honor it. The barons went home satisfied. The ink was barely dry when John wrote the pope asking him to annul it. In September, Pope Innocent obliged and condemned it in the name of God. (Anything to keep Richard fighting in the Crusades and to keep John quiet.)

In a few years, John and the pope were so hated that John was hunted down and poisoned. A contemporary writer, Matthew Paris, wrote that, "Foul as it is, hell itself is defiled by the foulness of King John."[3] The next Viking-become-Britain to be crowned was Henry III. He was dedicated to the papacy because the bishops clustered around the young king and gave him power to crush the people and damn their souls, if he was not obeyed. He remarked that, "At a time when we were orphaned and a minor, it was our mother, the Roman Church which placed us on our throne." He impoverished the people of England and gave a fifth of the revenues of the English Church to the pope. With most of the remaining revenues he bribed the bishops and the barons of Norman descent and engaged in frivolities. (He gave London its first zoo, including a polar bear, lions, a rhinoceros, an elephant,—and, of course, snakes.)

Meanwhile, Back in Rome...

Let's review and remember that the popes Leo I and Gregory had argued that the papacy of Rome was the official voice of the church in the world. Succeeding popes became the civil and religious heads of the governments carved out of the old Roman Empire. Since this book is not a review of the papacy itself, we will not continue recounting the escapades of the popes. There are numerous treatises on the history of the papacy. Suffice it to say their power culminated in the 1302 decree:

"Unum Sanctum" Bull (decree), November, 1302
"We declare, define, and affirm that every man must obey the Pope or forfeit his salvation." —The Roman Catholic Church

And their control of armies meant that they were not only willing, but able, to force their will on all men throughout the Mediterranean and Europe. The "Holy Roman Empire" now governed the Western world from Rome. Its leaders maintained control by virtue of strategically placed centers, including Londonium, that had a monopoly on the three basics:

1. Spiritual life
2. Education
3. Safety

The stance was, to coin a phrase, believe and behave like we want, or die. (Sounds like the Islamists today, doesn't it.)

In summary, let us briefly show the status of the "church" by quoting none other than the great historian, Edward Gibbon, commenting on the "Soldier Pope."

"Pope John XII, the bastard son, the grandson, and the great-grandson of Marozia, a rare genealogy, was seated in the chair of St. Peter, and it was at the age of nineteen years that the second of these became head of the Latin Church. His youth and manhood were of a suitable complexion; and the nations of pilgrims could bear testimony to the charges that were urged against him in a Roman synod, and in the presence of the Holy Roman Emperor Otho the Great.

"As John XII had renounced the dress and decencies of his profession, the soldier may not perhaps be dishonored by the wine which he drank, the blood that he spilt, the flames that he kindled, or the licentious pursuits of gaming and hunting. His open simony might be the consequence of distress and his blasphemous invocation of Jupiter and Venus, if it be true, could not possibly be serious. But we read with some surprise, that the worthy grandson of Marozia lived in public adultery with the matrons of Rome: that the Lateran palace was turned into a school for prostitution, and that his rapes of virgins and widows had deterred the female pilgrims from visiting the tomb of St. Peter, lest, in the devout act, they should be violated by his successor."[4]

If you get the picture, the pope in Rome had become a lecherous killer. He was a man guilty of all of the seven deadly sins of the New Testament, including raping and ravaging female pilgrims who were on a sacred trip to Rome! And he wasn't the first, or the last, of the perverted popes.

If you remember, the seed of all this was planted by Augustine in the third century from his unbiblical writings about the dualism of the person, which was Greek philosopher "stinkin-thinkin." The seed grew and became a mighty, poisonous tree from which the fruit was sin and crime on a massive scale. In some ways, it <u>still exists</u> within the hierarchy of the papal structure! Do priests still preach mass while being pedophiles, and is there any evidence that the hierarchy covers it up? Does the Roman church still insist upon celibacy, but turn its imperial head away from sexual sin?

Enough said. Along came a priest of the Imperial Church that disagreed with all that the imperial papacy had become from the debauchery in Rome to the slavery in Britain.

William of Ockham AD 1300

"Popes and councils may err. The Bible alone is inerrant.
A Christian cannot be held to believe anything not in the Scriptures.
The church is the community of the faithful. The Roman Church is not identical with it…The papacy is not a necessary institution."
—William of Ockham

William of Ockham (or Occam) postulated the first theory of "thinking." It has been called "Occam's Razor." This theory of thinking remains a standard rule of thumb in scientific thought to this very day. Basically, it is the theory of maintaining focus on the facts and the truth, with no superfluous, unproved, additions that delay a good solution to a problem. It states succinctly; "Among competing hypotheses, the one with the fewest assumptions should be selected." (In other words, if it walks like a duck, quacks like a duck, and swims like a duck, don't waste time wondering if it is anything other than a duck.) Why was this so controversial?

Roman priests of that day spent much of their time trying to convince the common people that God was too mysterious for them to understand and connect with, so the people needed "holy men" from the church to intercede for them; with, of course, payment to the Roman Church whose prelates would appease the spiritual world. Occam's Razor flew in the face of this blackmail and threatened this mafia-like hierarchical structure.

How? William of Ockham used his principle to preach that evidence of God is all around us and he is proven in nature, the nature of man, and man's creation, and that the common man could connect with God himself. (This was the definition of *humanism* during the fourteenth and fifteenth centuries. This is why Erasmus was called a humanist, not today's definition.) The Greek Bible William read said that the Roman hierarchy was not necessary. His Bible showed no need for papal authority, worship of Mary, and all the other money-making schemes of the "church."

One of William of Ockham's protégés was the uncle of one William Wallace, called BraveHeart. When BraveHeart was a lad, his priestly Culdee uncle said to William, "I tell you the truth, freedom is the finest of things. Never live under a servile yoke, my son."[5] And William never did. He died a free man,- and was hanged, drawn, quartered, and decapitated by King Edward of England; and this heinous action was supported by a monstrous papacy drunk with power.

A subsequent student of the writings of our Culdee, William of Ockham, was a young man named John Wycliffe. (We'll see him in detail in a following chapter.) "William was a devotee of St. Francis of Assisi and his vow of poverty. Ockham first taught at Oxford University, then went to France to live in a monastery. While living in France with the friars of St. Francis, he was condemned by the pope because this British priest questioned the extravagance of the bishops and cardinals. Threatened with imprisonment, he fled to Bavaria."[6]

At the Bavarian court of King Louis, William kept on writing. He said that, at most, the pope only had authority over the church and its beliefs, not over kings and their kingdoms. This went against Roman teaching. Reformers like Wycliffe, Hus, and Luther, who came after him, listened to William of Ockham's views.

But most remember him now because he, subsequently, developed tools of logic. He insisted that we should always look for the simplest explanation that fits all the facts, instead of inventing complicated theories or mystical allegories. This rule is still called "Occam's Razor."

Martin Luther called Ockham, "Without doubt the leader and most ingenious of the schoolmen" and called him his "dear teacher."

<u>Ockham was a priest, a scholar, and was called, by contemporaries, *Doctor Invincibilis*, the invincible doctor.</u>[7]

However, Rome and the imperial priesthood would not be challenged easily. The decrees kept coming from the seat of the vicars of Christ.

"As for the church itself, Rome is the mistress and mother of all churches. To obey her is to obey Christ… To the pope, it belongs to determine what is of faith. Yea, subjection to him is necessary to salvation."—Contra Errores, Reusch's edition, p. 9,

The true Church of Jesus Christ had been hijacked by Romanism, and corruption was rampant everywhere except the true Christian strongholds of northern Ireland, Wales, and Scotland.

The popes decided to take the law into their own hands. They claimed, based on their interpretation of 2 Peter 1:20, "authority to interpret" the Scripture. What they really did was to interpret based on allegorical eisogesis rather than historical and textual exegesis; reading into rather than from the Holy Writ.

The famous philosopher Kierkgaard said about vicars like them: "The scholar stuffs his britches with grammars, lexicons, and commentaries, and thus the Bible as God's Word never reaches his soul."

Undaunted, the Romans continued to build an impressive library of "church tradition." They said: "The Scriptures contain what is to be believed, but the authority of the Church establishes what these truths are. Our belief in the Scriptures rests ultimately on the authority of the Church."[8]

So, the religious mafia became a law unto itself. The "Catholic Canon

Law" (over 1,900 decrees in seven volumes) was established as the official body of law for the people. It legislated in detail all phases of human life. It protected the clergy in the commission of crimes by demanding that they be tried in ecclesiastical courts for all offenses. (They, thus, got away with a slap on the wrist in most instances.)

It also gave sanction to the principle of ecclesiastical compulsion, declaring that physical force is to be used to coerce ecclesiastical dissidents.[9]

In this effort, the popes and bishops of Rome were not true innovators. The Devil has always been allowed by God to tempt those who are evil, worldly, and selfish.

Human Tradition of 'Law' Over 'Relationship'

The Evil One, the Devil, is never very inventive. He began his deception of law over relationships with the earliest of "civilizations." In ancient Egypt, we find his fingerprints in their laws and traditions. If one was to be able to view the system of religious slavery existing in Egypt during the time of the Pharaohs, it would become very clear that it was of the Devil. The system of fear and symbols of death abounded. The control was by the Imperial Court, the aristocrats, and the priests. Just as it became for the Roman Catholic Church.

As we read Egyptian history, we find that this was so. From high person to low, an amulet of a dung beetle was worn around the neck at the heart. The heart was the embodiment of the person, so they employed the beetle as a symbol of their hope for a future eternal life. (The adult beetle was seen to roll mud and dung into a ball. The eggs placed in the ball fed on it and then hatched to life. For the average Egyptian right up to the Pharaoh, this represented rebirth.) On the back of the "heart scarab" was etched, "O my heart which I had upon earth…do not speak against me concerning what I have done."[10]

You see, the Weighing of the Heart was the scene of the great "judgment seat" for the Egyptians. When anyone died, they were subject to, according to the priests who made their living directing their "sheeple" toward heaven, a series of stations of death. The spirits of all Egyptians who died would have to ward off demons at up to 200 stations in order to proceed to the judgment scene. At each station, there needed to be an answer for the demon. For each offering to a priest while alive, there would be one talisman given, which was called an answerer. The average person collected all these throughout their life by paying off the clergy and scribes for the "answer" to take into death with them at their burial. They knew that they were not pure in heart, but this act would cover it over for them, buying their way to eternity.

"By the time of the New kingdom, 1550 BC, a person might be buried with as many as 365 Shabtis or Ushabtis to do the talking for them as they made their way to the great judgment scene."[11]

This way, the priestly hierarchy got paid every day of the year by everyone to make sure that they even got ushered into the great judgment scene. But this was important. Eternal life was at stake. So the people paid. There was a lot more to the religion and religious festivals of all the different gods. Anytime one wanted anything, the tradition was to go and pay at the temple, buy a talisman to a particular god, and get your message sent to the god of that need. (See any parallels to the Roman Church?)

The great judgment scene was the Weighing of the Heart. IF the dead managed to get their heart past all of the demons through their 'answerers,' they would find themselves in a chamber standing before the god Osiris. They were judged on their behavior during life. Now everyone knew that he would never be able to be perfect in truth all his life, so they had the answerers to just answer that he was pure and passable by what the religious scribe wrote for him in his stead.

Once in the great judgment hall, the god Osiris would ask the dead person if their heart was pure. There was a long list of questions brought by all the divine judges in the chamber. The dead must answer correctly that they had not left life while being in debt or offence to ANY of the main gods of Egypt.

"The proceedings were recorded by Thoth, the scribe of the gods, and the deity of wisdom and the scribal profession. He was often depicted with an ibis head, writing on a roll of papyrus. His other animal form was the baboon, sometimes depicted sitting atop the great scales of justice. The symbolic ritual that accompanied this trial was the weighing of the heart of the deceased on a pair of enormous scales. It was weighed against the principle of truth and justice, *Maat*, represented by a feather, the symbol of the goddess of truth, order, and justice. (Sound a little like Mary?) If the heart balanced against the feather then the deceased would be granted a place in the Fields of Hetep and Iaru. If it was heavy with the weight of wrongdoings, the balance would sink, and the heart would be grabbed and devoured by a terrifying beast that sat ready and waiting by the scales."[12]

THE DEAD PENITENT   HEART   MONSTER   FEATHER   THOTH

Of course, the whole secret to the religion was to have all the people live their lives in fear of their heart being eaten by the monster and never getting to eternal life where there would be no worries, pain, or hardships. This was the system preached daily and worked through by the entire Egyptian populace. Why do we think that they were more than happy to raid other nations and enslave them to manual labor so they could use the stolen booty and property to buy more answerers and go to more festivals to appease the gods; and the priests, who would surely report "bad behavior" to Osiris; and the divine judges. This also, conveniently, made every war a religious war. The priests were only too happy to absolve soldiers for their service as long as they paid the temple taxes and bought more answerers.

(See any parallels to modern religion?)

So What?

Do we see any pattern here? Think of the world's religions, great and small. They are "works" religions with many laws and traditions one must conform to in order to make it into eternal life. Only TRUE Christianity depends on a relationship wherein Jesus died for all sin and substitutes his purity before God for all our wrongdoing. The religious establishments hate the very idea. The implementation of it destroys their sweet system of lifelong slavery of the masses.

Before moving on, we should not ignore the Jewish system that Jesus fought against. Can you see the pattern even here?

A Kingdom of Priests

It is at this point that the author is reminded of the religious body of Jesus' day. Jesus taught that there should be a kingdom of priests, that each of his followers were to be priests that gave rather than took and loved rather than used people. His immediate followers wrote down the principles of relationship between mankind and God. These, in the original New Testament, were not and are not man's laws and rules but principles of relationship from the heart of God. The Jews as a whole were anything but godly and relational during the first century.

Fundamentally, the Pharisees continued a form of Judaism that extended beyond the Temple, applying Jewish law to mundane activities in order to sanctify the every-day world. Leaders were not determined by birth but by scholarly achievement. In general, the Pharisees believed that their ends would be achieved through *halakha* ("the walk" or "how to walk"), a corpus of laws derived from a close reading of sacred texts. This belief entailed both a commitment to relate religion to ordinary concerns and daily life, and a commitment to study and scholarly debate. The Pharisees believed that all Jews in their ordinary life, and not just the Temple priesthood or Jews visiting the Temple, should observe rules and rituals concerning purification.

The Oral Torah

The Pharisees believed that in addition to the written Torah recognized by both the Sadducees and Pharisees and believed to have been written by Moses, there exists another Torah, consisting of the corpus of oral laws and traditions transmitted by God to Moses orally, and then passed down by Moses and his successors over the generations. The Oral Torah functioned to elaborate on what was written, and the Pharisees asserted that the sacred scriptures were not complete on their own terms and could therefore not be understood. Thus, one may conceive of the "Oral Torah" not as a fixed text but as an ongoing process of analysis and argument in which God is actively involved; and by participating in this ongoing process rabbis and their students actively participated in God's ongoing act of revelation.

History then repeated itself in the Roman Church and its sacrilege of "Church Tradition."

"The Scriptures contain what is to be believed, but the authority of the Church establishes what these truths are...Our belief in the Scriptures rests ultimately on the authority of the Church."[13]

> E X A M P L E—"There is no salvation outside the Roman Church. All who refuse subjection to the Pope are heretics. From the pope's authority to loose and to bind no human being is exempted. Nothing is exempted from his jurisdiction."[14]
> —Deus nullum excepti, Reg., IV. 2

The Devil knows no originality. He just repeats the same pattern; the LAW over the person. What Moses tried to teach to the Egyptians was relationship over law. What Jesus tried to teach to the Jews was relationship over law. What Constantine the Great had set free by edict, the papists imprisoned by terror, tyranny, and inquisition. This proves the adage that as long as there is a specific code to obey, religious men and women can conform without a change of heart. Jesus called these sorts of people, "whitewashed sepulchers." (And, they can make a nice living out of it.)

During the period of years from AD 800 through AD 1500, with the exception of the Scottish and Welsh Church, there were 700 years of a worldwide debauched church power structure. People were born, lived, and died never knowing anything but a corrupt church, masquerading as the representatives of God for fifteen GENERATIONS! Dr. Craig Lampe, in his *The Forbidden Book*, gives us a disheartening list of the ANTI-Christian "official church" operating from Rome:

1. Over 100,000 prostitutes were in the employ of the Church as a universal acceptance of Augustine's proclamation of prostitution as a "necessary evil."

2. "Artifacts belonging to Jesus" were strategically enshrined for the purpose of drawing lay people into undertaking pilgrimages sponsored by the Church at exorbitant prices.

3. Indulgences were granted for crimes that ranged from adultery to murder and rendered the state powerless to prosecute the criminal. Indulgences were often granted for money paid in advance for a criminal act not yet performed.

4. Early in the sixteenth century, on the Continent, Bishop Tetzel, the special envoy to both Popes Julius and Leo, extracted enormous sums of money from the parishes for the construction of St. Peter's Basilica by granting pardon for penances in puragtory.

5. Julius and Leo declared the Holy Wars to justify the mass slaughter of the Jews in order to steal their money and possessions to finance the building of the Vatican, primarily the Sistine Chapel and St. Peter's Basilica.[15]

The Dark Ages (including Middle Age) lasted for over 700 years, until another Englishman came along who stood against the popish minions and decided the bastardized Latin Scriptures and the power-hungry practices of evil popes had held sway over Britain and Europe long enough.

We will introduce him, and others from "the rustic church," in chapter eight. But we must first introduce the devil's twin of Imperial Rome,

Islam, because its rise from the pits of Arabia caused seizures and trembling throughout the Holy Roman Empire. The Whirling Dervish-like Mohammedans came to power in the AD 600s and made it their goal to subdue the Western world from the south to the north even as rustic British Christians were attempting to evangelize Europe from the north to the south. The Imperial Church responded to the Islamic threat with the Crusades. But, finally, in God's providence, he used all of this to solidify the British Christians and to bring to them precious texts of the first centuries of the true church. Since the days of Constantine, the church at Constantinople had been storing up historic Greek and Hebrew texts of the Bible. In the next chapter, we see the reason that God chose to begin "leaking" them out into the true, rustic church of the future.

Sources

1. Janet Bately, "King Alfred and the Old English Translation of Orosius", *Anglia* 88 (1970): 433–60; idem, "'Those books that are most necessary for all men to know'. The Classics and late ninth-century England: a reappraisal", in The Classics in the Middle Ages, ed. Aldo S. Bernardo and Saul Levin (1990), 45–78, underline mine).

2. Opuscula, *hagiographica*, ibid. col. 657–742, Schaff, Philip, *History of the Christian Church*, vol. 4, 690.

3. Simon Jenkins, *A Short History of England* (Profile Books, 2011), 71).

4. E. Gibbon, *The History of the Decline and Fall of the Roman Empire*, 12 Vols., London 1813, IX 198–9, Ch. 49.

5. Edward J Cowan, *For Freedom Alone: The Declaration of Arbroath*, 1320, Dundurn Pub. 2003, p. 74.

6. Marilyn McCord Adams, *William Ockham* (University of Notre Dame, 1987).

7. *The Dialogue*, Ockam: Reisler, p 273/ Seeberg, p 271,278/ Werner, vol. III 120 & Schaff, *History of the Christian Church*, vol. VI, pp. 193).

8. *Libris canonici sacri*, Seeberg, p. 120.

9. Schaff, *History of the Christian Church* vol. V, 687, 768,769

10. Oakes & Gahlin, *Ancient Egypt* (Barnes & Noble Books, New York, 2003), 395.

11. Oakes & Gahlin, *Ancient Egypt* (Barnes & Noble Books, New York, 2003), 411.

12. Oakes & Gahlin, *Ancient Egypt* (Barnes & Noble Books, New York, 2003), 394, (parenthesis mine).

13. *Libris canonici sacri*, Seeberg, 120.

14. Schaff, *History of the Christian Church*, vol. V, 775.

15. Craig Lampe, *The Forbidden Book*, (2004), 30, used by permission. Copies may be obtained at greatsite.com

Images

Alfred, The Great, AD 849–899 ID 43373888 © Anthony Baggett | Dreamstime.com

Photos – Dreamstime.com

Chapter Seven

Hell on Earth

We begin this chapter with an excerpt from the collections of writings from historian Washington Irving.

A Letter From Muhammad
"Different prophets have been sent by God to illustrate his different attributes: Moses his clemency and providence; Solomon his wisdom, majesty and glory; Jesus Christ his righteousness, omniscience, and power—his righteousness by purity of conduct, his omniscience by the knowledge he displayed of the secrets of all hearts, his power by the miracles he wrought.
"None of these attributes, however, have been sufficient to enforce conviction. And even the miracles of Moses and Jesus have been treated with unbelief. I, therefore, the last of the prophets have been sent with the sword! Let those who promulgate my faith enter into no argument or discussion; but slay all those who refuse obedience to the law.
"Whoever fights for the true faith, whether he fall or conquer, will assuredly receive a glorious reward. The sword is the key to heaven and hell. All who draw it in the cause of the faith will be rewarded

with temporal advantages; every drop shed of their blood, every peril and hardship endured by them, will be registered on high as more meritorious than even fasting and praying.

"If they fall in battle, their sins will at once be blotted out and they will be transported to paradise, there to revel in eternal pleasures in the arms of black-eyed Houris."[1] —MUHAMMAD

THE APOSTLE OF THE SWORD

With the Koran in his hand, he came with a vast army of warriors and workers, spreading over the eastern half of what was once the Roman Empire. Their foundational work of torment lasted 150 years, but their horrific heritage exists to this day. His aim was "the sting of the Ishmaelite scorpion" in the name of God.

A descendant of the first-born of Abraham, Ishmael, Muhammad had the spirit of his ancestor, "wild, his hand against everyone and in hostility toward his brothers,"—just as God had said in Genesis. And his followers emulated him as they brought the scourge of their domination to Arabia, the Middle East, and beyond.

In the beginning, they were all on horseback as they pillaged, running down all who would stand rather than bow. This mighty movement had its origin in Arabia. The legions of war-mongers had long beards, long hair, yellow turbans, and horse-tail symbols on their banners. They rode under the dark green flag of the star and crescent. Their war cries were the origination of the saying, "Din of Iniquity," which is their rightful heritage. The Arabic word *din* means "practice." They practice iniquity. Their god was, and is, Allah, the god Satan invented.

Do we too harshly condemn Islam, the innovation of Muhammad and his immediate successors? Consider just two of eighty-two incidences during Muhammad's life which are on the record and admitted to by Muslim scholars.

In Mecca, Muhammad had hoped to be accepted as God's messenger by the Jews (living there) and to win them over by ordering his followers to turn in the direction of Jerusalem during prayer and adopt the Jewish

Day of Atonement, Ashura, as the Muslim holy day. However, he seems to have underestimated the Jewish tribes' allegiance to their scriptures and the effect that the many irreconcilable discrepancies between his own Kuranic pronouncements and the Jewish tradition would have on them.

When he moved on with his rag-tag group of mercenaries, his superficial, second-hand knowledge of the holy texts made it impossible for him to argue on par with the learned (Jewish) merchants of Medina, steeped in their tradition. The result of their unsurprising refusal to give it up in favor of the claims of a poorly educated refugee was that Muhammad's earlier, favorable pronouncements about the Jews evolved into an implacably hostile position. The perceived slight, as was customary with him, turned into rage. His warriors selected out the Jews and murdered them.

"In the attack against the [Jewish] tribe of Banu-'l-Mustaliq in 626, Muhammad's followers slaughtered many tribesmen and looted thousands of their camels and sheep; they also kidnapped some of their 'excellent women.' The night after the battle, Muhammad and his followers staged an orgy of rape. As one Abu Sa'id al-Khadri remembered, a problem needed to be resolved first: in order to obtain ransom from the surviving tribesmen, the Muslims had pledged not to violate their captives. One of the followers of the prophet gave witness about the captive women. 'We desired them, for we were suffering from the absence of our wives, but at the same time we also desired ransom for them. So we decided to have sexual intercourse with them but by observing '*azl*' (coitus interruptus). But we said: We are doing an act whereas Allah's Messenger (Muhammad) is amongst us; why not ask him? So we asked Allah's messsenger, may peace be upon him, and he said: It does not matter if you do or do not do it, for every soul that is to be born up to the Day of Resurrection will be born."

In telling his companions to go ahead and rape their captive married women without practicing al-azl, the only contentious issue was whether the victim's ransom value would be diminished or lost completely, if they were to return pregnant to their husbands.

Alarmed by the apparent consolidation of Muhammad's position, the Meccans decided to deal a crushing blow, once and for all, to the traitor who dared disrupt their commerce. In early AD 627, an army huge by

Arabian standards, some 10,000 men led by Abu Sufyan, advanced against Medina. Muhammad had prepared reserves, and after a siege of only two weeks, during which time Muhammad undermined the attackers' unity by sending envoys to different tribes of the coalition, they fractured, gave up, and withdrew.

In the flush of victory, Muhammad proceeded to attack the last Jewish tribe in Medina, Bany Qurayzah, which he accused of disloyalty and complicity with the Meccans. This time, mere expulsion and robbery would no longer do. Muhammad offered the men conversion to Islam as an alternative to death; upon their refusal, up to 900 were decapitated at a ditch, in front of their wives and children. Torches were lit so that the slaughter could be accomplished in one day. "Truly the judgment of Allah was pronounced on high" was Muhammad's comment.

"The women were subsequently raped; Muhammad chose as his concubine one Raihana bin Amr, whose father and husband were both slaughtered before her eyes.

"As for the captured husbands, fathers, sons, or brothers who were not decapitated, they were put in chains and crucified or boiling fluid was poured down their heads so that their skins melted. Some were hooked with rods of iron and kept in anguish until they died."[2]

Muhammad, An Evil Religion Man

Can it be argued seriously that Muhammad's Muslim brotherhood was anything less than a vicious, cruel, mercenary brood of human vipers—the Mafia of the sand dunes, bringing hell on earth to all whom they rode down upon. And Muhammad himself was a selfish, deluded warrior who had scant regard for human life, a thief who stole women and children, violating girls as young as nine years old, and was a murderer-perpetrator of genocide on the level of Hitler and Pol Pot. Ever since his time, Orthodox Islam's practice (din) continues in his hideous tradition of bloodshed by the sword. It is a Din of Iniquity to be confronted for what it is.

The Koran says: "A night spent in arms (fighting) is more precious in the sight of God than months of fasting and prayer. Whosoever dies in battle, his sins are forgiven. In the Day of Judgment, his wounds shall be resplendent as vermilion, and odoriferous as musk. In the Muslim's paradise, seventy-two damsels of sparkling beauty shall minister to the most humble of the faithful" (i.e., those who die in battle)

The favorite tool of the "night arms" was the din knife. This knife is a short sword that is curved. It is used for close combat, the blade against the neck of an infidel caught by surprise in the night. The French word for "din knife" is *boucan*, from which we get the word "buccaneer," for a pirate.

Islamic pirates would shout in the night, making a "din of iniquity" as they surprised their victims and hacked them to death with their knives. What did they shout? "*Allah u Akbar*," "God is the Greatest," meaning that nothing can supersede God or be better than him. But, which god are they shouting about? The God of life or the god of death? The Devil is the god of the din, the treacherous, secretive, slit the throat by surprise god, Allah. His most ardent followers continue to use this method today as they employ box-cutters, burst into airplane cockpits, and slit the throats of civilian pilots while shouting praise to the god of death, Allah. And, as they behead innocents captured in the Middle East today.

There are 199 references to jihad in the most authoritative Hadith collection. They ALL speak of jihad only as warfare.[3]

Where Does this Come Together?

Muhammad began his "comeback" in the south the same year that Boniface II became pope. One Sergius, a Nestorian Monk exiled to the Middle East, by Boniface II, is reputed to have written the Koran. Note that the Islamic flag has a star and a crescent on it, and not by accident, but by design.

Islamic history has it that Sergius and Muhammad met upon one of the caravan journeys Muhammad conducted for his uncle, and the two formed a pact. Sergius would use his knowledge of how the "Christian" leaders had gained all power in Europe with: religious writings, contracts with princes, and decrees. Muhammad, for his part, would use his charm and Arabic merchant contacts to begin to enact his plan for power over Arabia, of which he thought he had been robbed.

Sergius wanted a sign of their pact, and the two devised a flag that every Islamic army would take into battle for the next thousand years. It would have a star on it representing the Nestorian Sergius' God and a crescent on it representing the Moon gods that Mohammad's family had worshipped in the past.

Out of this collaboration between an outcast papal monk and an epileptic Arabian merchant, "wanna-be" prince, rose a hellish work that still threatens the civilized world. Muhammad learned his religious lessons well, though he could not read nor write. He and Sergius began to talk to those who were their friends and helpers in Mecca. They issued the doctrine claiming that Muhammad was a "prophet" and "received" the Koran at Mecca. This new religion was a religion of the sword, and their intent to terrorize was symbolized by the scorpion on their shields. The scorpion has always been the national symbol of the Ishmaelites of Arabia.

THE RELIGIOUS PLOT THICKENS

Meanwhile, back in Rome, the remnants of the once mighty Roman Empire were still crumbling. That very year the tyrant Phocas, Italy's emperor, granted liberty to the bishop of Rome to assume the title of universal pastor: pope. It is interesting to note that, at the time when the Roman Church was climbing to the summit of its impious dignity in the north, a deluded sheik was designing his own brand of slavery for the south. Could there be "Satanic Verses" north and south being forged as a double-edged sword to use against the innocents of the world?

At the age of forty, after completing the period of his probation in the "retreat," Muhammad assumed the title which Sergius had suggested for him: apostle of God. Sergius was becoming tired of waiting for his protégé to take action. It was time Muhammad tried his success with the public. However, during the four years following his debut as the apostle of God, the converts to his new religion were only nine in number.

Obviously, merely the fact that he proclaimed he was an apostle of God that upheld Jesus as a prophet and Abraham as their earthly progenitor, etc. was not enough to persuade many to follow him, to make him the pope of the south. What could he and Sergius do to compel more followers? Well, they thought, God could not possibly be happy with those who would not have "ears to hear." So, they inserted into the writings that those who would not hear were infidels and their lives, belongings, and land were forfeit to God (and, of course, were to be in possession of the prophet for proper distribution in his name).

In the year AD 626, Muhammad and his minions crushed and expelled the Jewish al-Nadir tribe from Arabia. In 627 he raided the Jewish Qurayzah tribe, killing all the men and taking plunder. In 629 he put the entire Jewish population of Khyber to death by the sword. He expressed that Allah was continuing to instruct him in how to handle the Jewish people. In the space of one year, all the Jews around Medina had been exterminated or exiled. Within three years, all the Jewish tribes in Arabia had been wiped out by the "holy army."

The entire life of Muhammad, after his flight to Medina, was one continued scene of butchery and conquest in the name of Allah. He, with his associates and followers, plundered every caravan of its valuable commodities. Including, at long last, the caravans of his own uncle! (His uncle had kept the young Muhammad as a feeder of his camels and under his thumb.) Sweet revenge it was. It would be an almost endless task to give even a catalogue of his numerous wars. This "prophet" reduced city after city to his religion by the power of the sword. Lust and ambition were his two powerful motives. In his unbounded physical lusts, it is clear that he had no less than fifteen wives at any one time. Many wives were little more than captives who were traded by their tribal leaders as a bribe for peace. For ten years, Muhammad's life exhibited nothing but highway robbery, plunder, and bloodshed, in which some historians estimate he exceeded even Alexander the Great in atrocity.

As he ruled and set down his decrees, he admitted the inspiration of the Old and New Testament and the divine mission of Moses and Jesus Christ. He thereby wooed the affections of unsuspecting or cowardly Jews and Christians. But he insinuated that God only designed his mission, Muhammad's mission, to be dominant. The world's choice was Islam "Submission" or death.

Following Muhammad's death, an oligarchy of imams took control of Islam. In the years of the Diwan imams following Umar and his successor, Ali, Christians were styled infidels and dogs, insulted, and treated shamefully. The cities and towns occupied were given three options: the Koran, crippling tribute, or the sword. They were prohibited from building new churches or attending the old ones. They were never to sound the bells. They were forced to admit scoffing Muhammadans into their community assemblies. Those returning to the Christian faith, once having taken the oath to Islam were given the penalty of death. The insults, injuries, oppressions, etc. are not to be described in squeamish company. In just ten years, from AD 634 to 644, the Muhammadan Saracens captured 3,060 cities, destroyed 4,000 churches, and erected 1400 mosques, using Christian and Jewish slaves to erect mosques from the ruins of their own former buildings of worship.

The Muhammadans took Damascus in 634, Jerusalem in 637, Egypt in 638, and westward to the banks of the Atlantic. They crossed the borders of Europe in 675, while at the same time crossing the Hellingspont and besieging Constantinople from all sides, but were driven back by great warriors upon the city walls. The Muhammadans simply went around the city and continued on into Greece.

On the western front, in 711 they crossed the straights of Gibralter into western Europe and conquered Spain. Their dominion now consisted of: western Asia, northern Africa, and southwestern Europe. It was a penalty of death to profess Christianity in that empire. The Bible was "killed" by burning and burying across the Mediterranean, right up to the gates of Rome itself. By the year 762, the Holy Scriptures were banned or destroyed systematically everywhere in the Western world except northern Britain and Wales. If we ever doubted why God had to have a plan and shelter for his Book and his chosen people, those doubts have surely passed away!

The first evil Islamic movement lasted from AD 612 to 762, exactly 150 years. The sting of the scorpion of Ishmael, bred in the Arabian sands, was severe. Anyone captured by the Muhammadans would suffer as severely as if a giant scorpion had stung him, so horrible were the atrocities committed by the followers of Muhammad. His sheiks sent messengers into towns and cities with the message of Islam:

"Ye Christian dogs, you know your option—the Koran, the tribute, or the sword. We are a people whose delight is in war rather than in peace, and we despise your pitiful alms, since we shall be speedily masters of your wealth, your families, and your persons."[4]

THE MUHAMMADANS CONFRONTED

Near the end of the 150-year reign of Islamic terror, the Ottoman hoards were in control of the East, Middle East, Mediterranean, and most of southern Europe. The Devil was ecstatic. The Ottoman Empire under Malek Shah was divided among his four sons at his death. It was divided into four parts: 1) Persia, 2) Syria, 3) Asia Minor, and 4) India. As the Islamic princes moved in conquest, the Turkish camp was soon seated in the neighborhood of Kutaieh in Phrygia, and his flying cavalry laid waste the country as far as the Hellingspont and the Black Sea."[5] They marched out of Baghdad in 1057, crossed the river, and the next century their conquest extended to the Hellingspont and embraced all Turkey and half of Greece.

Then came the mighty Crusades. For a while, the crusaders beat back the Muslim power mongers and recovered a portion of Turkey, between Europe and Asia. The contest lasted for two centuries. Europe, weary of its endless struggle, withdrew. The Turks reorganized and passed over into Europe. The eastern Christian empire was shorn of all its territories and reduced to only its fortified city of Constantinople.

In AD 1453, two hundred thousand Islamic Turks with cannons battered down the walls of the greatest city of Christendom. One hundred thousand of its citizens were slain upon her ramparts. This rapacious, licentious, bloodthirsty, brutal power educated in their religion to believe that all unbelievers (they call anyone who is not a Muhammadan an unbeliever or infidel) were fit for death. Each Pasha was an absolute lord in his own province. Their rule was intolerable to anyone but the ruling class.

"The myriads of Turkish horse overspread a frontier of six hundred miles from Tauris to Arzeroum, and the blood of one hundred and thirty thousand Christians was a grateful sacrifice to the Arabian prophet."[6]

But, God will not be mocked. In AD 1450, Christian Greek and Hebrew texts, some of the original writings of the early church, and many Roman histories were transported by ship to western Europe. During this time, as more Muslims attacked Constantinople and Christians fled in waves of humanity, they took many ancient copies of the Scriptures to the west, including to Britain's Oxford. Finally, in AD 1453, after over 1,100 years of Christianity, great Constantinople fell to the Muslims. The church of the Hagia Sophia was turned into a mosque. The entire city was Islamicized and is until this day.

Hagia Sofia in Istanbul

But, God Will Not Be Mocked

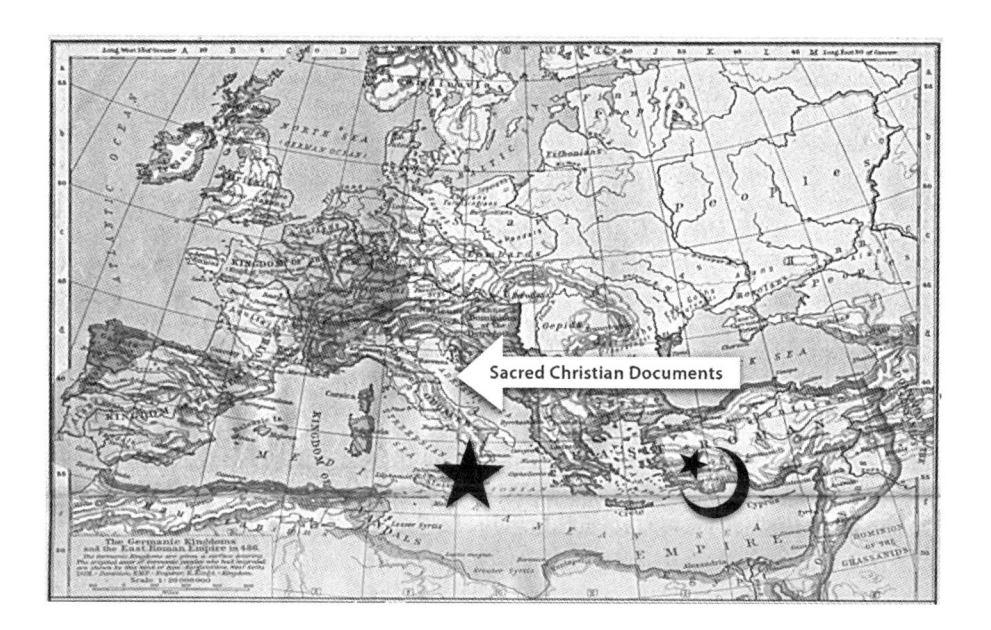

[Map with label "Sacred Christian Documents"]

Because of the fall of Constantinople, thousands of written manuscripts were brought out to Europe by the faithful before they could be confiscated or burned by the Muslims. Many made their way to the "Rustic Church."

(See appendix 4 for more history on the Muhammadans during the Dark Ages. Their rampant and atrocious killing of hundreds of thousands in the East was abominable.)

Why Is this Important to Christians Today?

Shall we, in the West, continue to be lulled into the stupor of the lie that Islam is a religion of peace? And, if we can speak to Islam's children, what can we offer as a way to true peace? We turn to one of the truly inspiring historians and philosophers of our day, Vishal Mangalwadi, for the answer: "The New Testament taught that God saw the misery of man and came as a man, Jesus Christ, to make human beings sons and daughters of God. But Islam denied God the right to become a man. According to Islam, for God to become a creature as lowly as man would violate his dignity…Far from violating God's dignity, the incarnation was to be the ultimate proof of man's dignity: of the possibility of man's salvation, of a man or a woman becoming a friend and child of God...Its [Islam's] failure to appreciate the value and dignity of human beings prevented Islamic civilization from developing the full potential of its people. It trapped the masses without the fundamental rights and liberties that made it possible for the West to overtake Islamic civilization."[7]

Today, it is for Muslims to decide if they will follow their history of crucifying their own people on the cross of humiliation under the heavy thumbs of their imams or free them within a framework of godly dignity. And, as with any other framework, the teaching begins with children. More than fifty years ago, Israeli prime minister Golda Meir gave a speech wherein she stated a great truth: "Peace will come when the Arabs will love their children more than they hate us."[8] So far, there is no peace in the Middle East—and the children, young and old, suffer.

Meanwhile, Back in Rome With The Evil of The North...

The power grab of the Roman See (L. = *sedes*, meaning "chair" where the ruler sits) continued to corrupt the so-called Christian Church. Throughout the centuries the results increased in hierarchy and made an imperial church that little resembled the church of Jesus Christ. Of course, there have always been individuals who have followed the teachings of Christ within the Roman Catholic Church. However, our opinion is that they continue to be victims of the Roman Imperial Church structure.

Do we think that the Roman Church of the middle ages is nothing like the Roman Catholic Church today? Look at just a few of the writings and subsequent decrees:

Pope Gregory VII, in AD 1075, defined the pope as universal monarch and not just the "vicar of Peter" but the "vicar of Christ, Christ's ambassador and representative on earth."

"If anyone receive not the whole of the said books, with all their parts, as holy and canonical as they have been wont to be read in the Catholic

Church, and in the old Vulgate translation, or knowingly despises the said traditions (decrees and writings of the popes), let him be accursed."

Council of Trent, April 1546

"Bible Societies violate the traditions of the fathers and the Council of Trent, by circulating the Scriptures in the vernacular tongues of all nations. In order to avert this pest, our predecessors have published several constitutions…tending to show how pernicious for the faith and for morals this perfidious institution [The Bible Society] is!" —Pope Leo XII, 1824 Encyclical epistle

Catechism of the Catholic Church, 1994

- "The sacraments confer the grace that they signify.
- The sacrament of baptism erases original sin.
- Sins committed through weakness after baptism are forgiven through penance and extreme unction.
- The sacrament of the Eucharist forgives sin for the living and the dead.
- The manner of Christ's presence is a miraculous corporeal presence.
- Holy orders are a sacrament.
- Marriage is a sacrament."

If an official representative of the Catholic Church does not "recognize" these sacraments by leading them, they are not in effect before God for the person or their families.

(By the way, if marriage is a sacrament, and all good Catholics must uphold the sacraments, why do the priests, bishops, and popes not have to engage in the sacrament of marriage?)

Perhaps most egregious of all from the standpoint of the Bible is this statement from the *Catechism of the Catholic Church*, 2nd edition, 1997 as given to us by Catholic theologian Dr. Ronald Witherup:

"Very basic to a Catholic approach to Scripture is the acceptance of two interrelated sources of knowing God's will, Scripture, and Tradition. At the very outset, then, Catholics have a basic stance that opposes the fundamentalist idea of sola scriptura. To quote Vatican II's Dogmatic Constitution on Divine Revelation: 'The Church has always venerated the divine Scriptures as she venerated the body of the Lord...to offer it to the faithful from the one table of the Word of God and the Body of Christ. She has always regarded, and continues to regard the Scriptures, taken together with sacred Tradition, as the supreme rule of her faith.'

"This quotation shows the essential connection between the Bible, as God's holy Word, and the magisterial Tradition of the Church. From a Catholic perspective, as important as the Bible is, it cannot serve alone as the sole source of revelation...the Catholic position implicitly acknowledges that not every teaching of the Church can be found in sacred Scripture... The Church's living magisterial office is charged with ultimately determining the meaning of Scripture where necessary, under the guidance of the Holy Spirit."[9]

We haven't the opportunity in this small volume to print all of the errors that this "magisterial office" of interpreting Tradition for the Church has caused. Let us take two as examples:

Again, quoting from Dr. Witherup:

"The Catholic position on the creation stories of Genesis is not to take them literally in every detail. In fact, Pope John Paul II has indicated clearly that the scientific theory of evolution is not necessarily incompatible with the Genesis stories of creation...Thus Adam and Eve need not be literal, historical individuals but representative figures of the first human beings. Catholic teaching only insists that at some point God placed within humankind a soul that distinguishes people from all other beings, something that need not contradict a theory of Evolution."[10]

"Catholics recognize the Gospels as a collection of oral, written, and edited traditions that developed in diverse contexts in the early decades of the Christian community...As they exist now, they are not eyewitness accounts of Jesus' ministry but theological presentations of the stories of Jesus of Nazareth."[11]

The reader must decide if this is a magisterium run amuck. Our opinion is that there is no better way for the Evil One to kill the Bible than to continue revising and redacting it throughout the centuries via a compromising and politically-correct Catholic magisterium.

Back to the Rustic Church, Our Heritage

The Roman Church could not and would not be accepted by the Christian family of faith in Britain. But, certainly right up to and across the English Channel all the way to the old Roman Walls, the popes held sway. Would God allow the true, rustic church to be swallowed up in Romanism or in Islam? Let's see his movement in chapter eight.

Sources

1. Irving Washington, *Mohammed and His Successors* (J. B. Lippencott, 1874), 156–157.

2. Trifkovic Serge, *Sword of the Prophet*, (Regina (Orthodox Press, 2002), 42–45, Muslim history book 8, Number 3371.

3. Douglas Streusand, *What Does Jihad Mean?*, Middle East Quarterly, Sept. 1997.

4. *The History of the Decline and Fall of the Roman Empire*, vol. 5, 315.

5. Gibbon, vol. 6, p. 24.

6. Gibbon vol. 6, p. 12.

7. Vishal Mangalwadi, *The Book That Made Your World* (Thomas Nelson, 2011), 70–71.

8. Statement to the National Press Club in Washington, D. C. in 1957, as quoted in Marie Syrkin, ed., *A Land of Our Own : An Oral Autobiography* (1973), 242.

9. Ronald Witherup, *Biblical Fundamentalism, What Every Catholic Should Know* (The Liturgical Press, 2001), 39–40.

10. ibid., 41.

11. ibid., 41–42.

Images

Hagia Sofia in Istanbul © Ionut David | Dreamstime.com

CHAPTER EIGHT

THE LIGHT AT THE END OF THE HORRID TUNNEL

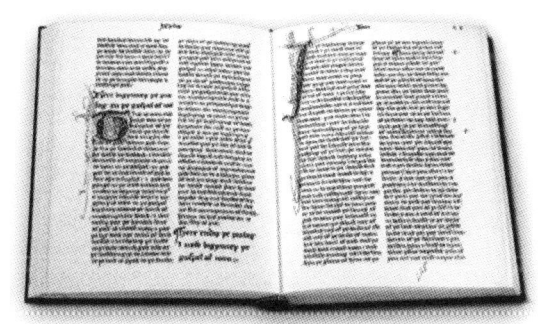

AD 1330–1384

JOHN WYCLIFFE, THE MORNINGSTAR OF THE REFORMATION, began to translate the Scriptures from Latin into English.

The first hand-written English language Bible manuscripts were produced in AD 1380s by Wycliffe, an Oxford professor, scholar, and theologian.

"The Bible is for the government of the people, by the people and for the people."

I'll bet that you thought Abraham Lincoln was the first person to come up with the; "of the people, by the people, and for the people" phrase. Well,

Lincoln was well read, and the Bible was one of his school books. He also read Bible history and was easily able to adapt John Wycliffe's quote about the Bible. We're glad Lincoln could appropriate from Wycliffe. There are more ideas about the Bible and the government that we also get from this giant of Bible teaching. Wycliffe was brilliant. He was educated in law, science, philosophy, logic, and theology. He would have been a perfect counselor to Robin Hood, if there had been any such person. John lived during the time of the supposed "steal from the rich and give to the poor" hero. His criticism of the Church attracted the admiration of the rulers of the day in Britain. King Richard was off fighting the one Crusade that Britain participated in. Richard's wife, Queen Anne of Bohemia, admired Wycliffe and kept him from Roman Church prosecution.

He called the instituted church a disgrace to God and to the people it instructed in his ways; all the while he was a professor at Oxford University. Wycliffe's penchant for translating passages of Scripture from Greek manuscripts, therefore showing the Latin Vulgate of the day to be dead wrong on many issues, caused him to be dismissed from Oxford. He was "exiled" to a post as the parish priest at Lutterworth in 1375. Students organized caravans of carriages and wagons to Lutterworth to hear the sermons. His followers became known by the name of "Lollards," and a campaign began to take portions of translated Scripture from village to village, to read and instruct the people who gathered in the village square. This sort of rebellion of the Roman hierarchy resulted in severe persecution.

We must keep in mind that Wycliffe and the Lollards were copying everything by hand. In those days, it took up to eighteen months to "write" a whole Bible. But Wycliffe finished his manuscript of the Bible in English. His loyal Lollard followers completed several copies by the time of his death, and almost nightly, they met for periods of prayer, study, and transcription of small passages to be given to the people who were starving for the hope of the Word. Their silent battle cry was, "If God be for us, who can be against us" (Rom. 8:31).

Wycliffe's papist opponents said, "The jewel of the clergy (the Bible) has become the toy of the laity."

In spite of the zeal with which the hierarchy sought to destroy it, there still exist about 150 manuscripts, complete or partial, containing the translation of Wycliffe in its revised form. From this, one may easily infer how widely diffused it was in the fifteenth century. For this reason the Wycliffites in England were often designated by their opponents as "Bible men." The pope's minions called them "Lollards" as a derisive term, meaning they were unlearned, young men "lolling about" and preaching.

At Wycliffe's funeral his epitaph was read; "He was as the morning star in the midst of a cloud, as the moon at the full, as the sun shining forth upon the temple of the Most High, and as the rainbow giving light in the clouds of glory." Ever since, Wycliffe has been known as the morningstar of the reformation.

He wrote such glorious truths to the English ear as:

"It is not necessary to go either to Rome or to Avignon in order to seek a decision from the pope, since the triune God is everywhere. Our pope is Christ." And,

"The church is the totality of those who are predestined to blessedness. It includes the church triumphant in heaven… and the church militant, or men on earth. No one who is eternally lost has part in it. There is one universal church, and outside of it there is no salvation. Its head is Christ. No pope may say that he is the head, for he cannot say that he is elect or even a member of the church."

"Wycliffe aimed to do away with the existing hierarchy and replace it with 'poor priests' who lived in poverty, were bound by no vows, had received no formal consecration, and preached the gospel to the people. These itinerant preachers spread the teachings of Wycliffe. Two by two they went, barefoot, wearing long dark-red robes, and carrying a staff in the hand, the latter having symbolic reference to their pastoral calling, and passed from place to place preaching the sovereignty of God. The bull of Gregory XI impressed upon them the name of Lollards, intended as an opprobrious epithet, but it became, to them, a name of honour. Even in Wycliffe's time the 'Lollards' had reached wide circles in England and preached 'God's law, without which no one could be justified.'"[1]

In writing to true followers of Christ, Wycliffe gave the bottom line regarding authority:

> "Believers should ascertain for themselves what are the true matters of their faith, by having the Scriptures in a language which all may understand. For the laws made by prelates are not to be received as matters of faith, nor are we to confide in their public instructions, nor in any of their words, but as they are founded in Holy Writ, since the Scriptures contain the whole truth…It is the pride of Lucifer, and even greater pride than his, to say that the teachers of man's traditions, made of sinful fools, are more profitable and needful to Christian people than the preachers of the Gospel."[2]

No matter how brilliant or correct John Wycliffe was, or should we say BECAUSE of how correct he was, the Imperial hierarchy of the Roman Church spoke out against him not only during his lifetime but well after it. Archbishop Arundel gave the general rebuttal of the Imperial Church:

> "It is a dangerous thing, as St. Jerome assures us, to translate the holy Scriptures, it being very difficult in a version to keep close to the sense of the inspired writers: for by the confession of the same father he had mistaken the meaning of several texts. We, therefore, decree and ordain, that from henceforward no unauthorised person shall translate any part of the holy Scripture into English or any other language, under any form of book or treatise: neither shall any such book, treatise, or version, made either in Wycliffe's time or since, be read, either in whole or in part, publicly or privately, under the penalty of the greater excommunication, till the said translation shall be approved either by the bishop of the diocese, or a provincial council, as occasion shall require."[3]
> —ARCHBISHOP ARUNDEL, BISHOP OF YORK, 1408

However, the Lollards were undaunted. Portions of Wycliffe's English translation were circulated far and wide. It is a little-known fact that the text became the textbook for the emerging English language. Many have been taught to think that Chaucer's prose and poetry was the basis of the language called "Middle English" and such is partly true. What is little known is that Chaucer was a Lollard sympathizer and honored Wycliffe secretly in the "Tale of the Parson" when he wrote *The Canterbury Tales*. Wycliffe's theological writings and philosophy formed the foundation that educated peasants and scholars for the next 100 years.

The church hierarchy never ceased to be furious with the "treasonous Wycliffe." The Council of Rome was called by Pope John XXIII in the year 1412. The last official act of the council on February 10, 1413 was to order the burning of Wycliffe's writings. This is the same pope who threatened to burn all of his rivals for the papacy, "if I could but lay hands on upon them." [4]

John was eventually deposed by the Council of Constance, (followers of the other, also reigning pope), and upon his forced return (from running away from the council), he was tried for heresy, simony, schism and immorality, and found guilty on all counts. The eminent English historian Gibbon, wrote, "The more scandalous charges were suppressed; the vicar of Christ was accused only of piracy, rape, sodomy, murder, and incest."[5]

This statue is located at the entrance of the harbor of Konstanz on Lake Constance. It depicts Imperia, a prostitute who during the Constance Council (1414–1418) served both the emperor and the pope. In her hands she holds both of them; both are naked, except for the crown and and the papal tiara. Photo was taken in July 2014.

The threat of the truth in the writings of Wycliffe was like acid indigestion for the papacy. Indeed, it was a growing ulcer in the belly of the beast. Finally, in 1428, forty-four years after the "Morningstar's" death, Pope Martin V ordered the bones of Wycliffe to be dug from his grave and burned. This was the height of silliness. But this is what we come to when we start down the road of lies and secrecy in order to retain power.

Burning Wycliffe's bones, from *Foxe's Book of Martyrs* (1563)

And, this is where we entered on our journey to understand the history of the true church and her British/Welsh mission for the world.

At the same time that the pope's minions were burning the bones of Wycliffe, a German entrepreneur was about to change everything for the slaves to religion and the revolution was, of all things, begun as a church tool of the Roman machine.

The Curious Case of Johann Gutenberg

Johannes Gensfleisch zur Laden Gutenberg
c. 1395 Mainz, Germany
Died: February 3, 1468 (age 70)
Nationality: German
Occupation: Engraver, inventor, and printer;
Known for the invention of the movable-type printing press
Religion: Catholic

His father worked with the ecclesiastic mint. Gutenberg grew up knowing the trade of gold-smithing. This is supported by historian Heinrich Wallau, who adds, "In the fourteenth and fifteenth centuries his [descendants] claimed a hereditary position as ...the master of the archiepiscopal mint. In this capacity they doubtless acquired considerable knowledge and technical skill in metal working. They supplied the mint with the metal to be coined, changed the various species of coins, and had a seat at the assizes in forgery cases."

Wallau adds, "His surname was derived from the house inhabited by his father and his paternal ancestors 'zu Laden, zu Gutenberg'. The house of Gänsfleisch was one of the patrician families of the town, tracing its lineage back to the thirteenth century."

Patricians (aristocrats) in Mainz were often named after houses they owned. Around AD 1427, the name zu Gutenberg, after the family house in Mainz, is documented to have been used for the first time.

For some historical context, let's remember the "holy wars" of Popes Julius and Leo X. One of those "pograms" cleared the Jews out of Gutenberg, (the *berg*, town, of the *Judens*, Jews), so that the friends of the popes could move in. The rich family of Johannes Gensfleisch was allowed to grab the property of the best Jewish family because they were goldsmiths to the papal rulers in Germany. The German word for "Jew" was *Guden*. Johannes father lived in a "Guden," house, on a hill that was atop a former small township, "berg," of Jews. There, the Guden-berg family continued their service to the prelates of the church.

Around 1439, Johann Gutenberg was involved in a financial misadventure making polished metal mirrors (which were promoted to capture holy light from religious relics) for sale to pilgrims. We guess that, after the holy pilgrimage, the duped buyers found only their own reflections in the mirrors and the light of truth dawned on them. Following this, and other business failures, Johann went to work as a jeweler again, in the family business.

Gutenberg's Revolutionary Press

But, something extraordinary happened in Germany while the Roman Dragon ruled and rampaged in England and on the Continent. Gutenberg had a side-business problem. Not only was he a goldsmith to the archbishop and the prince, but he owned a small business which employed "scribes," to write out indulgences for the Roman Church. In the early 1400s, so many German Catholics were in need of buying off the authorities based on paying the church penance, that Gutenberg was way behind in getting the paperwork done. His people could only write so fast.

The story goes that Johannes was visiting with a merchant who had just come from the Orient with precious metals for jewelry and other wares when the man showed him some "printing blocks" that the Chinese used to imprint a seal on their merchandise. Necessity being the mother of invention, an idea was born. Gutenberg wondered, "What if, instead of wooden blocks, metal could be used to imprint letters of the German alphabet. If these could be arranged into words and pressed into ink, then moved around to form new words for other offences that had been committed against God, then the work of writing indulgences could be done ten or twenty times faster."

Moveable Type Press

Johannes borrowed some money and crafted the first ever moveable type printing press. Gutenberg was able to convince the wealthy moneylender Johann Fust for a loan of 800 guilders. Peter Schöffer, who became Fust's son-in-law, also joined the enterprise at Hof Humbrecht, a property belonging to a distant relative of Gutenberg. Schöffer had worked as a scribe in Paris and is believed to have designed some of the first typefaces. By AD 1450, the press was in operation. They were printing out indulgences by the dozens every day and exceeding demand.

One day, when the time of Lent was near and German Catholics were going to attempt to be good, Gutenberg surmised the press would be idle. He got the idea to print and offer a Bible to the archbishop, his anchor client in the indulgences business. Back in those days, a Bible took about eighteen months to scribe and bind. Gutenberg figured that he could accomplish the project in three to four months. He went to work and produced the first moveable-type Bible, The Gutenberg Bible. The word got around that the archbishop was pleased with the work, and Johannes printers were tapped for many more Bibles; all in Latin of course. For the first time in his life, Johannes Gutenberg was making money. Lots of money. The Catholic machine was very good business.

Gutenberg Bible

At the same time, the press was also printing other, more lucrative texts. There is also some speculation that there may have been two presses, one for the pedestrian texts, and one for the Bibles.

Of course, the real profit-making enterprise of the new press was the printing of thousands of indulgences for the church, documented as beginning from 1454–55.

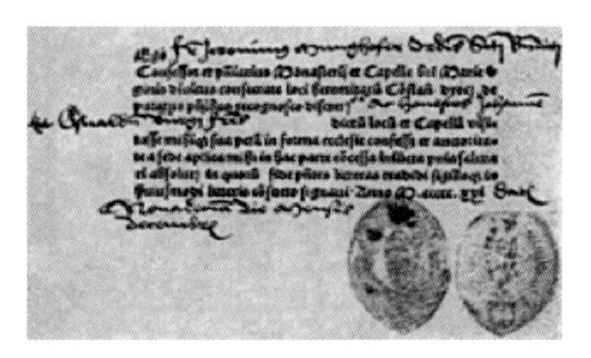

The first precisely datable printing is Gutenberg's 31-line indulgence, which is known to already exist on October 22, 1454.[6] It is a template for particularly popular sins and consists of 550 printed words or 3,500 pieces of type.[7]

The Mass of Saint Gregory. Engraving by Israhel van Meckenem of the Mass of Saint Gregory, 1490s, with, at the bottom, an indulgence of 20,000 years out of purgatory each time specified prayers were said in the presence of the picture. (For which, of course, there was a hefty charge by the church.)

An eighteenth-century printed absolution certificate granted by the Patriarch of Jerusalem and sold by Greek monks in Wallachia. (History Museum, Bucharest)

A vellum copy of the Gutenberg Bible owned by the U.S. Library of Congress.

However, nothing good lasts forever and in 1462, during a conflict between two archbishops, Mainz was sacked by Archbishop Adolph von Nassau and Nassau's army, and Gutenberg was exiled. An old man by now, he moved to Eltville where he may have initiated and supervised a new printing press belonging to the brothers Bechtermünze.

Ancient Italian Printing and Press

However, the Roman Church seized the moment to print indulgences to their heart's desire without giving the middleman, Gutenberg, a share. The capital of printing in Europe shifted to Rome and Venice. In Rome, the Pope now had a monopoly on the printing of indulgences and could make all the money for the church treasury. In Venice, visionary printers, like Aldus Manutius, ensured widespread availability of the major Greek and Latin texts in print. The claims of an Italian origin for movable type have also focused on this rapid rise of Italy in movable-type printing.

In January 1465, Gutenberg's achievements were recognized by the Roman Church and he was given the title Hofmann (gentleman of the court) by von Nassau. This honor included a stipend, an annual court outfit, as well as 2,180 litres of grain and 2,000 litres of wine tax-free. It is believed he may have moved back to Mainz around this time, but this is not certain.

Why do this for an old man? Probably because he possessed printing knowledge and was loved by the people. The archbishop couldn't kill him, but he could neutralize him. He made sure that Gutenberg didn't need money to keep printing "other writings."

Gutenberg died in 1468 and was buried in the Franciscan church at Mainz, his contributions largely unknown. This church and the cemetery were later destroyed, and Gutenberg's grave is now lost. However, God was able to use this German entrepreneur and Catholic to progress the Bible as never before. It was a round-about blessing, and the connection was made by several "rustic" scholars and a famous Italian printer who loved everything Greek.

Enter the Epic Work of Manutius

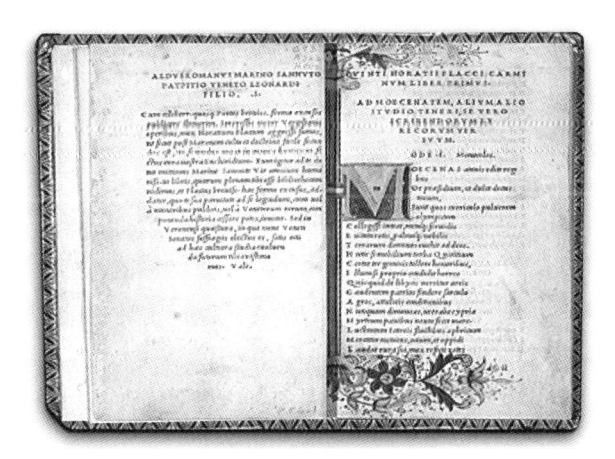

Hypnerotomachia Poliphili

By the end of the fifteenth century, Venice had become the European capital of printing, being one of the first cities in Italy, after Subiaco (45 miles east of Rome) and Rome, to have a printing press. Amazingly, there were 417 presses by 1500! The most important Renaissance printing office was the Aldine Press of Aldus Manutius, which in 1499 printed the Hypnerotomachia Poliphili, considered the most beautiful book of the Renaissance.

Aldus Pius Manutius (Bassiano, 1449 – Venice, February 6, 1515)

In addition to editing Greek classics from manuscripts, Manutius re-printed editions of classics that had originally been published in Florence, Rome, and Milan, at times correcting and improving the texts. Near the end of his life, Manutius had begun an edition of the Septuagint, the first to be published; it appeared posthumously in 1518.

In order to promote Greek studies, Manutius founded an Academy of Hellenists in 1502 called the "New Academy." Its rules were written in Greek, its members were obliged to speak Greek, their names were Hellenized, and their official titles were Greek. Members of the "New Academy" included Desiderius Erasmus and the British Christian Thomas Linacre.

Linacre

He was one of the first Englishmen to study Greek in Italy, and brought back to his native country and his own university the lessons of the "New Learning." His teachers were some of the greatest scholars of the day. Among his pupils was one—Erasmus—whose name alone would suffice to preserve the memory of Linacre, his instructor in Greek.

In the 1490s this Oxford professor was also the personal physician to King Henrys the VII and VIII. But he was not satisfied to be at court in England. Momentously, Thomas Linacre, decided to learn Greek. After reading the Gospels in Greek, and comparing it to the Latin Vulgate, he wrote in his diary, "Either this (the original Greek) is not the Gospel…or we are not Christians." He first read the Gospels in Greek in, of all places, Italy, lair of the Dragon.

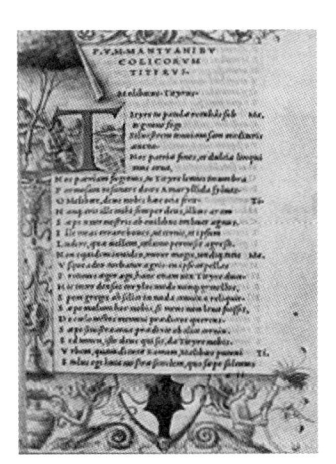

Examples of Greek Classics from the Aldine Press

The Aldine Press in Italy was started by Aldus Manutius based on his love of classics and at first printed new copies of Plato, Aristotle, and other Greek and Latin classics. He also printed dictionaries and grammars to help people interpret the books. While earlier scholars wanting to learn Greek employed learned Greeks to teach them directly, the Aldine editions, edited by Greek scholars, allowed many across Europe to study Greek. Historian Elizabeth Eisenstein claimed that the fall of Constantinople in 1453 had threatened the importance and survival of Greek scholarship, but publications such as those by the Aldine Press secured it.

Erasmus was one of the scholars learned in Greek that the Aldine Press employed.

When the press expanded to current titles, the New Academy group wrote some books themselves and, occasionally, employed other writers, including Erasmus. And he is the subject of chapter nine.

Sources

1. *Foxe's Book of Martyrs*

2. Henry C. Sheldon, quoted in Peabody, M.A., *History of the Christian Church*, vol 2, (Hendrickson Publishers, 1988), 411.

3. Archbishop Arundel, Bishop of York, 1408 (*Baxter's Hexapla 1841/ Colliers *Ecclesiastical History*, iii 280).

4. Philip Schaff, *History of the Christian Church*, vol. VI, 142.

5. *The Decline and Fall of the Roman Empire*, vol. 3, (New York: The Heritage Press, 1946), 2417.

6. Paul Needham, *The Changing Shapes of the Vulgate Bible in 15th Century Printing Shops*, (2009).

7. Bettina Wagner, *Early Printed Books as Material Objects*, (2010), 11.

Images

Imperia © Gunold Brunbauer | Dreamstime.com

Moveable Type Press © Yuriy Chaban | Dreamstime.com

Gutenberg Bible © Spaceheater | Dreamstime.com

Ancient Italian printing press © Lukeluke68 | Dreamstime.com

Chapter Nine

The New Testament's Man of Letters

Desiderius Erasmus in 1523
Other names: Desiderius Erasmus Roterodamus,
(Erasmus of Rotterdam)
Born: October 27, 1466, Burgundian Netherlands
Died: July 12, 1536 (aged 69), Basel, Old Swiss Confederacy
Main interests: Christian Philosophy, Renaissance Humanism

Talk about a less than desirable beginning, Erasmus began life as the bastard child of a Catholic priest and his mistress, Margaretha Rogers, the housekeeper of the curate house in Gouda, Holland. As we have mentioned, this was not totally frowned upon during the Middle Ages and the Renaissance. In fact, if a clergyman wanted conjugal relations with the opposite sex, she must be a mistress. Wives might produce heirs, and heirs would demand property of their fathers. This the church would not allow. All property of Roman clergy remained in the hands of the pope and bishops.

Erasmus Begins to Search

His family put him on the path to priesthood by sending him to a local Augustinian monastery in the town of Steyn, but Erasmus hated it. He was a very lonely young man, wanted by no one, the ultimate non-person in medieval Catholic Europe. There he found one faithful friend, a fellow monk named Servatius Rogerus. There are letters which survive wherein Erasmus expresses his "love" toward the only person who loved him back. No one knows exactly what the true relationship was between these two lonely young men in the monastery. Maybe it was a sexual relationship and maybe not. Suffice it to say that Servatius was transferred to another monastery and Erasmus went into a time of depression and soul-searching. (Critics should ask themselves if they can remember doing anything wrong during their hormonal youth.)

After some time, Erasmus convinced the leadership at Steyn to transfer him to the office of the bishop of Cambrai, many miles to the south. There, he polished his writing and his thinking as the secretary for the bishop. During this time, he developed the beginning of his "humanist ideas." Humanism is distinct from Secular Humanism, which is prominent today. Secular Humanism makes man the center of all things, without the need for God. Renaissance Humanism was understood as man's relationship with God through the realization that God could be seen in the laws of God's nature. This philosophy stated that since God is free and not bound by matter, and since man is made in his image, man must also be free. Man, therefore, was not created to be in a cycle of misery under any hierarchy's thumb, but to be free to follow his conscience.

Erasmus never returned to monastic life, but became an ordained priest in 1492. He soon became a roving international student, and that travel would cause him to cross paths with the rustic scholars from England, also studying at the Academy of Hellenists in Italy and whom he followed home. We do have a clue for the time of the total change in his life. It is his adopted name.

Desiderius is a Latin given name which means "the longed-for."

He adopted this additional "name" in 1499, during his time in England at Cambridge University. Some have suggested that this was because he had a salvation experience there and considered himself "longed for" by God after Jesus' expression in Luke 22:14, using the Greek word, *'epithumio'*—to long for.

Erasmus was not only a scholar but a personal friend of Sir Thomas More, a court lawyer and statesman for King Henry VIII. However, there was something that they strongly disagreed on. Erasmus had the audacity to translate much of the Greek New Testament into English. When some of his students reported that he was reading and teaching theology in English, Erasmus was expelled from the university. He promptly went to Basel, Switzerland, where there happened to be a printing business that would gladly help him print lots of copies of Latin New Testaments from his Greek translation, along with notes of the meanings he had devised by using the picture language called English.

This new Latin New Testament revealed how "spun" the original Latin Vulgate had been as translated by Jerome and, more importantly, how corrupt the Vulgate had become since Jerome. Most important, it proved that the major "mysteries" of the pope as Christ's vicar, Mariology, penance and other favorite church "coffer-fillers" had no basis in Holy Scripture. One of these new, New Testaments found its way into the hands of a young English scholar named William Tyndale. The year was 1520, and things were heating up in the political and theological arena. The pope decreed that possessing Scriptures that were in any language but Latin was heretical and outlawed, and the existent Latin Scriptures must be ones officially recognized by "the Holy See." Anyone rebelling against this decree would be severely punished. One wonders if the pope and his minions might have been just the least bit afraid that the "jig could be up" for their corrupt money-train if people knew the truth of the Bible.

The Catholic Counter-Reformation movement often condemned Erasmus as having "laid the egg that hatched the Reformation." He countered by originating the phrase, "Pandora's Box" when he retorted that the bishops accused him of opening the Bible to the masses. He said, "But one thing the facts cry out, and it can be clear, as they say, even to a blind man, that often through the translator's clumsiness or inattention the Greek has been wrongly rendered; often the true and genuine reading has been corrupted by ignorant scribes, which we see happen every day, or altered by scribes who are half-taught and half-asleep."

Erasmus also wrote his own summary of "protestation" against the prevailing church, to wit:

"Christ has not died in order that wealth, abundance, arms, and the rest of the pomp of an earthly kingdom which was formerly possessed by the heathen should now be in possession of a few priests not unlike heathens."

In 1499, while in England, Erasmus was particularly impressed by the Bible teaching of John Colet. This prompted him, upon his return from England, to master the Greek language and translate the New Testament. On one occasion he wrote to Colet:

"I cannot tell you, dear Colet, how I hurry on, with all sails set, to holy literature. How I dislike everything that keeps me back, or retards me."

In the year 1516, the now middle-aged scholar, working in the lowlands of Germany, produced his Greek New Testament with accompanying commentaries for the scholarly reader. As stated, Johan Froben, with his printing presses in Basel, Switzerland, printed the work.

Though Erasmus admired Jerome's early attempt in the Latin Vulgate, he made hundreds of changes in the text based on his scholarship of the Greek language. This amounted to a full-scale attack on the Imperial Church in Rome. To change Jerome was to attack the structure of the Imperial Church.

"Most notorious was Erasmus's retranslation of Gospel passages (especially Matthew 3:2), where John the Baptist is presented in the Greek as crying out to his listeners in the wilderness, '*metanoeite*'. Jerome had translated this as *poenitentiam agite*, 'do penance', and the medieval church had pointed to the Baptist's cry as biblical support for its theology of the sacrament of penance. Erasmus said that John had told his listeners to come to their senses, or repent, and he translated the command into Old Latin as '*resipiscite*'. Indeed, throughout the Bible, it was difficult to find any direct reference to penance or purgatory, as orthodox theologians had been pointing out to Westerners since the thirteenth century."[1]

In Erasmus' prologue to his New Testament translation, he said that he wished to see the "countryman chant the Bible at his plough, the weaver at his loom, the traveler on his journey, and even women," to read his text. (This was later translated into English by young William Tyndale, who would blurt out his version of the sentiment to a Roman clergyman several decades into the future.) He also wrote many other commentaries on Christianity and the Christian life. In 1504, he wrote a best-seller called *Enchiridion Militis Christiani: The Dagger for the Christian Soldier*. This was a treatise on Christ-centered faith.

In this short work, Erasmus outlines the views of the normal Christian life, which he was to spend the rest of his days elaborating. "The chief evil of the day" he said, "is formalism—going through the motions of tradition without understanding their basis in the teachings of Christ. Forms can teach the soul how to worship God, or they may hide or quench the spirit."

By the 1530's, the writings of Erasmus accounted for 10 to 20 percent of all book sales. He is credited with coining the adage, "In the land of the blind, the one-eyed man is king." (Speculation is that he meant his contemporaries in the clergy keeping the masses blind by design.)

The third edition of Erasmus' Testamentum (New Testament), 1522, was used by Martin Luther in his German translation of the Bible, written for people who could not understand Latin. This translation aided Tyndale as he translated the first English New Testament, (Worms, 1526), and was the basis for the 1550 Robert Stephanus edition used by the translators of the Geneva Bible and the King James Version of the English Bible.

Incidentally, here is another crucial example that is a doctrinal divergence from the Latin Vulgate of the Imperial Church. Here is the current reading of 1 Corinthians 15:51, found in our Protestant Bibles.

"Behold, I tell you a mystery: We shall not all sleep, but we all shall be changed."

The Vulgate read, "We all will rise but we shall not all be changed."[2]

This was a doctrinally and contextually critical verse. The Imperial Church used this verse in support of offerings and prayers for those in purgatory and the litany of other heresies perpetrated by the hierarchy. Their threat? If we shall not all be changed, it will be because we were not prayed for in purgatory; therefore, all should be changed who are in purgatory before the coming of the great white throne judgment.

Contextually, the apostle Paul's meaningful story of resurrection was changed. In properly rendering the critical texts, Protestant Bibles share the story of Paul correctly. Paul says that, not everyone will die, but that some believers will be alive in the flesh when Jesus comes again for his church. But, Paul says that the spiritually saved, both the dead (those who sleep) and those alive at that time, will be changed into imperishable bodies. This revelational mystery from Paul has nothing to do with so-called purgatory or hell, except in an eisogesis (reading into) of the text that Rome was so famous for.

Another very interesting aside comes from the time of Erasmus. From rustic Ireland, Erasmus was provided and edition of the Codex Britainnicus, which was originally written in the thirteenth century. This Greek codex had 1st John 5:7 in it as we have in the critical text today, and the King James Version of 1611. Erasmus did not have it in any of his medieval references, but he included it in his third revision of the New Testament after this find. The precious, and sometimes excluded, verse follows: "For there are three that bear witness in heaven, the Father, the Word, and the Holy Spirit and these three are one" (NKJV).[3]

This example shows that we continue to find the "true New Testament" in the rustic and the original church. Indeed, since then, textual critics have discovered that this verse was attested to by Cyprian in AD 250 and Athanasius in AD 350, as well as the German TEPL Codex translated from the classic Latin before Jerome's Vulgate.

Erasmus' Later Work

Erasmus published a definitive fourth edition of the New Testament in 1527 containing parallel columns of Greek, Latin Vulgate, and Erasmus' Latin texts. He used the then available Polyglot Bible to improve this version. In this edition Erasmus also supplied the Greek text of the last six verses of Revelation (which he had translated from Latin back into Greek in his first edition). In 1535 Erasmus published the fifth (and final) edition which dropped the Latin Vulgate column but was otherwise similar to the fourth edition. Versions of Erasmus' Greek New Testament were based on the Textus Receptus, or the Greek Byzantine version of the Bible, of which there were many that came out of Turkey and Greece during the Muhammadan invasion. This is the reason that, sometimes, Erasmus' translation is considered the Textus Receptus.

Erasmus New Testament, 1516

"Christ desires his mysteries to be published abroad as widely as possible. I would that [the Gospels and the epistles of Paul] were translated into all languages, of all Christian people, and that they might be read and known." —Erasmus

"Truly, it is not meet to declare ourselves Christian men by killing very many but by saving very many, not if we send thousands of heathen people to hell, but if we make many infidels Christian. Not if we curse and excommunicate, but if we, with devout prayers and with our hearts desire their health, and pray unto God to send them better minds."[4] —Erasmus (speaking of the pope's Crusades)

Erasmus did not quarrel as much with Luther's theology as with his attitude and tone. In a letter to Luther, he expressed the wish, "May the Lord Jesus grant you daily more of his spirit for his glory and the general good."[5]

Erasmus knew and corresponded with Martin Luther after the German priest was excommunicated by the pope. Erasmus' local prelate's men encouraged him to confront the errant German hothead. In 1524, he wrote *A Diatribe on Free Will*, emphasizing that the initiative of grace was with God alone. However, this tract only served to bring the discussion to a new level of exposure of the Roman hierarchy. The parties both began to realize that Erasmus was a consensus builder and not a spear-wielding soldier of the accepted church.

Erasmus did follow up to Luther's reaction to his *A Diatribe*, with two volumes of lectures on Free Will so that the Church would apprehend that he saw their side of the equation. In these writings he accused Luther of forcing him back to the "imperfect structure of the old Church." "Therefore, I will put up with this Church until I see a better one; and it will have to put up with me, until I become better."[6]

Later, the Roman Inquisition attempted to ban all his writings, but, as we know, Pandora's Box was already wide open, never to be shut again.

Meanwhile, Back in Britain: The Secret Breakout

While Gutenberg was printing Bibles and indulgences for the archbishop of Germany, back in England, a Christian physician and fellow member of the Academy of Hellenists, named Thomas Linacre, was moved by the Spirit of the Lord to go around the Roman clergy's constrictions of the time and create an English grammar book based on Greek. He was somewhat protected in so doing because he was the personal physician to King Henry VIII. Isn't it marvelous how God positions his people to do his work? And, oftentimes, they are supported, unknowingly, by ungodly and tyrannical rulers.

Thomas Linacre

Linacre's English-Greek grammar book was widely copied, and it taught young school students the elements of Greek and how it was translated into the English language. This set the stage for the populace to understand the Bible in Greek. The years of this development were AD 1460-1470.

Twenty-five years later one of those young Greek grammar students, who happened to be the son of the lord mayor of London, began to teach at Oxford. John Colet was also protected from the Roman Church because of his status. His father had saved King Henry VII's life in battle and was a respected leader in the realm.

John Colet

John was a very academically gifted man, and he began to lecture on the apostle Paul's writings as read directly from the Greek texts. The newest generation of students, who understood Greek grammar from their Linacre Greek/English schoolbooks, attended Colet's lectures in record numbers.

You see, at Oxford during this time, students were not allowed to speak or to read any language but Latin while on campus. The faculty at Oxford was afraid of the Roman hierarchy and implored John Colet to desist from teaching from the Greek text. He refused to do so and was ordered to leave the campus for preaching. They exiled him to the mostly empty and cavernous St. Paul's Cathedral where he preached from the same material. Soon, there was standing room only in the great building. Over ten-thousand people from all walks of life were hearing the apostle Paul's words in their own tongue from an unpolluted text for the first time in over a thousand years. It was heresy to the Roman Church—and they had facilitated it!

As we have mentioned, one of the priests in the area, Erasmus, heard John Colet, and he couldn't wait to return to his post as a teacher at Cambridge University to do the same.

And a young, brilliant scholar, one William Tyndale, was coming onto the scene.

We will examine the impact to the rustic church of this theological giant in chapter eleven, but first we must have a chapter on the impact of that Catholic priest who shook the world from the town of Wittenberg, in Germany. God's magnificent plan was coming together for freedom of the captives.

Sources

1. Diarmaid MacCollough, *Christianity, The First Three Thousand Years*, (Penguin, 2009), 596.

2. Donald L. Brake, *A Visual History of the King James Bible*, (Baker Books, 2011), 145.

3. Donald L. Brake, *A Visual History of the King James Bible*, (Baker Books, 2011), 136–137.

4. *Enchiridion Militis Christiani*, Methuen's edition, (1905), 8.

5. Philip Schaff, *History of the Christian Church*, vol. VII, 424.

6. Dairmaid MacCollough, *Christianity, The First Three Thousand Years*, (Penguin Books, 2009), p. 614

Images

Photos – Dreamstime.com

Desiderius Erasmus as depicted by Hans Holbein, the Younger © Grafzero | Dreamstime.com

Chapter Ten

The Wittenberg Door

Martin Luther (Statue at Wittenburg)

On October 31, 1517, Luther posted the ninety-five theses, which he had composed in Latin, on the door of the Castle Church of Wittenberg.

On the same day, Luther sent a hand-written copy, accompanied with honorable comments, to the Archbishop Albert of Mainz and Magdeburg, responsible for the practice of indulgence sales, and to the Bishop of Brandenburg, the superior of Luther. He enclosed in his letter a copy of his "Disputation of Martin Luther on the Power and Efficacy of Indulgences."

Museum copy of Martin Luther's 95 Thesis'

German priest Martin Luther lived in the heart of the Holy Roman Empire ruled by Friedrich of Saxony. Friedrich was one of seven electors who decided on who the emperor would be. His Wittenberg Castle and the adjoining church had a large collection of holy relics for pious visitors to come and worship. In the year 1513, Luther began to lecture at the local college on the Psalter and to encourage his parishioners to reflect on their spiritual life. This caused the lecturer himself to also consider his inner life. By the year 1515, Martin began lecturing on the Apostle Paul's letter to the Romans.

When he turned to the book and studied that faith was primarily essential to salvation—as it was written, "He who through faith is righteous shall live"—he began to reflect. Why, he thought, was so much of the tradition of the church based on pilgrimages and penance; i.e., works religion? Through prayer and meditation, Luther came to the realization that the doctrine of purgatory, with all its attendant structures of intercessory prayer for the dead designed to work for self or others to improve heavenly prospects after death, was unscriptural. He saw it for what it was, a lie told by clergymen in the guise of ultimate truth.

He also saw indulgences, grants remitting punishment from crimes, as officially sanctioned graft of the same church. As a priest, he had heard that Pope Leo X had raised funds from the German faithful to finish rebuilding St. Peter's Basilica in Rome. These injustices in the name of God had been going on for centuries, enslaving Christians. Luther was called to stop the madness of the Imperial Church. Through a series of called meetings and denunciations, the discussion became a groundswell of people who realized they had been and were being swindled in the name of God; and Luther was the reluctant leader.

As the inquisition of priest Luther ran on, his refutations included the booklets titled: *Address to the Christian Nobility of the German Church*, *The Babylonian Captivity of the Church*, and *The Freedom of a Christian*. He was told to revoke these by the archbishop of the Catholic Church. Martin replied, "If then I revoke these books, all I shall achieve is to add strength to tyranny, and open not the windows but the doors to this monstrous godlessness, for a wider and freer range than it has ever dared before." He was excommunicated.

During his exile and while in hiding, Martin Luther translated the Bible into German for all the people to understand it for themselves, so that through faith they could approach salvation.

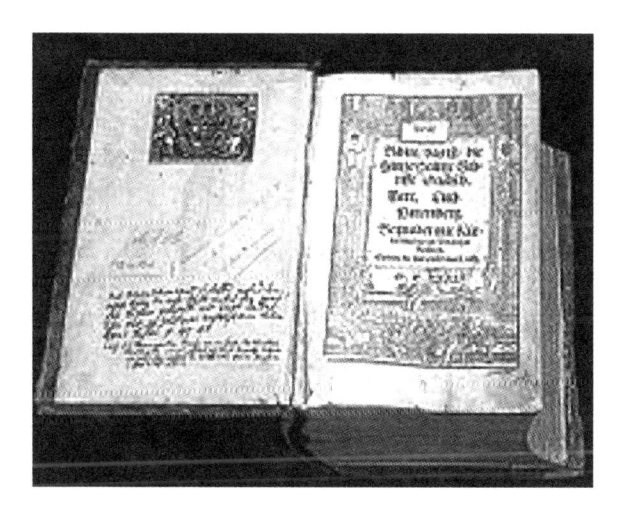

Luther wrote, "The papists must bear with us, and we with them. If they will not follow us, we have no right to force them. Wherever they can, they will hang, burn, behead, and strangle us. I shall be persecuted as long as I live and most likely be killed. But it must come to this at last; every man must be allowed to believe according to his conscience, and answer for his belief to his maker."[1]

Arguably, Luther's deepest impact on Christianity was his preaching from the Bible on the "Priesthood of the Believer." It was the powder-keg that ignited all of Europe. Why? Because this teaching negated a priest's vocation as being superior to all other believers. This teaching challenged class distinctions. We will see that the seed planted by Luther about this Bible truth will bring the greatest harvest in the American colonies.

During his protestation, Luther reported that he often disputed in private with the Devil in the night, about the state of his soul, so earnestly that he himself perspired and trembled. Once, the Devil told him that he was a great sinner. "I knew that long ago," replied Luther, "Tell me something new."[2]

As the common people flocked to Lutheran Churches, the Prince of Saxony protected them. Apparently, he, too, had become fed up with the extortion of the official church of the empire. Luther befriended all who would come and seek Christ, free from the Roman hierarchy. One of those was a former nun, Katherina Von Bora.

As Protestantism spread across Germany, many monks and nuns sought freedom. Those who walked away from their convents and monasteries and were caught were severely punished. However, twelve nuns from the local Nimbschen Convent decided to chance it and got word out to Luther. He arranged for their escape. On the evening of April 5, 1523, a loyal Lutheran drove a wagon full of barrels into the convent, put each nun into a barrel, and drove away. According to Lutherans, Von Bora was in the first barrel.

Luther became friends with Von Bora, and she became the housekeeper for the monastery turned "Lutheran Headquarters" where Martin lived. For several years, he tried to match her with local men who desired to wed her. She demurred and stated to those in the household that only someone as wonderful as Martin could win her heart. Finally, he caught the clue bus and asked her to marry him. He wrote to a friend, "If I can swing it, I'll take Kate to wife ere I die, to spite the Devil."[3] They married and carried on the work of nurturing the new protesting church and their six children. Some in the Roman Church voiced the thought that when Luther married Katherina, "Antichrist must be the fruit of such a union," for it had been predicted that he would be the offspring of a monk and a nun. This caused Erasmus to utter that biting sarcasm, "If that prophecy be true, what thousands of Antichrists the world has before now seen."[3]

Katherina von Bora Luther

Katherina is often considered one of the most important participants of the Reformation because of her role in helping to define Protestant family life and setting the tone for clergy marriages. She always called Luther, "Doctor Luther." He called her *Selbander* which is German for "better half." Katherina kept cows for milk and butter, and she started a piggery because Martin liked pork. She turned a neglected field into a thriving garden and planted an orchard nearby. Martin pointed to all her accomplishments and remarked to friends, "Have I not a fair wife, or shall I say boss?"

The Luthers would arise at six each morning and pray with the children, recite the Ten Commandments, the Apostles' Creed, and the Lord's Prayer, then sing a psalm. Martin would hurry off to preach or meet and Katherina would manage the household. On February 18, 1546, Martin Luther entered into Glory. A year later, Katherina had to flee Wittenberg because of war. She never was able to live in her home again. After years of war, the family returned to Wittenberg to find everything destroyed. Then, the plague hit the area and they had to flee to the countryside, working for their keep in various places for years. She and the children lost almost everything, and she died surrounded by them on December 20, 1552. On her deathbed, she is quoted to remark for others not to worry because, "I will stick to Christ as a burr to cloth."[5] And, she encouraged her children to do the same, which, by all accounts, they did.

OTHER PROTESTANTS AND THE BIBLE

There are so many other Fathers of Protestantism that we could speak of, but for our purposes in this book, we need to mention the Reformed Protestants. Why? Because as brave and wonderful as Martin Luther was, he just never was able to break totally away from some of the trappings of Roman Church doctrine and practice. This is why leaders like Zwingli and John Calvin rose up to lead the Protestants away from Roman Catholicism. Luther was once chided by a friend for allowing the mass trappings in Lutheran churches and for allowing images in church. Martin remarked, "Remember, the Catholic Church may be a prostitute, but she is still our mother." He told followers that they should get married and have their children baptized in Catholic churches if there was not a Lutheran church in the area.

The Reformed Church held no such view. The leaders of those congregations held the Bible as their only reference and the traditions of the popes as heresy. Though Luther would allow for the sacrament of the Eucharist to be celebrated under the "truce" of what he called Consubstantiation rather than Transubstantiation, Zwingli would have no compromise. He said that the Eucharist was not to be a magical talisman of Christ's body. It was a community pledge, expressing the believer's faith and thankfulness by a Christian to God, a way of commemorating what Jesus had accomplished on the cross. And, what was true for it was also true for baptism. He said that baptism was a "welcome into the family of God and not a magical washing away of sin."

John Calvin, in his monumental work, the *Institutes of the Christian Religion*, rebuked the Lutheran idea of Consubstantiation in the Eucharist. This is the idea that, though Christ is not bodily in the bread and the wine, he is capable of being everywhere, so he "comes" to the service. Calvin preached more than a "sign" of dedication to Christ, but it was certainly not eating the actual body and the blood of the Lord, as the Romans insisted. He referenced the venerated Augustine of Hippo, the church writer that Luther quoted so frequently, "To what purpose dost thou make ready teeth and stomach? Believe, and thou hast eaten already."[6]

What Is the Point?

The importance of all this to our premise is that the old English and Scottish churches had none of this rancor. To them, the Gospels and Paul's letters were simple and easy to understand. These rustic, Celtic people said that the Eucharist was a rite that when observed gave power to the individual through the truth of belief it symbolized, which is God's Word through the Spirit nourishing the believer. And, baptism symbolized a new Christian's entrance into eternal life through his or her heart's belief on Jesus Christ as Savior sent by God; i.e., Celi and Yeshua spiritually alive for all men.

There is so much more that could be covered about the Christian Protestant movement in Europe, but that will need to wait for another time. Suffice it to say that the Roman Imperial Church and the Protestants were then and are now at war for the hearts and minds of the faithful. Hot war then, cold war now.

The Reformation in England

The early Reformation gained a sort of victory in England during the time of King Henry VIII. As most history buffs will know, Henry wanted to rid himself of his first wife, Catherine of Aragon, so he could have a male heir. If there ever was a 'crooked stick with which to make a straight lick,' it was Henry VIII. We must realize that that time was not equivalent to ours for the rights of people. It was a time when selfish monarchs ruled by obliged oligarchy and military power. If one was inside the king's court, he had some power, and the lust for that power from those of the king's court, gave the king power to rule as he saw fit.

King Henry VIII was defined by caprice and lust. He used the monarchy and the custom of a male heir to divorce and remarry at will. However, when he began this "male-heir" journey, God was able to work within it to wrest England from the bloody, Imperial Roman Church. When Henry was threatened by the pope with excommunication if he divorced his first Spanish Catholic wife, Catherine of Aragon, Henry declared that the Church of England was his church and was separate from the Roman Church, with him as the head of it. He was the first king in Europe to do so, and this reversed the religious direction of a thousand miserable years. After all, there was a great deal of English and Scottish Church history before and after the Catholics entered the picture.

Something was happening here in the British Isles that most leaders of the world did not realize. God was unleashing his power to resurrect the Christian "rustic people" to whom Jesus had passed the torch of his true church from the rebellious Jews. The seed had broken through the ground and a mighty oak in diminutive form sought the sun. Within a few years, all the Roman monasteries, nunneries, and friaries in England and Wales were closed and the inhabitants invited to join the Church of England or become the citizens of another country.

These were the days of the famous prime minister to Henry, Thomas Cromwell. Cromwell was a pendulum swung too far "right," but he had a monumental job to do. As he did it, he grabbed too much of the king's power and paid for it with his head. However, the Protestant archbishop of Canterbury, Thomas Cranmer, was more diplomatic, and his work was much more long-lasting.

Cranmer wrote *The Book of Common Prayer.* This was not only a book of prayer, but a customs and rite-of-passage manual which still exists today. The words of his prayer book have been recited by Englishmen far more frequently than Shakespeare. The phrases used during marriage ceremonies, funeral services, and regular church gatherings congealed a Christian nation, and the small clerical book became companion to the English Bible for generations. At the time it was written, English was a marginal language on the edge of the world. The British nation was a gadfly on the rump of the powerful nations of the world: France, Spain, Germany, Italy, North Africa, and the Muslim Emirates. BUT, within a scant three-hundred years, it would rule the world and take the English Bible in translation to the nations that had become its footstools. But, we have gotten ahead of ourselves. Let's get back to a seminal moment for the translation of the English Bible.

For Such a Time as This, Anne

Today's modern dramatists and movie makers have besmirched the memory of Anne Boleyn. Sure, she wanted to be queen. Sure, she had Henry VIII wrapped around her little finger. However, she was not only an intriguing queen in a provocative situation, but a Protestant sympathizer. She did something that no one else could do. She ushered the idea of true Christianity back into the throne room of the king of England. How she did so is a really good story.

Through one of her maids in waiting, Anne received a copy of William Tyndale's book, *The Obedience of a Christian Man*. This was a manual intended for the king of England to use in order to break totally free of Romanism. Tyndale had written it after leaving Oxford and intended for it to be offered to King Henry as he broke from Rome. However, Tyndale was a lonely scholar and not a court lawyer. No one in power at London would give him the time of day. So, God worked through another route.

Queen Anne actually began reading the Tyndale book to Henry and was rebuffed by Roman bishop Tunstall for bringing it into court. Henry loved it because it was a roadmap to freedom from the Roman Church, giving religious evidence of the Roman Church's deviation from Holy Scripture. However, when she came to the part where Tyndale said, "The king should devote himself to the service of his people, the meanest of whom is the equal with him in the kingdom of God" that tore it with Henry. He would read no more. That, combined with the inability of Anne to produce a male heir, sealed her fate. She was beheaded as the king considered another womb to continue his legacy.

But the damage to the Roman Imperial Church was done. Anne was gone, but *The Obedience of a Christian Man* had done some good work in Henry's devious mind. From this time on, Henry would use excerpts of the "freedom manual" in convincing his bishops and cardinals that they should be and would be leaders of The Church of England, leaving the pope without a valuable English and Scottish cow to milk. However, the "crooked stick" that was Henry VIII, did not become straight. It simply was a means to the ends of God.

Even to his death, a few years later, Henry would not let the average man have a Bible in English, even though he broke from Rome. He authorized his clerics of the Church of England to have an English Bible in all churches, but was troubled that the "irresponsible thumbing through its pages could give the people radical thoughts." Still, only the royally accepted clergy could have unfettered access to the Word of God. The Oxford-educated priest and genius, Tyndale, would not be silenced. It was he, more than any other man, who changed everything for the rustic, English believers in the era of the Reformation.

That story is in chapter eleven.

Sources

1. James A. Froude, *Short Studies on Great Subjects*, (Charles Scribner and CO, 1871), 118.
2. Philip Schaff, *History of the Christian Church*, (Charles Scribner's and Sons, 1910), 336.
3. *Luther's Letters*, Vol. 2, p. 655, 1525, DeWette's Collection.
4. Desiderious Erasmus, *Letter to Franciscus Sylvius*, 1526.
5. Meurer, *The Biography of Katharina von Bora*, 1854.
6. Augustine, Bishop of Hippo, *Commentary on John*, 25:12.

Images

Martin Luther (Statue at Wittenburg) © Christina Hanck | Dreamstime.com

Chapter Eleven

Every Plowboy…

Though Henry VIII wanted to break away from Rome, he took his time and tried, through much intrigue, to "win" over the papacy rather than fight it. Intertwined within his country and his court were those who could see no other choice than to stick with the Imperial Church. In God's good timing, William Tyndale came along and was a true genius. He practically grew up at Oxford. He had entered the university in 1505, when he was twelve. He earned his master's degree by 1515 at the age of twenty-two. When we consider that attaining a master's degree during that day required a year each of grammar, rhetoric and logic; a year each of music, arithmetic, geometry, and astronomy; a year of philosophy, including natural, moral and metaphysical expertise; and, finally, at least full command of Latin and one other language, it was a great feat of mental strength for anyone at any age to attain it, much less a teenager. But William Tyndale was also a genius at linguistics. He was able to read, write, and speak in no less than eight languages: English, German, Hebrew, Greek, Latin, Italian, Spanish, and French.

A few years after William Tyndale graduated and began to teach at Oxford, a horrible scene took place which would ever after change him. In 1519, in a small village called Little Park in Coventry, England, five men and two women were found guilty by the Roman bishop of teaching their children to recite the Lord's Prayer and the Ten Commandments in English. The Papal Court of Inquisition actually called up the children during trial and had them recite the Lord's Prayer for the court, which then condemned their parents to death. The "Little Park Seven" were taken out and burned at the stake for their heresy. That day Tyndale made himself a promise to be the enemy of this debased church and the monarchy that supported it in order to get its pound of flesh in taxes.

The next year, 1520, he decided to put his mind to work on translating a New Testament into English for the common man. (This was the same year that priest Martin Luther was excommunicated by the pope for his rebellion in Germany.) By the next year, Tyndale's English New Testament was done and circulated. And by 1522, Tyndale found himself a victim of the inquisition.

During his trial, Tyndale quoted the writings of the Church Fathers in Latin, he used some of the writings of Erasmus which had been accepted by previous popes and insisted that he would rather follow God's laws than the current pope's laws. A judging Roman priest taunted Tyndale.

"We would be better to be without God's laws than the pope's," he screamed at Tyndale. William responded, "I defy the pope and all his laws. If God spare my life ere many years, I will cause the boy that drives the plow to know more of the Scriptures than you."

Tyndale was put under arrest for a while and, upon his release, self-exiled to Europe in 1524. All copies of his New Testament in English were confiscated and burned. He made his way straight to Wittenberg, Germany and met with Martin Luther. The two hit it off, and Luther gave Tyndale permission to use his writings translated into English if it would help the cause in Tyndale's island nation home. By the year 1525, the translation was ready. AND, lo and behold, there just happened to be a print shop in the Continental lowlands which was owned and operated by the grandson of the partner of, guess who, Johannes Gutenberg. His name was Peter Schoeffer.

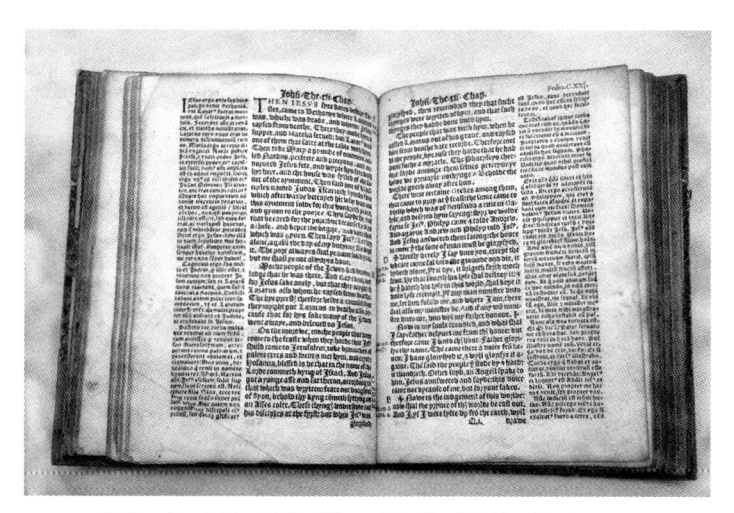

William Tyndale's 1538 edition of the English New Testament, which showed the English text and Erasmus' Latin text. From the Reed Rare Books Collection in Dunedin, New Zealand.

In 1526, he printed 2,000 copies of the complete Tyndale New Testament in English, and Lollards (Culdees) smuggled them into England by ship, concealed in bags of flour and bales of cloth.

However, the enemy was relentless. Most copies were found, and the owners were punished while the Bibles were burned. Only three original copies of Tyndale's first New Testament remain today. But God is relentless, too. There are many stories of God's providential aid to the men of England as they struggled to bring the Bible to the English-speaking peoples. One such great story is of the sailing man, Augustine Packington.

Packington was a merchant and trader of renown in the British Empire. King Henry and the archbishop of London, Bishop Tunstall, knew him well and had a "holy mission" for the merchant sailing man. They wanted him to go to the Continent and buy all the copies of Tyndale's English New Testament as they came off the presses. Then, Packington was to bring them to England where they would be promptly burned at the port of entry.

What the archbishop didn't know was that Packington was a secret Lollard (Culdee), and a friend to William Tyndale. Packington reported his task to Tyndale as soon as he reached the Continent. Tyndale told Augustine that he had a new and revised translation of the English New Testament which was better than the old one. Packington asked what it would take to print such a translation. It so happened that the price for 2,000 copies was exactly what the English archbishop had paid Packington to buy the remainder of the old copies in supply. Packington took the rest of the inventory of old Tyndale New Testaments and dutifully delivered them to the archbishop to be burned. Meanwhile, Tyndale used the church's money to print the new, revised translation in English. When Packington's ship arrived in port at Brussels after delivering the "bad Bibles" to the bishop, Tyndale's revised copies were ready. Packington took them back to England and, since he was so trusted by the archbishop, his cargo was not inspected and 2,000 brand-new English New Testaments were delivered all over the English countryside,—courtesy of the archbishop of the Roman Church. Bishop Tunstall couldn't figure out where he went wrong! But we know that God will not be mocked.

The following is how John Foxe, Christian historian, documented it shortly after the time:

"After this, Tyndale corrected the same New Testaments again, and caused them to be newly imprinted, so that they came thick and threefold over into England. When the bishop perceived that, he sent for Packington, and said to him, 'How cometh this, that there are so many New Testaments abroad? You promised me that you would buy them all.' Then answered Packington, 'Surely, I bought all that were to be had, but I perceive they have printed more since. I see it will never be better so long as they have letters and stamps: wherefore you were best to buy the stamps too, and so you shall be sure,' at which answer the bishop smiled, and so the matter ended."[1]

By the year 1529, Tyndale had printed a third and better revised edition. This version was also transported to England by the thousands and was secretly read by churchmen and their congregations. In 1531, he had translated all of the Pentateuch into English and distributed that also. The proverbial cat was out of the bag. There were English Bibles all over England, and the pope's minions were furious. They sent spies to find Tyndale and eradicate his nest of rebellious and dangerous heretical theology polluters.

What was so threatening about Tyndale? Well, let's see as we reveal the writings of this exceptional Christian.

Tyndale's Writings and Faith

William Tyndale, English Scholar
Born: 1490, England
Died: October 6, 1536, Vilvoorde Castle, Belgium
Education: Oxford, Cambridge

He is frequently referred to as the "Architect of the English Language," (even more so than William Shakespeare) as so many of the phrases Tyndale coined are still in our language today.

From the languages he studied, Tyndale could see that English and Greek were the most "inflected" languages of the world. They were in the same heritage and a translation purer than Latin would be more faithful than any previous versions, especially the now polluted Latin of Jerome, the Vulgate.

From Tyndale we get such popular phrases as:

- lead us not into temptation but deliver us from evil
- knock and it shall be opened unto you
- twinkling of an eye
- a moment in time
- fashion not yourselves to the world
- seek and you shall find
- eat, drink, and be merry
- ask and it shall be given you
- judge not that you not be judged
- the word of God which liveth and lasteth forever
- Let there be light (Luther translated Genesis 1:3 as: *Es werde Licht*, "It will be light.")
- the powers that be
- my brother's keeper
- the salt of the earth
- it came to pass
- gave up the ghost
- the signs of the times
- the spirit is willing, but the flesh is weak
- live and move and have our being

Tyndale brought to the English New Testament the meaning of the Greek without the bombastic formalism of Latin. He also used linguistic forms to express the meaning from the writer that had never crossed the minds of Englishmen before:

"Even so then at this present time also, there is a remnant according to the selection of grace. And if by grace, then it is no more of works: otherwise grace is no more grace" (Romans 11:5-6 KJV).

"Comparative Frames of Reference" are prominently used in Greek and in English in order to clarify the message. In this case, Tyndale saw that the apostle Paul wanted to drive home the point that Israel's election (and the Christians of his day) was based on grace and not on works. Oftentimes, the Latin translation of the Roman Church offered emphasis instead of frames of reference. This lack of linguistic word order has the effect of deemphasizing what is most important in the message and allowing the pope to clarify it with his decrees.

Here is another example. "Judge not, that ye be not judged. For with what judgment ye judge, ye shall be judged: and with what measure ye mete, it shall be measured to you again" (Matthew 7:1–2).

The call of Jesus is not to avoid judging, but to judge in the way you would want to be judged; that is, equitably.

Frame of Reference provides the basis of comparison and "focus" of the message. This linguistic "form" is easily translated directly from Greek into English because English was and is from an oral and rhetorical heritage most like Greek. "Filling in the blanks" rhetorically clarifies. It could be read as, "You know how you judge others? That's how you will be judged."

Latin is "orderly" and does not often allow, as English does, for emotive frames of reference that clarify. These English/Greek word context formulations, called "anchoring relations," provide focus for the mental picture being created. They are a good match.

We take this linguistic clarification for granted today, but in sixteenth-century England, it was revolutionary. The ruling English/Roman hierarchy would not stand for it. It upset the mafia-like apple cart.

The Mafia Will Not Go Quietly

There were three main characters in the English king's court during this time of Tyndale.

They were Archbishop Wolsey, Bishop Tunstall, and Sir Thomas More. These were the unholy trinity who harassed and plagued the rustic church of God. Of course, they had their spies and minions, who sought out and trapped the Culdees as they could. There was a network of monks, friars, and priests who worked to expose the rustic Christians. Those who are familiar with Nazi Germany will realize the similarity. It was a fearsome time, but God was not to be mocked or deterred. He worked around this titanic and tyrannical trio for his glory as he has done for thousands of years across the world and under the radar of the Evil One's soldiers.

Spiritual Masters of England During the Reign of Henry VIII

Cuthbert Tunstall

Master of the rolls, and bishop successively of London and Durham, Cuthbert Tunstall, born in 1474, was the eldest and illegitimate son of Thomas Tunstall of Thurland Castle, Lancashire.

Cardinal Wolsey at Christ Church (1510)

Tyndale thought of Wolsey as a wolf in sheep's clothing. He is quoted as saying, "Wolfsey, is the falsest and vainest cardinal that ever was."

During the infiltration of the domain of the Imperial Church in England, Tunstall, Wolsey, and Sir Thomas More were the rulers of the rulers, the heads of the snakes.

Thomas More

- Thomas More wrote *Dialogue*, a work against, "the pestilent sect of Luther and Tyndale."

    He also wrote *Confutation*, a work against Tyndale in three volumes, analyzing and refuting EVERY LINE of Tyndale's writing with the orthodox Roman Catholic position of his day.

- More was canonized as a Saint in 1935.

- "The Church is the Word of God unwritten while the Scripture is the Word of God written. The Word of God unwritten is of as great authority, as certain, and as sure, as his word written in the Scripture." —Sir Thomas More

More was the foremost Roman apologist of the sixteenth century. From the court of Henry, he pressed the official position of the church, while Henry watched and positioned for power. More hated Tyndale's New Testament and wrote that it was "well worthy to be burned."

More also hated Luther for parting with the Roman Church and for marrying the ex-nun Katharina de Bora. Yet, all around him were bishops, abbots, friars, and monks who lived openly with their concubines and mistresses. AND, the popes were renowned for this. More hated the evangelical brethren. In his *Confutation* he complained that too few had been burned: "But there should have been more burned by a great many than there have been within this seven years past."[2]

Not a principle he has written has been officially refuted by the Catholic Church to this day.

Even though these monsters were ruling the Church in England, God was always working through his people, his Culdees, the rustic representatives of the true church and, yes, the priests and scholars trained in the clergy's official universities. One great story gives us an example of this. Once again, let's reference the great Christian historian of the day, John Foxe:

"George Constantine [a Protestant, was] apprehended by Sir Thomas More, which then was lord chancellor of England, of suspicion of certain heresies. Master More said in this wise to Constantine: 'Constantine, I would have thee plain with me in one thing that I will ask of thee, and I promise thee I will show thee favor, in all the other things, whereof thou art accused to me. There is beyond the sea Tyndale, Joye, and a great many more of you. I know they cannot live without help—some sendeth them money and succoureth them, and thyself being one of them, hadst part thereof, and therefore knowest from whence it came. I pray thee, who be they that thus help them?'

'My lord,' quod Constantine, 'will you that I shall tell you the truth?'
'Yea, I pray thee,' quod my Lord.
'Mary, I will,' quod Constantine. 'Truly,' quod he, 'it is the Bishop of London that hath holpen us, for he hath bestowed among us a great deal of money in New Testaments to burn them, and that hath and yet is our only succour and comfort.'
'Now by my troth,' quod More, 'I think even the same, and I said so much to the bishop, when he went about to buy them.'[3]
Constantine was jailed, and no one knows his eventual fate. But, my what a legacy in a few words from the "rustic rich" preaching to the "prelate poor."

Tyndale's Work

Tyndale wrote to readers of his translation and his writings:
"Let it not make thee despair, neither yet discourage thee, O reader, that it is forbidden thee in pain of life and goods, or that it is made breaking of the king's peace, or treason unto his highness, to read the Word of thy soul's health—for if God be on our side, what matter maketh it who be against us, be they bishops, cardinals, popes."

Published Works

- *A Pathway into the Holy Scripture*
- *The Parable of the Wicked Mammon* (1527)
- *The Obedience of a Christian Man* (1527–1528)
- *The Practyse of Prelates* (1530)
- The New Testament (1526–1534 three editions)
- The Pentateuch

All these works and more were written during those mysterious years, in places of concealment so secure and well chosen that neither the ecclesiastical nor diplomatic emissaries of Wolsey and Henry VIII, charged to track, hunt down, and seize the fugitive, were able to reach him. Under the false idea that the progress of the Reformation in England rendered it safe for him to leave his deep concealment, he settled at Antwerp in 1534, and combined the work of an evangelist with that of a translator of the Bible.

On the practical Christian side, Tyndale spent five days each week in translation and two days doing Christian work. On one of the two days, he preached in a secluded location. On the other, he went incognito to the slums and brought food to the people. Unlike most religious men of his day, William sought not to live in the ivory tower trappings of the pious but to live out his faith as he had seen the Gospels reveal. On Tyndale, Drs. Craig and Joel Lampe have said it best on their "greatsite.com" cataloguing the history of Bible workers:

"His translations are made directly from the originals, with the aid of the Erasmus 1516 Greek-Latin New Testament, and the best available Hebrew texts. The Prolegomena in Mombert's William Tyndale's Five Books of Moses show conclusively that Tyndale's Pentateuch is a translation of the Hebrew original. His translations, it would turn out, became decisive in the history of the English Bible, and of the English language. Nearly a century later, when translators of the Authorized, or King James Version, debated how to translate the original languages, eight of ten times, they agreed that Tyndale had it best to begin with. Tyndale's place in history has not yet been sufficiently recognized as a translator of the Scriptures, as an apostle of liberty, and as a chief promoter of the Reformation in England."[4]

The End—of the Beginning

Tyndale's execution from Foxe's Book of Martyrs

Tyndale was betrayed by a friend, named Philips, the agent either of Henry or of English ecclesiastics, or possibly of both. Tyndale was arrested and imprisoned in the castle of Vilvoorde for over 500 days of horrible conditions. He was tried for heresy and treason, in a ridiculously unfair trial, and convicted.

Burning Charges against Tyndale. Heresies:

- ∞ He maintains that faith alone justifies.
- ∞ He maintains that to believe in the forgiveness of sins and to embrace the mercy offered in the Gospel was enough for salvation.
- ∞ He avers that human traditions cannot bind the conscience, except where their neglect might occasion scandal.
- ∞ He denies the freedom of the will.
- ∞ He denies that there is any purgatory.
- ∞ He affirms that neither the Virgin nor the Saints pray for us in their own person.
- ∞ He asserts that neither the Virgin nor the Saints should be invoked by us.[5]

Tyndale's Murder

After eleven months of privation and starvation, he was brought out of prison and tied to the center post in the castle courtyard. He was given the choice of "kindness" because he was a clergyman. Kindness meant that the executioner would strangle the victim with a cord prior to lighting the wood for the heretical burning. Tyndale opted for the kindness and said his last words, "Oh God, open the eyes of the king of England." He was then strangled to death with a cord from behind the post and his body burned at the stake. He was forty-two years old. One year after his murder, King Henry VIII rebelled against the pope and officially created the Church of England. The king vowed there would be no more burnings of Englishmen by Rome. Tyndale New Testaments were brought out into the open and read at will by order of the king.

By the time of Tyndale's martyrdom in 1536, some sixteen thousand New Testaments had passed into England and Scotland.

In a few years, fifty-four clergymen brought together by King James would use Tyndale's Pentateuch, New Testament, and the partial translations of other Old Testament books, which had been completed by Tyndale's disciples, to compose 90 percent of the King James Bible.

The burning of Latimer and Ridley, from John Foxe's Book of Martyrs (1563).

William Tyndale Was Not the Only Victim

It is estimated that the "church" under the popes, and royalty who catered to them, martyred over a <u>million</u> Christians for their faith during AD 1000—1800, exiled a <u>million</u> more, <u>and</u> confiscated their properties and goods for the "Roman Church."

"Orthodoxy had no more zealous champions than the Franciscans and Dominicans. In southern France, they wiped out the 'stain of heresy' with the streams of blood which flowed from the victims of their crusading fanaticism. They were the leading instruments of the Inquisition."[6]

"As early as 1282 Pope Gregory IX confided the execution of the Inquisition to the Dominicans, but the order of Francis demanded and secured a 'share' in the gruesome work… In time, (the Franciscans) gained the unsavory reputation as collectors of papal revenues." [7]

"The annals of the Inquisition give to the Dominican Order large space. The Dominicans were the most prominent and zealous 'inquisitors of heretical depravity.'[8]

"[In England] the parliamentary act for burning heretics, passed in 1401, was directed against the followers of Wycliffe and the Lollards. It was not until the days of Henry VIII [Tyndale's lifetime] that the period of prosecutions and burnings in England for heresy fully began." [9]

History is replete with the gruesome tales of the Imperial Roman Church during the thousand years of darkness wherein they ruled. We do not libel them, we only recall for our readers the true history of the actions during that day. Why recount it? Because the religious descendants of the dragons and monsters are still with us today. They continue to victimize the faithful the world over. Are they more tame during the twenty-first century? Of course they are. Burning at the stake can be shown on Facebook for what it is. And, try telling the tame and kindly public relations story to the thousands of boys who have been raped by Roman priests in the last century, and repeat the "tisk-tisk" words their families hear who have felt the sting of cover-up by bishops, cardinals, and popes—the Vicars of Christ. But, God will not be mocked and his plan develops through it all.

A "Rustic" Story

It is not often that this author copies an entire story from another work; however, this one requires the cited privilege. In *Foxe's Book of Martyrs* is the story of Walter Milne. Foxe does a brilliant job of documenting the correct answers to the false sacraments of the Roman Church hierarchy. And, it's a great story. It took place during the time we are documenting in this chapter and the struggle between the rustic church of Scotland and the Roman Church in the British Isles. It reads as follows:

"Among the martyrs of Scotland, Walter Milne was pivotal, for out of his ashes sprang thousands of others holding the same opinions, which forced the church of Scotland to debate true religion with the French and Catholic Church.

Milne was a parish priest of Lunan who embraced the doctrines of the Reformation and was condemned in the time of Beaton. He was able to escape safely from prison and hid in the country of Scotland until the leniency of the queen dowager allowed him to resume his preaching. Forced into hiding a second time, he was captured and tried for heresy at St. Andrews at the age of eighty-two.

The following dialogue took place between Milne and Andrew Oliphant, one of the bishop's priests, at his April 1551 trial.

"What do you think of priests marrying?" Oliphant asked Milne.

"I hold it a blessed bond; for Christ himself maintained it (allowed it), approved of it, and made it available for all men. But you don't think it's available for you. You abhor it while taking other men's wives and daughters, (prostitution and mistresses) not respecting the bond God made. You vow chastity and break it. St. Paul would rather marry than burn, which I have done, for God never forbade marriage to any man."

Oliphant—"You say there are not seven sacraments."

"Give me the Lord's Supper and baptism, and you can divide the rest among yourselves. If there are seven, why have you omitted one of them, marriage, and given yourself to immorality," replied Milne.

"You are against the sacrament of the alter. You say the Mass is idolatry."

"A lord or a king calls many to a dinner, then when the hall is ready, he rings a bell to summon the crowd, turns his back on his guests, eats alone, and mocks them. This is what you do, too."

Oliphant—"You deny the sacrament of the alter is the actual body of Christ."

"The Scripture of God is not to be taken carnally, but spiritually, and stands in faith only. As far as the Mass, [transubstantiation] it is wrong. Christ was offered once on the cross for man's sins and will never be offered again. He ended all sacrifice."

Oliphant—"You deny the office of bishop."

"Those you call bishop don't do a bishop's work as defined by Paul's letter to Timothy. They live for sensual pleasure and don't care for their flock. They don't honor the Word of God but seek honor for themselves."

Oliphant—"You speak against pilgrimages."

"They are not commanded in Scripture. There is no greater immorality committed in any place than at your pilgrimages."

Oliphant—"You preach secretly in houses and openly in the fields."

"Yes. And on the sea, too, in a ship."

Oliphant—Will you recant? If not, I will sentence you."

Milne - "I am accused of my life. I know I must die once and therefore, as Christ said to Judas, what thou doest, do quickly. I will not recant the truth. I am corn, not chaff; I will not be blown away with the wind or burst by the flail. I will survive both."

After this trial, Bishop Andrew Oliphant ordered Milne given to a secular judge (see any parallel with Christ at his trial?) to be burned as a heretic, but the provost of the town, Patrick Learmont, refused to be Milne's secular judge, as did the bishop's chamberlain. The whole town was so offended at the sentence that they wouldn't even sell the bishop's servants a rope for tying Milne to the stake or a tar barrel for round him. Finally Alexander Summerwail, more ignorant and cruel than the rest, acted as a secular judge and sent Milne to the stake.

When Milne was brought up to be executed, Oliphant ordered him to climb up to the stake.

"No," Milne replied, "You put me up there and take part in my death. I am forbidden by God's law from killing myself. But I go up gladly."

Oliphant put the old man up himself. Then Milne addressed the crowd.

"Dear friends, I suffer today for the defense of the faith of Jesus Christ, set forth in the Old and New Testaments. I praise God that he has called me to seal up his truth with my life, which, as I have received it from him, I willingly offer to his glory. If you would escape eternal death, do not be seduced by the lies of priests, monks, friars, priors, abbots, bishops, and the rest of the sect of Antichrist. Depend only on Jesus Christ and his mercy to save you."

There was great mourning and crying among the crowd as Milne died, and their hearts were so inflamed by his death that he was the last religious martyr to die in Scotland."[10]

The preceding is just one of many similar stories of Roman Church persecution of the faithful. Foxe produced three massive volumes of martyr stories of the true church.

Are Things Different In Today's Progressive Societies?

Today, many areas of the world have succumbed to violence against Christians. It has really never stopped, even though the Catholic Church finds it politically correct to demure from lethal violence. Today, the Roman hierarchy prefers to clandestinely enslave live victims.

Islam is on the rise too. But this evil pulls no punches in the fight to enslave. In Africa, *Boko Haram*, meaning "Western education is forbidden," is intending to make all of Nigeria an Islamic nation. The group is composed of bandits in the name of Allah. They kidnap and kill Christians on a massive scale, just as the Middle East buccaneers called, ISIL, The Islamic State in the Levant, do.

Their leader, Abubakar Shekau said,

"As for killing, Allah says we should decapitate, we should amputate the limbs, we should mutilate. We are fighting a religious war…we are fighting Christians."[11]

These are just a few of the examples of the Devil's work in the world today. Consult your world news to find more of his handiwork in the name of God.

However, as always, God will not be mocked. He is always watching and working. Today, every "plowboy", every working man and woman, boy and girl, can freely read the Holy Scriptures in English, which has become the language of the world.

Sources

1. *Foxe's Book of Martyrs*, chapter 12.
2. Brian H. Edwards, *God's Outlaw* (Evangelical Press, 1976), 126–129.
3. *Foxe's Book of Martyrs*, chapter 12.
4. Greatsite.com.
5. Brian H. Edwards, *God's Outlaw* (Evangelical Press, 1976), 166–167.
6. Gibbon, *The History of The Rise and Fall of the Roman Empire*, ch. XVI / Grotius, Dutch Martyrs/ Pope Alva, C.
7. Philip Schaff, *History of the Christian Church*, vol. VI, 386–387, 418.
8. Philip Schaff, *History of the Christian Church*, vol. VI, 424.
9. Philip Schaff, *History of the Christian Church*, vol. VI, 533.
10. *Foxes Book of Christian Martyrs*, (Barbour Publishing, 2010) Barbour Publishing, 88–90.
11. *Voice of the Martyrs Magazine*, October, 2014.

Images

William Tyndale's 1538 edition of the English New Testament, from the Reed Rare Books Collection in Dunedin, New Zealand. © Awcnz62 | Dreamstime.com

Thomas More © Georgios Kollidas | Dreamstime.com

CHAPTER TWELVE

BIBLE WORK GOES ON

TWO OF THE DISCIPLES OF TYNDALE who escaped when he was captured were named Rogers and Coverdale. They carried the printing press and copies of the Tyndale New Testament to the interior of Europe, where they continued to organize, print, and bind both Tyndale's translation and his commentary.

Myles Coverdale

John Rogers

In the year 1541, they were invited to come back to England and supervise the version called The Great Bible which was commissioned by King Henry VIII. Henry not only commissioned and sponsored the English Bible in that form, but he also commanded that a copy be put in every parish and a reader appointed for those who could not read. What a turn-around in a few scant years after hundreds of years of persecution. The pope was livid. Henry was no true Christian according to history, but he hated the pope and was happy to tweak the papal nose by allowing and supporting his own brand of church. (The Bibles were chained to the pulpits. This, not out of fear of theivery, but so that only the priest of the Church of England would read the words and interpret for the people.)

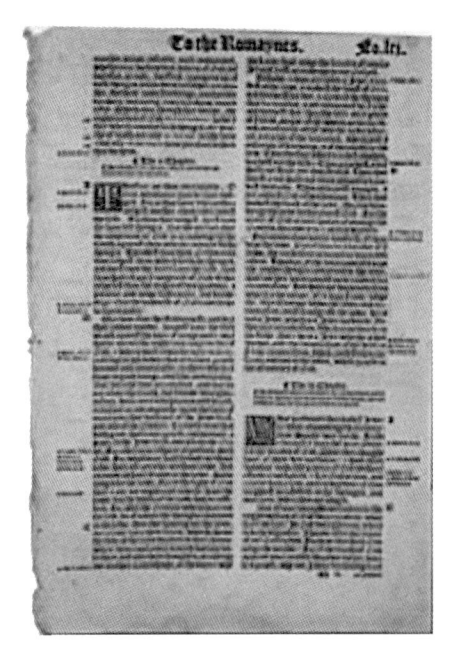

Leaf from the Great Bible

The Evil One Tries One Last Desperate Effort in the British Isles

King Henry VIII died just six years later in 1547. Edward VI ascended to the throne, but he died after only five years and all hell broke loose. In-fighting began between loyalists of the king's court and Queen Mary, called Bloody Mary. However, with the aid of Catholic officials and much palace intrigue, she attained the throne a year later.

Bible Work Goes On

Mary I "Bloody Mary"

She was called "bloody" because she was Roman Catholic and ordered that the papal co-regency return to her shores and the Church of England destroyed. She outlawed (once again) the Bible in English and burned at the stake 282 Protestants in five years, including John Rogers, and beheaded many others of royal rank. Once again, the true church had to go underground to survive. The dragons were back to kill the Bible. The burnings returned with them. For five long years, reformers were martyred, and the fires burned Scriptures as well as flesh.

Upon Mary's ascension, Coverdale immediately fled to Geneva, Switzerland, where he could further study Bible manuscripts and worship in freedom. During their exile, English Protestant leaders were aided by famed John Calvin who gave them the money to print a new Bible. In 1560, they published The Geneva Bible. This version of the Bible was essentially the Tyndale Bible with the addition of thousands of explanatory notes that promoted learning and understanding of the text. It was the first "study Bible."

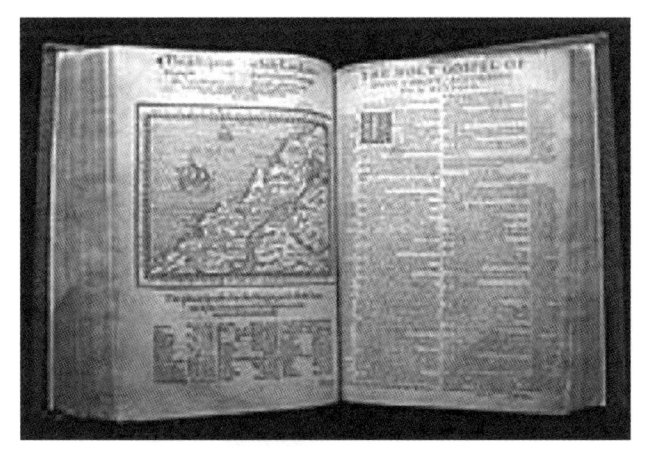

The Geneva Bible, 1560

William Whittingham

Reverend William Whittingham is one of the unsung heroes of the faith. He, single-handedly, composed the Geneva Bible as the first "study Bible" for believers. He placed maps of the Holy Land and explanations of the times of the Bible within the text for visual aids. He separated and numbered the books and verses for Bible recitation and memory aid. He put pictures of artist renderings of the apostles and famous Christian characters of the Bible—in the Bible. Christian families, for the first time, could home-school their children and communicate the love of God in Jesus Christ <u>without</u> the aid of an official clergyman. Christians loved it and clung to it. The official church went ballistic!

The Geneva Bible

By 1560, Queen Elizabeth I gained the throne of England. She approved of the Church of England and the Reformation. Coverdale was allowed to bring the Geneva Bible back to England. It became the Bible of choice for writers of all types. Shakespeare, Spenser, John Bunyon, John Milton and John Newton all quoted from this version of the Tyndale Bible. It was also the favorite Bible of the Puritans and was the Bible that came over to America on the Mayflower with the Pilgrims. It was the Bible of Americans for the first 100 years of the nation's infancy and childhood.

The Geneva Bible was immediately accepted by the Culdees of Scotland, who designated it to be read in all the churches. It was during this time that a foundational law book was written by one Theodore Beza. *The Right of Magistrates*, published in 1573, was the progenitor of the American Bill of Rights. It was Beza's thesis that the Church council could depose a pope, since Christ was the true head of the church. Beza also stated that a civic leader's duty was to the kingdom and not to the king. The impeachment of any American president by Congress was an idea from the principles in Beza's book.

More than this, he wrote that, "the very idea of unalienable human rights makes no sense without the biblical principle of the unique worth granted to all individuals by their Creator. Also, human rights become powerless ideals without magistrates exercising their right to enforce them over the abuse of authority by rulers."[1]

If You Can't Beat Em...

During this time, the Roman Catholic Church was beside itself that the Bible was available in the English tongue. It had lost the battle to keep the Bible from the people, but decided that two could play the game of translation. While the priests were not happy that the commoners had access to a Bible that allowed private and personal interpretation, they were forced to support a translation that the pope could live with.

The first Catholic Bible in English was the Rheims Bible, published in 1582 at the English College in Rheims, France. The translators were led in their work by Gregory Martin. They translated directly from the Latin Bible, not the Greek. It had no notes or study helps and, thus, was "The Pope's English Bible."

The "Genesis" of the Catholic Bible

Back in the year 1563, Archbishop Parker was selected by the queen as the chief editor of the Bishops' Bible. This Bible was translated by a number of English scholars who had "gone over" to the new Anglican Church inaugurated a few years earlier by King Henry VIII. The Bishops' Bible indeed used as a reference the Greek New Testament, but it was a 1550 translation which could hardly be seen as an official, antiquarian Greek source. Mostly, they used Pagninus's Latin version. They omitted any margin notes that "could cause offense." Which means, any note that questioned the church hierarchy or the monarch's power.

The educated, Anglican clergy preferred The Bishops' Bible, of course. In an attempt to fully convert the Crown to the new translation, the Anglican group sent Queen Elizabeth a copy of the Bible on September 22, 1568. The cover page displayed a prominent portrait of the queen. She was not fooled, but she allowed it to remain. For more than thirty years after that day, the feud was on between Protestant ministers and Anglican priests considering the Geneva Bible versus the Bishops' Bible.

The Simple-Complex King

The story ramps up in England with the advent of James to the British throne. King James was a complex man. He disliked the Geneva Bible because it had notes which diminished the monarchy. So, he appointed fifty-four English scholars and prelates to make a translation he could approve. The story begins like this.

James VI and I of England and Scotland
(June 19, 1566 – March 27, 1625)

Upon Elizabeth's death, March 23, 1603, her appointed successor was James I of Scotland. King James was the son of Mary Queen of Scots, not Bloody Mary, who was also a committed Catholic. Back during Elizabeth's reign, Catholics had made several attempts to place her on the throne. Elizabeth had her imprisoned and beheaded in 1587. James was subsequently placed in the care of the Earl of Mar, who raised him within the national Protestant Church of Scotland (led by Culdees).

James was taught French, Latin, and Greek so that he could discern between the Latin Vulgate and ancient Greek texts the Culdees held. He grew to have a distrust of Catholic hierarchy, of course. However, in his own self-interest, he made use of all the theological parties in his realm. He placated thousands of Protestant ministers by allowing the Geneva Bible to flourish while giving powerful positions in local government to Anglican bishops who were devoted to the new English hierarchy of church and state, [the leaders of the non-rustic religious sophistry].

As we look at his background, we see that James was greatly influenced by Scottish Protestants. These men were not fully enamored by the monarchy, but it was a frying pan much preferred to the fire of the papacy. So, they groomed young James to boost the English monarchy to the point that it could tame the dragon. Unfortunately, monarchy became its own stumbling block in due time.

The King James Bible

In only one year after the king's inauguration, he became the royal referee in the growing conflict between theological rivals. In 1604, he convened court in Hampton to discuss the feud. The king was critical of Protestant minister individuality on the one hand, and of Anglican hierarchical impudence on the other. The Geneva Bible's margin notes had stated on numerous verse studies that any monarch is subject to God and that the people of God had independence under God to make decisions of faith. James hated those devious notes. They disputed his absolute rule and jeopardized his monarchy. However, he also was suspect of the Anglican bishops who would rule with him through use of the Scriptures and through the name of Christ and thus overpower him with the people.

Eighteen Anglican bishops were invited to court and four Puritan ministers. The scholarly, Geneva-toting, ministers knew that they were hopelessly outnumbered. However, they had the ear of the monarch and were determined to appeal to his Scottish, Protestant heritage for a hearing of their grievances against an Anglican hierarchy who had, in many ways, used the Bishops' Bible to abuse the people just as had the papacy.

One of their number, John Rainolds, a Puritan, stood up in the court as the men hushed to hear. "May your majesty be pleased," he began, "May a <u>new</u> translation be made that will answer to the intent of the original rather than allowing for the corrupt interpretations of Henry VIII and Edward VI."[2]

Rainolds knew exactly what he was doing. He was pleading that James' Stuart line of kings make its mark over the Tudor linage of Elizabeth who had beheaded James' mother and ruled roughshod over the Scots for a hundred years. King James was called out by the only reasoning that he could not ignore without discounting his own heritage and reign!

The Lord Bishop of London, head of the Anglican delegation, rose in opposition, to cut off the deft move. "My Lord, if every man's humor be followed, there would be no end of translating." But it was too late.

King James stared at the group and rose to the occasion. He could not ignore the challenge, but he could not give in to the Puritans either.

"I would that England had one uniform translation, but I have never yet seen a Bible well translated in English, and I think the Geneva is the worst of all. This new translation must not be burdened with marginal notes that are partial, untrue, seditious, and treacherous toward kingship, but rather must spread the idea of divine rule by monarchs."

The King James translation would be His Majesty's version of the Holy Scriptures. One of the best examples of this preferential treatment is found in Psalm eight and the fifth verse. Speaking about mankind, the Hebrew text clearly stated; "You have made humans only slightly less than divine, adorned with glory and majesty, and yet given them responsibility for the world created beneath their feet." The translators knew that this would not do. They translated the verse, "For thou hast made him a little lower than the angels, and hast crowned him with glory and honor. Thou madest him to have dominion over the works of thy hands; thou hast put all things under his feet."

The "spin" toward the monarchy made the average man and woman to be lower than the angels, a layer in between them and divinity. And, the hierarchical language of the sixth verse allowed the king to be rightly the ruler of all "his" subjects—under God, of course. King James was pleased. The Anglicans smiled. The Puritans winced. Because, of course, now the average man could not go directly to God with petitions as a divinely inspired individual. He and she, as the angels, worshipped God with no will of their own, and all the king's men were at the head of the line and at the ear of God's representative on earth, the king. See how this worked?

However, the Puritans had begun the process of getting something of what they wanted. It was better than the "nothing" they had walked into court with. They were now positioned to wear down the Anglicans through many years of protest over Latinized text that had the approval of the pope, who was loathed by the king. James proclaimed that "scholars throughout the land should participate."

But, there were rules, the king's rules:

Instructions to the Translators

1. The ordinary Bible read in the church, commonly called the Bishops' Bible, to be followed, and as little altered as the original (languages) will permit.

2. The names of the prophets and the holy writers, with the other names in the text, to be retained, as near as may be, accordingly as they are vulgarly used.

3. The old ecclesiastical words to be kept, as the word church, not to be translated congregation.

4. When any word hath divers significations, that to be kept which hath been most commonly used by the most eminent fathers, being agreeable to the propriety of the place and the analogies of faith.

5. The division of chapters to be altered either not at all, or as little as may be, if necessity so require.

6. No marginal notes at all to be affixed, but only for the explanation of the Hebrew or Greek words, which cannot, without some circumlocution, so briefly and fitly be expressed, in the text.

7. Such quotations of places to be marginally set down as shall serve for the fit reference of one Scripture to another.

8. Every particular man of each company to take the same chapter or chapters; and, having translated or amended them severally by himself where he thinks good, all to meet together to confirm what they have done, and agree for their part what shall stand.

9. As any one company hath dispatched any one book in this manner, they shall send it to the rest, to be considered of seriously and judiciously; for His Majesty is very careful on this point.

10. If any company, upon the review of the book so sent, shall doubt or differ upon any places, to send them word thereof, to note the places, and therewithal to send their reasons; to which if they consent not, the difference to be compounded at the general meeting, which is to be of the chief persons of each company, at the end of the work.

11. When any place of special obscurity is doubted of, letters to be directed by authority to send to any learned man in the land for his judgment of such a place.

12. Letters to be sent from every bishop to the rest of his clergy, admonishing them of this translation in hand, and to move and charge as many as, being skillful in the tongues, have taken pains in that kind, to send their particular observations to the company, either at Westminster, Cambridge, or Oxford, according as it was directed before in the king's letter to the archbishop.

13. The directors in each company to be the Deans of Westminster and Chester, for Westminster, and the king's professors in Hebrew and Greek in the two universities.

14. These translations to be used, when they agree better with the text than the Bishops' Bible: Tyndale's, Coverdale's, Matthew's [Rogers'], Whitchurch's [Cranmer's], Geneva.

These fourteen rules assured that there would be no surprises and no diminishing of the king's power over the Church of England and over his subjects. But, it was light years better than Imperial Roman domination.

In the ensuing years, the Catholics in England would try to assassinate King James several times for his support of a new translation which incorporated some of the ideas, mostly sourced by ancient Greek translations, of the Puritans.

How the KJV Process Worked

The bulk of the King James translation of the Bible was on the shoulders of fifty-four men divided into six companies. An affable Anglican, Lancelot Andrews, became chairman of the translation committee. Some thought him to be a Culdee sympathizer, but none dared voice the suspicion. He was gracious to all. Andrews was with Queen Elizabeth when she died and preached her funeral. He then participated in the coronation of King James. Andrews had mastery in fifteen languages and knew the finer points of Hebrew and Greek grammar. There was a one-two punch to the secret of a more knowledgeable text. The committees which had a Puritan on each, demanding change via the original languages, and the chairman, who would not willingly keep the Latin over the Greek in many passages once the light of true scholarship landed upon them. He was gracious to all. Andrews grew up a Puritan and entered the Anglican church as the most able linguist of his age.

Miles Smith edited the collected version of the KJV. Smith was a scholar in classical studies, which included; Chaldean Syriac, Arabic, and Hebrew. He was bishop of Gloucester and a professor at Oxford. He recognized the Geneva Old Testament as a fine translation from the Hebrew and used it to edit the work. And, when it came to the New Testament, he bowed to the superior New Testament translation committee which had a vociferous voice in John Harmer who was regius professor of Greek and warden of St. Mary's College in Winchester. Harmer was a strong supporter of the Geneva Bible and was one of the editing team of twelve who made the final revisions of the whole Bible in 1610.

Concerning the times of the King James translation, biblical historian Donald Brake says, "Historical and cultural circumstances converged to bring the world's finest scholars, the most gifted linguists, and the most experienced biblical writers of the time to the work of translating the Bible for the King James Version."[3]

However, it is noteworthy that in the seventeenth century, theological scholars only thought of the Bible's New Testament as using Classical Greek. They used Greek texts and sometimes got the meaning of the biblical text wrong because of the usage of these translations into English.

"It was not until Adolf Deissmann discovered Papyri in Egypt in the nineteenth century that New Testament Greek was demonstrated to be the common (*Koine*) language of the day."[4]

Another Example of The Faulty King James Authorized Text

Sin by omission has been called as great as sin by commission. In the case of the Book of Job, the translators deliberately omitted an entire verse that was plainly given in the Greek Septuagint. It seems that the KJV translators could not find a reference for what it said. Their sponsor had decreed that if there wasn't a plain reference for the statement, it was not to be included. Here is the passage from the last verses of the book:

"16. After this, Job lived a hundred and forty years; he saw his children and their children to the fourth generation. 17. And so he died, old and full of years."—Job 42:16–17

BUT, the Septuagint had an additional sentence to verse 17, which was;

"And it is written that he shall rise up again with those whom the Lord raises up."

Because the translators could not find where "it is written" in the rest of the Old Testament, and because Christ had not yet come and been "risen," at the time of the OT writing, they decided to simply leave the second part of the verse out. Many scholars believe that the phrase, "it is written" refers to a connotation about Job's name being written in the "Book of Life." However, the king's rules were to be obeyed, and it was safer to just leave the mention of the verse out of the King's Bible.

In summary, it is important to realize that:

Ninety percent of all the English translated texts were from Tyndale's translation. Therefore, 95 percent of the KJV ended up being more or less correctly formed from the original languages. The differences changed little of the original Hebrew and Greek intent, but succeeded in "winking an eye" to the monarchy and the established church oligarchy. Finally, the Pilgrims rejected the King James Version, kept the Geneva Bible, and boarded ships, first to the continent, then, in 1620, to America.

It is an amusing footnote that in 1649, after James' death, the King James Version was printed in England, <u>including the Geneva Bible notes</u>, due to declining sales and interest by the people.

However, by then, thousands of Geneva Bibles were being read in America. Bibles that placed God firmly separate from and above the rule of the monarchy and promoting individual Christians as being endowed with the "priesthood of the believer" over the state church.

Sources

1. Vishal Mangalwadi, *The Book That Made Your World* (Thomas Nelson, 2011), 347.
2. Donald L. Brake with Shelly Beach, *A Visual History of the King James Bible*, (Baker Books, 2011), 16.
3. Donald L. Brake, *A Visual History of the King James Bible*, (Baker Books 2011), 110.
4. Donald L. Brake, *A Visual History of the King James Bible*, (Baker Books, 2011), 107.

Images

Photos | Dreamstime.com

CHAPTER THIRTEEN

America the Beautiful

The Geneva Bible

America Founded on the Bible

THE FOUNDING FATHERS OF AMERICA primarily used the Geneva Bible. When the American colonies rebelled, King George embargoed the King James Bible and made it a crime to print anything else. (Satan, back to his old tricks.) The Geneva Bible was used in the Continental Congress and had profound influence on English and American common law and democratic government, finding expression in the Bill of Rights, the

Declaration of Independence, and the U.S. Constitution. But, let's back-up and relate to the story of the "rustic nation" of the "rustic British," the kingdom-bearers for God.

But, how did the shift from Britain to America come about? What was the "tipping point?"

Elizabethan era England reached the point of no return for the British to be the primary voice of men's salvation in the year 1628. According to historians,

"That was the year that William Laud, the Church of England's 'enforcer,' was made bishop of London, the most important bishopric in the country. That year also marked the beginning of the Great Migration. This lasted some sixteen years, and saw more than twenty thousand Puritans embark for New England, and forty-five thousand other Englishmen head for Virginia, the West Indies, and points south."

"No sooner had Laud become bishop of London in 1628, than Laud presented the king with a list of English clergy. Behind each name was an *O* or a *P*—if Orthodox, they were in line for promotion; if Puritan, they were marked for suppression.[1]

Of course, seven years earlier, the pioneers of separatism, the Pilgrims, had already landed on Plymouth Rock in America.

"They stood on the deck of the Mayflower breathing that fresh air, too exhausted to think beyond thanking God that their three-month ordeal was over… Finally on December 6, 1620, they went ashore." Not long after, as they were praying over breakfast, they heard a strange cry, and arrows came flying into the camp. There was a brief skirmish that was ended by one of the Pilgrims firing his musket at a tree that was shielding a brave. The tree bark shattered and hit the face of the brave, who shrieked and ran off. The other braves followed. Later, Governor Bradford also wrote in his journal:

'Yet by the especial providence of God, none of their arrows either hit or hurt us, though many came close by us and on every side of us, and some coats which were hung up in our barricade were shot through and through. So, after we had given thanks for our deliverance, we went on our journey and called this place 'The First Encounter,' [which name it bears today.]"² The Pilgrims had been the vanguard and they grew in faith and numbers as God blessed them. By the next decade, the Christian tide was coming in as Puritans left Old England for what they hoped would be the New England. A land of religious freedom under God.

Two Movements

From even before this time there was a dualism in American morals. There were those who were sent by English merchants to use and strip the land for its valuable resources and there were the Pilgrims and Puritans who came to be free to worship God as they felt the Bible taught.

The Pilgrims were not Puritans. Pilgrims were separatists from all the trappings of the established Church that had been polluted through the centuries by the Romans and the crowned heads of England. The Puritans were seeking freedom from being persecuted by the official church, too, but they were mostly about trying to "properly establish" it and conform it from within. Their leaders felt that if they could get their primary message of the "denial of self" through to the leadership of the Church of England, by example from the new world, that truth would transform it from within. However, both Pilgrims and Puritans could live side by side with the main thing they held in common, the Holy Scriptures in the form of the Geneva Bible, which both groups considered to be the best translation from the original languages of God. (And, up until that time, it was.) And then there were the English secularists, who were coming to America for an entirely different purpose.

To the south, The Virginia Company was made up of Englishmen too. They were not about religious freedom or settlement, but, for the most part, greed. They had a charter from King James, and they were in search of booty and fame. It was they who had incited the original Americans, the Indians, and caused them to be afraid enough to attack at the first sign of Englishmen anywhere along the coast.

Both of the two movements would, one day, begin to meld into Americans against the world and the worldly. However, for now, they were very different. Historian Perry Miller wrote:

"Winthrop (Puritan leader) and his colleagues believed that their errand was not a mere scouting expedition: it was an essential maneuver in the drama of Christendom. The Massachusetts Bay Company was not a battered remnant of suffering Separatists thrown up on a rocky shore; it was an organized task force of Christians, executing a flank attack on the corruptions of Christendom. These Puritans did not flee to America; they went in order to work out that complete reformation which was not yet accomplished in England and Europe."[3]

Satan Rises Up

A favorite few of the Indians of the East Coast of America were friendly and helpful to the new colonists. However, (sorry Hollywood) the vast majority of the Native Americans were in the firm grip of Satan and they showed this from the very beginning. The tribes of the northeast were in a constant state of war with each other. They barbarically killed, scalped, and robbed any other tribe that they could. The true documentation of the era is undisputed.

The Bible makes it clear that there is a constant war between Satan and God's people. Supernatural powers were at work in the Bay Colony. As the seventeenth century droned on in the new wilderness, the affluent Christianity of the Puritans allowed Satan to attack and manifest his power within the Indians and within some of the Puritan families. One of these families was of William Morse of Newberry. Cotton Mather was one of the few pastors who stood up to the powers of darkness, and he documented some of the attacks of the Evil One.

Reverend Cotton Mather wrote about the state of affairs:

"The New Englanders are a people of God, settled in those which were once the Devil's territories, and it may easily be supposed that the Devil was exceedingly disturbed, when he perceived such a people here accomplishing the promise of old made unto our blessed Jesus—that he should have the uttermost parts of the earth for his possession. The Devil, thus irritated, immediately tried all sorts of methods to overturn this poor plantation… Wherefore the Devil is now making one attempt more upon us—an attempt more difficult, more surprising, more snarled with unintelligible circumstances than any that we have hitherto encountered. The houses of the good people there are filled with doleful shrieks of their children and servants, tormented by invisible hands with tortures altogether preternatural."[4]

Contrary to modern dramatic writings, most of the Puritan clergy were not involved in the trials which took place at Salem. Matter of fact, the trials were stopped when the majority of the clergy appealed to Governor William Phips to curtail them. American historians Peter Marshall and David Manuel sum up this episode of the decade in which these things happened:

"In light of the modern tendency to judge the Puritans as sin obsessed bigots, who went berserk hunting imaginary ghosts and executing innocent people on trumped-up charges of witchcraft, it should be kept in mind that many contemporary accounts of this period document dozens of cases similar to those at (Newberry and Salem). Indeed under such tremendous pressure from the Enemy, the real wonder is that the Puritans acted with as much restraint as they did. During the five months in which the furor lasted, from May of 1692 to October of that same year, twenty people were actually executed for witchcraft, before the trials at Salem were brought to a halt. During that same year in Europe, many hundreds of witches were put to death."[5]

It is evident that the Puritan elders were not totally innocent in this matter. Some of the leaders were well versed in their theology but not well-related to their God. However, the historic records about the Salem witchcraft trials do not reveal but a few isolated incidents during one spring and summer in one area of New England. Though tragic, these compared to the vast human tragedy brought on by the warring Indian tribes upon themselves and upon the strangers from abroad, this was a tiny, yet sad, blip on the radar of American history.

Skirmishes with the Indians continued on throughout the colonies, but also the immigration continued to the tune of thousands arriving in search of freedom and independence—UNDER GOD.

Many early American settlers arrived believing they were a part of the

"New Israel," and that they would be instruments for Christ's triumphant return to earth. *Freedom* and *liberty* were both political and religious terms. They helped not only preserve fundamental human rights but also sustain loyalty to Christ and to "*sola Scriptura*."

The greatest pamphlet of the Revolutionary era, Thomas Paine's *Common Sense*, was the runaway best seller of the American Revolution, noting that:

"Monarchy, like aristocracy, had its origins among ruffians who enforced their 'superiority' at the point of a sword." Paine traces in elaborate detail Israel's "national delusion" in requesting a king as did other nations, and God's subsequent displeasure at a "form of government which so impiously invades the prerogative of heaven."

"We Owe Allegiance To No Crown"

Thomas Paine

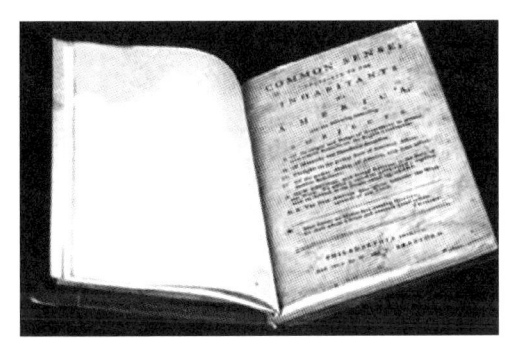

Paine painted the word-picture of a young tree which would grow huge and, with it, freedom throughout the world.

"We have it in our power to begin the world over again. A situation similar to the present hath not happened since the days of Noah until now. The birthday of a new world is at hand, and a race of men, perhaps as numerous as all Europe contains, are to receive their portion of freedom. How trifling, how ridiculous do the little paltry cavillings of a few weak or interested men appear when weighed against the business of a world."

The "American Spirit" holding the Bible and traveling in advance of the pioneers.

"For most American ministers and many in their congregations, the religious dimension of the war was precisely the point of revolution. Revolution and a new republican government would enable Americans to continue to realize their destiny as a 'redeemer nation.'[6]

For those who would make the argument that America was not founded as a Christian nation, we reply that it is our opinion America was founded by Christians as a free, republican nation. There are volumes of

Amerian History that can attest to the Christian heritage of the United States. We have only room to highlight that heritage here. Let's hear from our Founding Fathers for ourselves:

"Our Constitution was made only for a moral and religious people. It is wholly inadequate to the government of any other." –John Adams

John Jay, original chief-justice of the U.S. Supreme Court said, "The Bible is the best of all books, for it is the Word of God and teaches us the way to be happy in this world and in the next. Continue therefore to read it and to regulate your life by its precepts."

United States Declaration of Independence

"We hold these truths to be self-evident, that all men are created equal, that they are endowed by their Creator with certain unalienable rights, that among these are life, liberty and the pursuit of happiness."

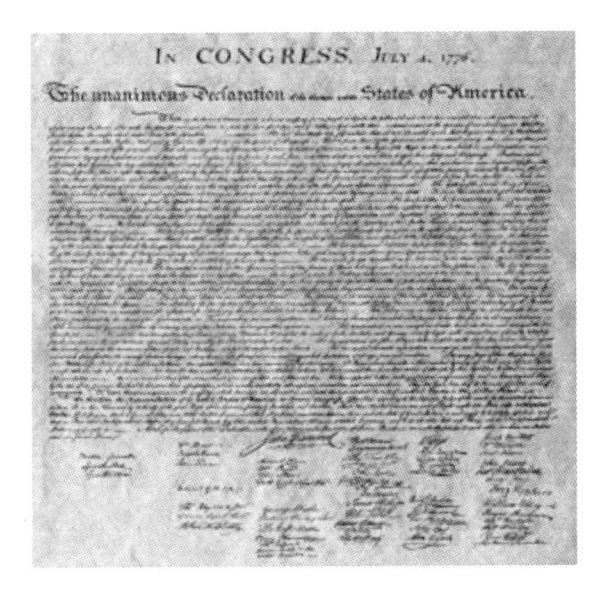

What Additional Evidence Do We Have?

- Clergyman Jacob Duche was appointed the first chaplain to Congress and offered prayers and performed Scripture readings every day at 9:00 a.m. Between 1776 and 1787, Congress had five chaplains.
- The military also had a clergy presence: on July 29, 1775, the Congress created the Chaplain Corps in the Continental Army and about a year later decided to appoint a chaplain to each regiment in the army.
- In 1777, Congress endorsed Robert Aitken's printing of the Bible in America, and on September 12, 1782, congressional Chaplains William White and George Duffield praised the project, and the Congress as a whole recommended Aitken's edition to the inhabitants of the United States.[7]

George Washington, first president of the U.S.

Washington's own contemporaries did not question his Christianity but were thoroughly convinced of his devout faith—a fact made evident in the first-ever compilation of *The Writings of George Washington*, published in the 1830s.[8]

George Washington's adopted daughter, having spent twenty years of her life in his presence, declared that one might as well question Washington's patriotism as question his Christianity.[9]

More sources of George Washington as a Christian:

- George Washington, The Writings of George Washington, Jared Sparks, editor (Boston: Ferdinand Andrews, Publisher, 1838), Vol. XII, pp. 399–411.

- George Washington, *The Religious Opinions of Washington*, E. C. M'Guire, editor (New York: Harper & Brothers, 1836).

- William Johnson, *George Washington The Christian* (1917).
- William Jackson Johnstone, *How Washington Prayed* (New York: The Abingdon Press, 1932).
- James D. Richardson, editor, *The Messages and Papers of the Presidents* (Published by the Authority of Congress, 1899), Vol. I, pp. 51–57 (1789), 64 (1789), 213–224 (1796), etc.
- George Washington, *Address of George Washington, President of the United States, Late Commander in Chief of the American Army, to the People of the United States, Preparatory to His Declination* (Baltimore: George & Henry S. Keatinge, 1796), pp. 22–23.
- George Washington, The Maxims of Washington (New York: D. Appleton and Co., 1855).

Washington, A Christian

In the Yale University Divinity School Library, there is a small book written by William Johnson titled, *George Washington, The Christian*. This book documents twenty-four pages of a manuscript written in George Washington's own hand. They speak for themselves:

"Let my heart, therefore, gracious God, be so affected with the glory and the majesty of thine honor that I may not do mine own works, but wait on thee, and discharge those weighty duties which thou requirest of me…"

"Direct my thoughts, words and work, wash away my sins in the immaculate blood of the Lamb, and purge my heart by thy Holy Spirit… daily frame me more and more into the likeness of thy Son, Jesus Christ."

We rest our case as to whether our first president was a devoted Christian!

John Adams, second president of the U.S.
Signer of the Declaration of Independence

"Suppose a nation in some distant region should take the Bible for their only law book and every member should regulate his conduct by the precepts there exhibited! Every member would be obliged in conscience, to temperance, frugality, and industry; to justice, kindness, and charity towards his fellow men; and to piety, love, and reverence toward Almighty God ... What a Eutopia, what a Paradise would this region be."[10]

John Adams has been called a deist. And, there is some evidence to the rumor. However, there is great evidence to believe that he also thought Christian morality to be the height of mankind.

While serving as president, he told the officers of a Massachusetts militia brigade, "Our Constitution was made only for a moral and religious people. It is wholly inadequate to the government of any other."[11]

Thomas Jefferson, Third President of the U.S.
Drafter and signer of the Declaration of Independence

"God who gave us life gave us liberty. And can the liberties of a nation be thought secure when we have removed their only firm basis, a conviction in the minds of the people that these liberties are of the gift of God? That they are not to be violated but with his wrath? Indeed, I tremble for my country when I reflect that God is just; that his justice cannot sleep forever; that a revolution of the wheel of fortune, a change of situation, is among possible events; that it may become probable by Supernatural influence! The Almighty has no attribute which can take side with us in that event."[12]

"I am a real Christian—that is to say, a disciple of the doctrines of Jesus Christ."[13]

Note: Thomas Jefferson was a young man when the Congress first met and when the nation's independence was in doubt. Eventually, he became a Unitarian, believing only in God and not the Holy Trinity. He really seems to have been an agnostic, but also an idealist. This religious/secular combination allows one to see the depravity of man and become depressed. Such a man must blind himself to the bankruptcy of his philosophy and go through life carefully avoiding the reality of mankind's sinfulness. This seems to describe the presidential and the elder Jefferson. He is lauded today by Progressives, but true American history shows that he was stunted by comparison to Washington and Adams.

Patrick Henry

Patrick Henry is best known for the speech he made in the House of Burgesses on March 23, 1775, when he argued in favor of mobilization against the British.

"Is life so dear, or peace so sweet, as to be purchased at the price of chains and slavery? Forbid it, Almighty God! I know not what course others may take; but as for me, give me liberty or give me death!"

"It cannot be emphasized too strongly or too often that this great nation was founded, not by religionists, but by Christians…not on religion, but on the Gospel of Jesus Christ."

Benjamin Franklin

In the course of mediating a quarrel in the Congress during the summer of 1787 on states rights, Franklin suggested that the members of the convention consider the "thought of humbly applying to the Father of lights to illuminate our understandings." In the course of the proposal, Franklin asked the members to consider the role that "daily prayer" had played in Congress during the American Revolution. At that time, Franklin reminded his fellow delegates, "Our prayers, Sir, were heard, and they were graciously answered." Franklin asked his colleagues if they had not "forgotten that powerful friend? Or do we imagine that we no longer need his assistance?"[14]

THE BIBLE ENDORSED BY THE AMERICAN CONGRESS

In 1776, the Continental Congress wanted to sponsor Bibles to soldiers. In 1777, 20,000 copies were printed by Congress, and George Washington wrote a letter of gratitude for Congress' efforts at raising the money and causing the printing to happen. A printer in Pennsylvania named Aitkens did the work, and it was called the Aitkens Bible, but it was the Geneva Bible of Tyndale, Rogers, Calvin, and Coverdale—without most of the extensive study notes. Soldiers reading and carrying that Bible won the war of American independence against all odds. In America's infancy, the Bible was the textbook for liberty that Jonathan Edwards, George Whitefield, and John Wesley preached from.

From 1376, the date that John Wycliffe was exiled for being the first Englishman to translate the Bible into his native tongue, until 1776, the birth of our nation, was 400 years. Four hundred years of struggle to read the Word of God as God intended for us to do since the first century. Four-hundred years during which the greatest forces of mankind endeavored to kill the Bible, to no avail.

THE 1800S IN AMERICA

"Nineteenth-century Americans, who believed that the United States had a special place in God's plan, first appealed to divine providence. The success of the American Revolution confirmed it. Second, they argued that the founders were Christians and thus had set out to create a nation that reflected their personal beliefs. Third, they made the case that the U.S.

government and the documents upon which it was founded were rooted in Christian ideas. Today's Christian nationalists have a good portion of American history on their side."[15]

"Writing in 1855, church historian Philip Schaff quoted an Austrian writer who observed, 'The United States are by far the most religious and Christian country in the world…because religion is there most free.'

When Thomas Jefferson (later in life and after being verbally accosted by Congregational preachers because he wouldn't give up his slaves) claimed smugly that Unitarianism would soon be "the religion of the majority from north to south." He could not have been more wrong. Apparently Jefferson did not leave Monticello very much during the final years of his life, for America was fast becoming the most evangelical Christian country on the face of the earth."[16]

John Knox Witherspoon

Scots Presbyterian minister, president of Princeton, and a signatory of the Declaration of Independence, John Witherspoon said, "Except a man be born again, he cannot enter the kingdom of God. True religion must arise from a clear and deep conviction of your lost state by nature and practice, and an unfeigned reliance on the pardoning mercy and sanctifying grace of God."[17]

Samuel Adams
Member, 1st and 2nd Continental Congress

Samuel Adams said, "The Massachusetts Bay Colony was God's new Israel." "Revelation assures us that 'Righteousness exalteth a nation' —communities are dealt with in the world by the wise and just Ruler of the Universe. He rewards or punishes them according to their general character."[18]

John Jay
First Chief Justice of the Supreme Court and Governor of New York

Our first chief justice said, "A proper history of the United States would have much to recommend it: in some respects it would be singular, or unlike all others; it would develop the great plan of Providence, for causing this extensive part of our world to be discovered, and these 'uttermost parts of the earth' to be gradually filled with civilized and Christian people and nations. The means or second causes by which this great plan has long been and still is accomplishing, are materials for history, of which the writer ought well to know the use and bearings and proper places."[19]

Leaders and the People were Christian

Not only were the leaders of Independent America Christians, but the people were decidedly of that persuasion also. Representative of that is a tradition started in the homes of Christians that continues to be used in a practical way today all over the country.

The Six-Panel Door
American's Second-Most Popular Unknown Symbol of Our Christian Heritage.
Originated by Quaker Brethren as the "Cross and Open Bible Door."

America the Beautiful 253

One dollar bill

America's <u>most</u> popular unrecognized symbol of our Christian heritage, The Great Seal.

The FRONT side of our Great Seal is the pyramid. The seal was designed by Christian scholar, Charles Thompson, clerk of the Continental Congress. It was approved by Ben Franklin and Thomas Jefferson (the committee) and by the entire Congress unanimously on the first vote.

The pyramid is topped by the words Annuit Coeptis—To nod assent to our endeavors.

Then, the all seeing eye of God. This means, according to the congressional committee, "Providence is favoring (our) undertakings."

Novus Ordo Seclorum. A new order of the ages, and above it—1776; with the understanding of the Continental Congress that this "new order" was a democratic republic under God.

This was indeed, a new order, as it was something heretofore never known on earth.

Noah Webster

HISTORY OF THE UNITED STATES: TO WHICH IS PREFIXED A BRIEF...

Noah Webster

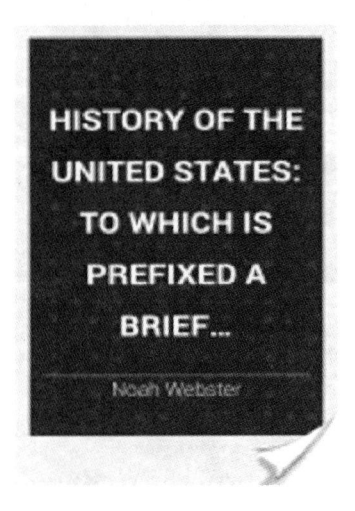

While Noah Webster, just a few years after producing his famous *Dictionary of the English Language*, would produce his own modern translation of the English Bible in 1833, the public remained too loyal to the Geneva and the King James Version for Webster's version to have much impact.

In 1832, he wrote *History of the United States*. It begins with a chapter called "Origins of the Human Race" that provides an exposition of the Genesis creation story. The book ends with an appendix titled, "Advice to the Young." In it he says the following:

"When you become entitled to exercise the right of voting for public officers, let it be impressed on your mind that God commands you to choose for rulers, 'just men who will rule in the fear of God.' The preservation of [our] government depends on the faithful discharge of this duty; if the citizens neglect their duty and place unprincipled men in office, the government will soon be corrupted; laws will be made, not for the public good so much as for selfish or local purposes; corrupt or incompetent men will be appointed to execute the laws; the public revenues will be squandered on unworthy men; and the rights of the citizen will be violated or disregarded. If [our] government fails to secure public prosperity and happiness, it must be because the citizens neglect the divine commands, and elect bad men to make and administer the laws."[20]

When Noah Webster died in 1843 he was considered by the Congress and the people an American hero.

Growth of the Bible in America

During the 200 years, 1786–1986, the King James Version became the most widely used Bible the world over. With archeological discoveries and new textual information, infused throughout the years, we Americans now have literally hundreds of versions and applications of the Bible in English that are more accurate to the ancient texts than ever before.

America was destined to become the most influential nation in history. Americans also exported the most precious commodity of all time—the Bible, interpreted correctly from the earliest manuscripts and translated from the best pictorial and textual languages into hundreds of other languages. In 1836, Frenchman Alexis de Tocqueville wrote in his book, *Democracy in America*, that this country was a nation wholly committed to the principles of Holy Scripture.

It was not really until 1885 that England's own planned replacement for their King James Bible, the English Revised Version (E.R.V.) would become the first English-language Bible to gain popular acceptance as a post-King James Version modern-English Bible. Greek experts Wescott and Hort consulted on the ERV and corrected much of the original KJV inaccuracies.

At the same time that religious skepticism and toleration were growing in the West, so too were revival movements that sought to return the masses to genuine faith in Christ and the gospel of salvation.

The Great Awakening

God had said in Scripture:

"And in the last days it shall be, God declares, that I will pour out my Spirit upon all flesh, and your sons and your daughters shall prophesy, and your young men shall see visions, and your old men shall dream dreams; yea, and on my menservants and my maidservants in those days, I will pour out my Spirit…" (Acts 2:17–18 KJV)

A premonition of the last days was what happened during the Great Awakening of America in the 1730s and 40s. We believe that this was a miraculous work of God that prepared the way, spiritually, for American Independence. In Massachusetts, Puritan preacher Jonathan Edwards began to see what he called "surprising conversions." At the same time revival began to break out in the independent churches of Mother England. Young evangelist, George Whitefield preached in the area of Wales, and the descendants of the Cymric Celts flocked to hear him, converting by the thousands and energizing the area for Christ.

However, Whitefield was convicted about America. He felt that his preaching to the colonies would help create "one nation under God." He was in communication with Christians in New Jersey and Pennsylvania who wrote to him about the Holy Spirit's work there. For instance, an educator named William Tennent and his four sons were discouraged at the cold relationship to God at Yale and Harvard. These schools were begun in order to prepare Gospel preachers to lead churches throughout the colonies, but they had grown lethargic through the previous generation. The Tennents started a new school that the teachers of those schools called the "Log College." This school would become so popular among the people that it eventually became what is now Princeton University.

These sorts of "awakenings" were happening over all of New England and down into Virginia. It would only take a man with God's own Spirit and great oratorical gifts to tie them all together. When Whitefield began to ride the preaching circuit, the fire burst forth for a life led by Jesus. He united, under the banner of Christ and his love, the thirteen colonies like they had never been before. From Boston to Charleston, people were discovering that they were worthy of God's love no matter their position. If they were separated by cultural background and lifestyles, they were no longer separated by religion. They were all Christians.

George Whitefield preached that America was not just to be a "city on a hill" but an eternal light of hope in a dark world. "Now, through the shared experience of coming together in large groups to hear the gospel of Jesus Christ, Americans were rediscovering God's plan to join them together by his Spirit in the common cause of advancing his kingdom."[21]

One terrific story recalled during this time is of Whitefield's effect on Benjamin Franklin. Franklin's grandfather had been a devout Puritan, but Ben had rejected the evangelistic fervor of his heritage. During the years of the Great Awakening, he began to come to hear George Whitefield's sermons while the preacher was speaking in Philadelphia. Franklin was astonished by "the extraordinary influence of the oratory on his hearers."[22]

Matter of fact, on one occasion, Franklin was so moved that he put four gold sovereigns, all the money in his pockets, in the collection plate, even though he had planned to only give no more than a shilling. Franklin subsequently wrote:

"It was wonderful to see the change soon made in the manners of our inhabitants. From being thoughtless or indifferent about religion, it seems as if all the world were growing religious, so that one could not walk through the town in an evening without hearing psalms sung in different families of every street."

The two men became fast friends, and Franklin wrote about the movement in *Poor Richard's Almanac*, his published newspaper. Incredibly, George Whitefield preached more than fifteen thousand sermons during the years 1739 through 1770! When he died, just a few years before the conflict began in earnest with Great Britain's crown, his dream had come true. America had become a nation—under God. They would recognize "No king but Jesus."

George Whitefield arrived in the colonies from England in 1739, and experienced wide success with his revival sermons.

THE DECLARATION OF INDEPENDENCE BEGINS

Just six years after the death of Whitefield, Benjamin Franklin, John Adams, Thomas Jefferson and several other Congressmen wrote their, and our, declaration.

"We hold these Truths to be self-evident, that all Men are created equal...We therefore, the representatives of the United States of America, in general congress assembled, appealing to the Supreme Judge of the World for the rectitude of our intentions, do, in the name and by the authority of the good people of these colonies, solemnly publish and declare, that these united colonies are, and of right ought to be, free and independent states… and for the support of the declaration, with a firm reliance on the protection of divine Providence, we mutually pledge to each other our lives, our fortunes, and our sacred honor."

Preachers of Freedom and Faith for America

- Jonathan Edwards was famous for his quiet but firm sermons in which he described in detail the torments of those who do not have personal faith in Jesus Christ.

Jonathan Edwards

- John Wesley was a revivalist preacher and personal friend of Whitefield. Wesley founded a small group of preachers and Bible students who focused on holy living and came to be called the "Methodists." Wesley spent some time in America and went home to Britain inspired that more should be done for the common man.

John Wesley

In his ground-breaking book of Christian philosophy, author Vishal Mangalwadi, gives us a great summary of John Wesley's life-work that launched the British Empire toward its godly destiny after it shook-off its pretensions to enslave America. There became a great awakening from the clutches of a closed English Church existing in bigotry. And, it shows how taking the Bible seriously, rather than smothering it, can do great good. He writes;

"The impact of the Bible via Wesley's work is evident in the lives and labors of the social emancipators during the nineteenth century. Wilberforce and Clarkson fought against the slave trade, Lord Shaftesbury and Sadler championed industrial emancipation, Elizabeth Fry and John Howard reformed prisons, Plimsoll focused on ships' safety regulations, Hannah More and Robert Raikes launched Sunday schools, and many more were to follow. The biblical revival resulted in the nineteenth-century preaching tradition. Finny, Moody, Spurgeon, Nicholson, Ryle, Moule, James Danny, Chavass, and others were popular preachers who expounded on the Bible rather than telling man-made stories. The Great Awakening…opened up the intelligent study of the Bible to the masses. It restored the Bible's position as the Book of books of the Anglo-Saxon peoples. Their biblical revival held in check the character-destroying consequences of atheism that corrupted other European nations like France…When the work of biblical revival had become established, many missionary societies were formed, all within a few years of each other—The Baptist Missionary Society, the London Missionary Society, the Wesleyan Mission Society, and the China Inland Mission."[23]

Supreme Court Building, Washington D.C.

The Supreme Court did formally declare the United States to be a "Christian Nation" in 1885 in its summation of the case, Church of the Holy Trinity vs. United States.

Justice Brewer said, "The United States is not a Christian nation in the sense that Christianity is the established religion or that the people are in any manner compelled to support it…Yet, America is a Christian nation in a historical sense."

But the Devil is still the prince of this world. He threw Darwin, Huxley, Holmes, Marx and others into our path in order to destroy what the founders had dreamed of and worked to produce: a nation built on Christian principles. (See the author's booklet and DVD, *The Light of Truth*.) for more on this.

(Can you name some in our government and "church" today who are not on God's side, but can be found to side with secular political priests and atheists?)

We have a great example of the sort of person that early Protestant Christian America produced. Of course there were many others, but let's take a moment to review the heritage of Cyrus McCormick as a typical example.

Cyrus McCormick's Legacy

Cyrus McCormick

The McCormick Reaper

Cyrus McCormick was the son of an industrious Christian couple, Mary Ann and Robert. Dad Robert was also an inventor and entrepreneur with a strong Christian work ethic. They had come from American Puritan stock and encouraged Cyrus to work and create. Cyrus disliked the backbreaking manual labor of harvesting by hand with a scythe. He decided to invent a more efficient and fast way for the average farmer. He came up with a culture-changing machine called the McCormick Reaper. This marvelous invention enabled the average farmer to save one hundred dollars for every dollar he spent on the machine.

In time, Cyrus married, and wife Nancy helped him in the business of building and selling reapers to the public. (A direct result of the biblical belief that women are equally able to create and work with their husbands.) Their factory eventually became one of the biggest enterprises in the U.S.A. The work was billed as: "McCormick conquers nature to the benign end of civilization and brings bread to the mouths of the poor."[24]

The Pilgrim work ethic in America taught the habit of saving and investing, not hoarding or throwing away one's money. Belief in and preaching of the Bible generated a moral culture that both inventors and investors could trust. Cyrus and Nancy took full advantage of this existing climate and biblical principles to market the reaper.

"Cyrus McCormick was not merely an inventor; he was also an innovative marketing strategist. His goal was to make the best and most affordable reaper available to as many people as possible. Following the teachings of the Bible as expounded by Luther, Calvin, and other reformers, McCormick believed that the business of selling his reaper was God's will for his life. So he strove to become the best salesman possible. *The Dictionary of American Biography* records that McCormick was among the first to introduce the use of field trials, guarantees, testimonials in advertising, and financing via cash and deferred payment.[25]

"McCormack invited farmers to take the reaper in May, before the harvest, without paying for it. Over the summer, his salesmen would train the farmers how to use the machine. During the harvest, McCormick's salesmen were readily available with spare parts. The farmers didn't have to pay for the reaper until December—when they were sure that the reaper was cost effective."[26]

The "So-What"

The American Puritan ethic and the Christian belief system of the Bible enabled the people to work within an infrastructure that was (and is) crucial to growth of an economy. Not only that. But it reached out to a hurting and underprivileged world. After Cyrus died, Nancy supported many causes that raised the unfortunate. One example: she supported Presbyterians as they created Allahabad Agricultural Institute in India, which was and is a blessing to tens of thousands of the poorest people in the world.

There is a great challenge today in America and Great Britain. The question is, will we continue to be the fruit-bearer to the nations that wehave been, in the name of God? As some have said, "We are only one generation away from godlessness."

We can trace the gospel of Jesus Christ going to all the world during the twentieth century. At the vanguard has been the Bible in English brought by British "rustic" missionaries and American "rustic" missionaries; and, then, translated into the languages of the world. We have seen that God's plan came together for freedom of the world's religious slaves via a blessed nation under his loving hand. The blessing was designed to come through America. It did not come through Jerusalem or the Jews. They are still enslaved. The blessing did not come through Rome or the Roman Church. Its masses in their Masses are still enslaved. It came and still comes through Protestant and independent People of the Way in America! Because of this, the followers of the Evil One have come out in force during the 21st Century to kill the Bible, to kill our way of life, and to kill us. But God will not be mocked. He has provided His Spirit movement to the world through His people. An outline of this is in our final chapter, fourteen.

Sources

1. Peter Marshall and David Manuel, *The Light and the Glory,* (Revell, 1977), 148, 152.

2. Peter Marshall and David Manuel, *The Light and the Glory,* (Revell, 1977), 122, 123.

3. Percy Miller, *Errand Into the Wilderness*, Essay, 11.

4. Cotton Mather, *The Wonders of the Invisible World,* 185,186.

5. Peter Marshall and David Manuel, *The Light and the Glory,* (Revell, 1977), 238.

6. *Christian History Magazine*, no. 50, 17.

7. John Fea, *Was the United States Founded as a Christian Nation?* (Westminster Knox Press, 2011), 127.

8. Jared Sparks, *The Dictionary of American Biography.*

9. Christiananswers.net.

10. Diary and Autobiography of John Adams, vol. III, 9.

11. John Fea, *Was the United States Founded as a Christian Nation?* (Westminster Knox Press, 2011), 200.

12. Notes on the State of Virginia, Query XVIII, p. 237.

13. The Writings of Thomas Jefferson, p. 385.

14. John Fea, *Was the United States Founded as a Christian Nation?* (Westminster Knox Press, 2011), 151.

15. John Fea, *Was the United States Founded as a Christian Nation?* (Westminster Knox Press, 2011), 4.

16. John Fea, *Was the United States Founded as a Christian Nation?* (Westminster Knox Press, 2011), 6.

17. John Fea, *Was the United States Founded as a Christian Nation?* (Westminster Knox Press, 2011), 230.

18. John Fea, *Was the United States Founded as a Christian Nation?* (Westminster Knox Press, 2011), 241.

19. John Fea, *Was the United States Founded as a Christian Nation?* (Westminster Knox Press, 2011), 235.

20. Noah Webster, *History of United States.*

21. Peter Marshall and David Manuel, *The Light and the Glory,* (Revell, 1977), 251.

22. Peter Marshall and David Manuel, *The Light and the Glory*, (Fleming H. Revell Co., 1977), 248.

23. Vishal Mangalwadi, *The Book That Made Your World,* (Thomas Nelson, 2011), 271.

24. William T. Hutchinson, *Cyrus Hall McCormick: Seed Time,* (Century Publishing, 1930), 271.

25. *The Dictionary of American Biography,* (Charles Scribner and Sons, 1946).

26. Vishal Mangalwadi, *The Book That Created Your World,* (Thomas Nelson, 2011), 331.

IMAGES

George Washington, first President of the U.S. © Georgios Kollidas | Dreamstime.com

Thomas Jefferson, third President of the U.S. © | Dreamstime.com

Benjamin Franklin © Andrey Arkusha | Dreamstime.com

Samuel Adams © Jesse Kunerth | Dreamstime.com

John Jay © Georgios Kollidas | Dreamstime.com

History of the United States © Georgios Kollidas | Dreamstime.com

Cyrus McCormick, courtesy of Christianity.com

McCormick Reaper, courtesy of mainlesson.com

Chapter Fourteen

Rustics to All the World

Jesus Christ's last public message before his ascension was:

"All authority in heaven and on earth has been given to me. Therefore go and make disciples of all nations, baptizing them in the name of the Father and of the Son and of the Holy Spirit, and teaching them to obey everything I have commanded you. And surely I am with you always, to the very end of the age" (Matthew 28:18–20 NIV).

The rustic Americans and the British took this command seriously, and the devout have sent others, gone themselves, and supported the world evangelization mission. One of the first to officially be sent off in the nineteenth century was William Cary.

William Cary

In 1792, as a young Baptist pastor in Leicester, he published *An Enquiry into the Obligations of Christians, to Use Means for the Conversion of the Heathens*. This missiological pamphlet argued that Christians should undertake evangelistic missions overseas. Expecting "great things" from God, he urged the leaders of the Northampton Baptist Association to found a "society for propagating the gospel among the heathen." Thus was born in 1792, the Baptist Missionary Society (BMS).

Carey, the first Baptist missionary of the modern era, arrived in colonial Calcutta in November, 1793 without any travel permits. His family managed to survive because he accepted employment as manager of an indigo plantation in the interior of Bengal.

Carey is an example of what one dedicated Christian can do when they enter the world in the name of Jesus Christ. During over four decades of service to India and her people, he was a:

Botanist—Wrote the three-volume, *Flora Indica* and brought Linnaean Gardening to India, and was founder of India's Agri-horticultural Society.

Economist—Introduced savings banks to India.

Printer—Fathered printing in India, Mission Press at Serampore was the largest in India,

Leper Healing Champion—Advocated human care and industry for leprosy victims.

Bible Translator—Translated the Bible into Bengali and 40 Indian tribal languages, which encouraged average people to read.

Educator—began dozens of schools for children of all castes.

Women's Champion—wrote and worked against: female infanticide, child marriage, widow burning.

All of this work was done by a man who had no more than an elementary school formal education and a love of the Bible.

American Rustic, Lottie Moon

The first missionary woman of American missionary acclaim was Lottie Moon. She travelled from the East Coast of the United States to China as a single Christian woman with one passionate goal: to seek to make

Christians of the Chinese. She spent her adult life in China and passed on to Glory on board a steamer ship back to the United States as an elderly woman.

There are soo many missionary stories to recount. Almost every one of them is about a "rustic" person, from Britain or America, who was a simple, believing soul, burdened for others. We immediately think of Hudson Taylor (to China), and Dr. Livingston and Henry M. Stanley (both to Africa). Here is a textual taste of Protestant Christian work in Africa, beginning through them.

In the 1850s and 1860s, slavery to the Orient, the West Indies, and America was still occurring on a massive scale. This was enabled mainly because dominant African tribes captured other tribes, floated many of them down the Congo, Nile, and Zambezi rivers, and herded them into the ocean ports as captive prey for the slavers. Protestant Christian, Dr. Livingstone believed that it was his job to find the "great inland sea" and set up a mission there to fight slavery. In his quest, he had already discovered the largest wonder of the modern world, the giant and thunderous Victoria Falls. And, he had discovered the deepest sea on any continent, Lake Tanganyika.

(On one of my journeys into Africa, during the 1980s, I actually swam in this lake. It was so wide that it looked like an ocean. There was, and is, on the eastern shore, a sandy beach with three foot waves that come ashore, just like at the ocean, but right in the middle of Africa.)

Dr. Livingstone had mapped the headwaters of the Congo. He had followed the Zambezi past the great falls and down to the ocean at Mozambique. After his wife's death, he headed again to Lake Tanganyika. He felt that, either that lake or one <u>north</u> might be the lake that was the headwater of the legendary Nile. Turns out that the "one north" was Lake Victoria, later discovered as the true headwater of the Nile.

Well, he had been missing for almost five years when Henry Stanley finally found him on the northern shore of Lake Tanganyika. This is the scene where the famous understated greeting was uttered, which can only be fully understood by an Englishman. Stanley wrote later about the meeting:

"My heart beats fast, but I must not let my face betray my emotions, lest it detract from the dignity of a white man appearing under such extraordinary circumstances. So I did that which I thought was most dignified. I pushed through the crowds, and, passing from the rear, walked down a living avenue of people, until I came in front of the semicircle of natives and Arabs, in front of which stood the white man with the grey beard.

"As I advanced slowly toward him I noticed he was pale, looked wearied, had a grey beard, wore a bluish cap with a faded gold band round it, had on a red-sleeved waistcoat and a pair of grey tweed trousers. I would have run to him, only I was a coward in the presence of such a mob—would have embraced him, only, being an Englishman, I did not know how he would receive me; so I did what cowardice and false pride suggested was the best thing—walked deliberately to him, took off my hat, and said,

'Dr. Livingstone, I presume?'

'Yes,' said he, with a kind smile, lifting up his cap slightly.

I replaced my hat on my head, and he puts on his cap, and we both grasp hands, and I then say aloud, 'I thank God, Doctor, I have been permitted to see you.'

He answered, 'I feel thankful that I am here to welcome you.'

I turn to the natives and Arabs, take off my hat to them in response to the saluting chorus of 'Yambos' I receive, and the doctor introduces them to me by name."

Well, that's how Stanley met Livingstone, and his report was in all the papers the next year, along with stories of exploration and evangelism on the "Dark Continent."

Dr. Livingstone remained in south central Africa for another year, and in 1873, he died there, alone in the night in a hut on the north shore of the great lake; less than a week's walk from the headwaters of the Nile. Nothing in the area is named after him today. On the morning after his death, his porters found his body kneeling beside his cot, hands folded in prayer. Few other missionaries had come to evangelize Africa, yet. No true "headwaters of the great rivers" had been found. Relatively few natives had been evangelized, and many were still being taken into slavery, even though England and America had now abandoned it. It seems that Dr. David Livingstone was something of a failure.

According to his wishes, the natives cut out his heart and buried it under a great baobab tree near the lake. They wrapped his body in strips of cloth and transported it to the South African mission. The mission sent it to London where it was buried in Westminster Abbey with other icons of the faith, and it lies there today beneath an unassuming slab.

What a sad story. But wait.

There had been something else happening while the good doctor was healing native Africans, traveling, and reporting his exploits back to the London Missionary Society. Three men, two British and one American, took up the abolitionist and the evangelical cause. Maybe you've heard of Charles Spurgeon. Because of Livingstone, he began a Bible teaching college for pastors and missionaries. It has been sending missionaries to Africa for over 150 years. Dr. Livingstone birthed a Bible College, even though he did not know it.

George Muller, the leading global evangelist of the day, and his church, supported 187 missionaries during his lifetime and helped translate and send Bibles to Africa, mainly through the South African mission of Robert Moffat and David Livingstone. Mrs. Livingstone's family was one of the main conduits of this.

Dwight L. Moody, from Chicago, used Livingstone's life lessons in his sermons. He brought revival to the United States and Great Britain and his voice was a primary mouthpiece for American abolition of racism and African evangelism for fifty years. Can Dr. Livingstone have had no part in that Bold Destiny work? I say, <u>Yes he Could and Did</u>!

David Livingstone died on his knees in prayer to God. He probably felt that he was something of a failure. But, he knew that his God was a Victor. His favorite verse of Scripture, written over and over again in his diary was, "Surely, I am with you always, to the very end of the age"(Matt. 28:20). One Dr. Livingstone commentary in the diary immediately following this verse, in stately English style, said, "It is the word of a gentleman of the most strict and sacred honor, so there's the end of it."

The apostle Peter, in 1 Peter, chapter 2, verses 4-6 says, "As you come to him, the <u>living Stone</u>—rejected by humans but chosen by God and precious to him, you also, like <u>living stones</u>, are being built into a spiritual house to be a holy priesthood, offering spiritual sacrifices acceptable to God through Jesus Christ. For in Scripture it says, 'See, I lay a stone in Zion, a chosen and precious cornerstone, and the one who trusts in him will never be put to shame."

Living Stone, Livingstone. He had a plan that, even though seemingly unrealized, gave him strength and became a great Christian legacy.

Amy Carmichael

One last story we would also like to mention here is of Amy Carmichael. She was born in Scottish-Ireland, during the last days of the year, 1867. She came from "Covenanter" stock (The Covenanters were so named because in a series of bands or covenants they bound themselves to maintain the Presbyterian doctrine and policy as the sole form of religion of the country of Scotland during the last struggle between the Church of England and the papacy.)

From an early age, Amy had the gift of reducing the burdens of others. In 1886, at the age of eighteen, she accepted Christ as Lord and Savior. She immediately began to work for better conditions at the mills of the country. She raised money for a building erected for the "welcoming" of the girls who worked day and night. Many girls came to know Christ and were protected from lives of sin.

On March 3, 1893, Amy sailed to the Orient under the banner of the British Keswick Movement. She became very ill and almost died, but recovered on a ship bound for home. Not to be defeated, Amy again left

Britain for the Orient and landed in India in 1895. She bound herself to the English Missionary work of the Zenana Missionary Society. However, she was concerned that the missionary community was separated from the people to whom they wished to share the gospel. One day in 1901, a seven-year-old girl named Preena fled the local temple, entered the missionary compound, and begged Amy to protect her.

It was only then that Missionary Carmichael learned the ugly secret that young girls were often sold by their parents to the temples as prostitutes for their gods. Infuriated that this atrocious practice was happening right under their noses and no one in the compound was willing to do anything about it, Amy began her own ministry for the bodies and souls of these children. It was slow-going and fraught with danger, but within three years, she had rescued seventeen such girls. They called her *Amma*, "mother." Reaching out, Amy decided to go to the source; poor parents who needed money and could not, or would not, take care of their girl babies. She began the "babies" ministry in 1904, and in 1918 she began work to rescue boys from certain temples, too.

Amy never solicited funds. When people asked to sponsor a child, she refused and asked the Lord for help in a general fund for the work. Many workers traveled to join Carmichael. They were never paid by the ministry. The ministry never borrowed funds or went into debt. And, once again the oddball in ministry, Amy encouraged her workers to "leave a margin" in their lives. She warned them to "beware of the barrenness of a busy life." She also worked on translations of the Bible into different Indian tongues, which to her was relaxation time. In 1931, she fell and was confined to her room and an occasional stroll, but that didn't stop her ministry. She wrote thirty-five books and many letters, all the while running the administration of the ministry.

Amy Carmichael's Dohnavur Fellowship continues to minister effectively in southern India today. God spoke to her through the Word. Her Bible was "dog-eared" throughout. She labored for sixty years, never returning to her homeland again.

As the passing cavalcade of missionaries, both British and American went to the world, they brought the Bible in the form of the King James and the Revised Version to many nations. At the same time, Bible Societies were sending missionary archeologists to seek out the earliest documents of the Christian faith. It is encouraging to see what they have collected and to hear some of the stories of those early explorers from Britain, the Continent, and America.

(For an excellent video summary of the movement, please see the author's DVD and booklet, *The Light of Truth*.)

The sheer number of Bibles produced in the last 150 years is staggering. For instance, between the years 1808 and 1901 one Protestant agency alone, the British and Foreign Bible Society, produced more than 46 million complete Bibles and nearly three times as many New Testaments and sections of the Bible. Since then, through the year 2000, the total numbers from all Bible-producing agencies have been unable to be counted. However, the best news is that scholars have been able to nurture and construct the most accurate translations of all time through the discovery of Middle Eastern and Egyptian papyri from antiquity. Let's be encouraged for a few moments together.

THE PAPYRI DOCUMENTATION

Beginning in the late 1800s and continuing today, great storehouses of papyri have been collected from the Middle East and North Africa. We would like to highlight just several of the discoveries and their explorers now. The believer should be greatly encouraged that the Christian Bible is the happy descendant of the most documented collection of evidence in the world. We begin with the oldest papri/parchment evidence: the Dead Sea Scrolls.

The Dead Sea Scrolls are a collection of 981 texts discovered between 1946 and 1956 at Khirbet Qumran in the West Bank. They were found inside caves about a mile inland from the northwest shore of the Dead Sea, from which they derive their name. Nine of the scrolls were rediscovered at the Israel Antiquities Authority (IAA) in 2014, after they had been stored unopened for six decades following their excavation in 1952. The texts are of great historical, religious, and linguistic significance because they include the earliest known surviving manuscripts of works later included in the Hebrew Bible canon, along with deuterocanonical and extra-biblical manuscripts which preserve evidence of the diversity of religious thought in late Second Temple Judaism.

The texts are written in Hebrew, Aramaic, Greek, and Nabatean, mostly on parchment but with some written on papyrus and bronze. The manuscripts have been dated to between 408 BC and AD 318 Bronze coins found on the site form a series beginning with John Hyrcanus (135–104 BC) and continuing until the First Jewish-Roman War (AD 66–73).

The initial discovery, by Bedouin shepherd Muhammed Edh-Dhib, his cousin Jum'a Muhammed, and Khalil Musa, took place between November, 1946 and February 1947. The twelve-year-old shepherds discovered 7 scrolls) housed in jars in a cave at what is now known as the Qumran site. John C. Trever reconstructed the story of the scrolls from several interviews with the Bedouin. Edh-Dhib's cousin noticed the caves, but Edh-Dhib himself was the first to actually fall into one. He retrieved a handful of scrolls, which Trever identifies as the Isaiah Scroll, Habakkuk Commentary, and the Community Rules, and took them back to the camp to show to his family. None of the scrolls were destroyed in this process, despite popular rumor. The Bedouin kept the scrolls hanging on a tent pole while they figured out what to do with them, periodically taking them out to show people. At some point during this time, the Community Rule was split in two. The Bedouin first took the scrolls to a dealer named Ibrahim 'Ijha in Bethlehem. 'Ijha returned them, saying they were worthless, after being warned that they might have been stolen from a synagogue. Undaunted, the Bedouin went to a nearby market, where a Syrian Christian offered to buy them. A sheikh joined their conversation and suggested they take the scrolls to Khalil Eskander Shahin, "Kando," a cobbler and part-time antiques dealer. The Bedouin and the dealers returned to the site, leaving one scroll with Kando and selling three others to a dealer for a total of seven Great British Pounds (equivalent to US$37 in 2014).

Two examples of the pottery that held some of the Dead Sea Scrolls documents found at Qumran.

Nash Papyrus, Second Century BC (150 BC)

NASH PAPYRUS is a second-century (150 BC) papyrus fragment written in square Hebrew script, containing the Decalogue and the Shema. The Nash Papyrus was the oldest biblical text known before the discovery of the Dead Sea Scrolls. A single sheet, not from a scroll, was purchased from an Egyptian dealer by W. L. Nash, secretary of the Society of Biblical Archaeology in England, and published by S. A. Cooke in 1903.

There is so much information and so many true stories of light upon our Holy Scriptures during the last one-hundred years. We have only space to recount several which we think were directly orchestrated by God for and by his rustic chosen people.

The Story of the Magdallen Papyri

While we are talking about ancient manuscripts, we would be remiss not to mention the Magdallen Papyri. (The word *papyri* is from whence we derive the English word "*paper*.")

Charles Bousfield Huleatt

The papyri texts of the New Testament in Greek were discovered in the year 1900 in Luxor, Egypt by the "Christian Indiana Jones," a.k.a. Charles Huleatt. This is a fascinating story. Rev. Huleatt was an English military chaplain, but his hobby was archeology and paphyrology. He found three "scraps" of ancient texts of the New Testament and sent them home to England. He mailed them to his alma mater of Magdallen College at Oxford.

What the texts reveal are portions of Matthew's Gospel which have been dated to between the years AD 50 and 66. The text is written on both sides, like a book rather than a scroll. That means it was a book copied from earlier originals by perhaps twenty years, with time to be carried from the northern Middle East to Egypt. The papri also have what scholars call *"nomina sacra,"* sacred abbreviations, which only occurred as readers already knew what the abbreviations meant. In other words, they had heard these stories before and the new copies could abbreviate sacred names and descriptions without fear that the reader knew and could relate to what was described.

For instance, papyri fragment number three is of Matthew 26:22–24. This is the scene of the Lord's supper. Verse 22 says, "They were very sad and began to say to him one after the other, 'Surely you don't mean me Lord.' In this text, the Greek is the nomina sacra of *KE* for *Kyrie* which is "Lord." And the same fragment has Matthew 26:31 which says, "Then Jesus told them, 'This is the very night you will all fall away on account of me.' The text has the word "Jesus" as the nomina sacra *IS*, which is the abbreviation of *Iesous*, Jesus.

These precious papyrus fragments exist at Oxford today and are definitive proof that the Gospels were written within the time of the Lord's first disciples. The copies are dated from AD 50-66, so the originals must have been written by AD 40-45, while the original disciples were still alive and in their prime, less than ten years after Jesus' death and resurrection.

Here are some additional examples of first through second century papyri.

Papyrus 1

Papyrus AD 1—100 (in the Gregory-Aland numbering) designated by [1], ε 01 (von Soden), is an early copy of the New Testament in Greek. It is a papyrus manuscript of the Gospel of Matthew dating to the early second century. It is currently housed at the University of Pennsylvania Museum (E 2746) and was discovered in Oxyrhynchus, Egypt.

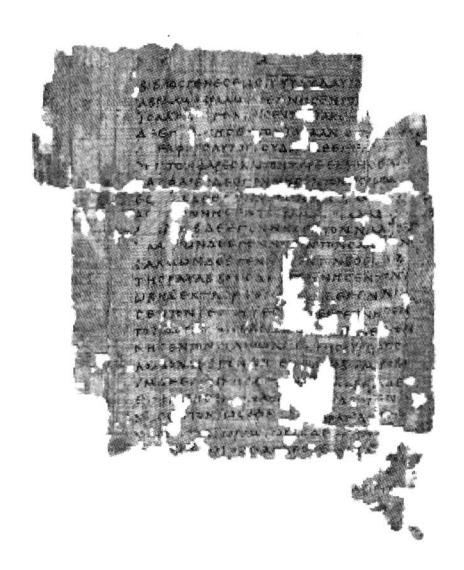

According to scholars P1 has close agreement with Codex Vaticanus.[1]

Probably originally written during or shortly after the apostle John was living in Ephesus!

P-52 Fragment

the Jews, "For us it is not permitted to kill **anyone," so that the w**ord of Jesus might be fulfilled, which he sp-
oke signifying what kind of death he was going to
die. Entered therefore again into the Praeto-
rium Pilate and summoned Jesus **and sai**d to him, "Thou art king of the **Jews?"**

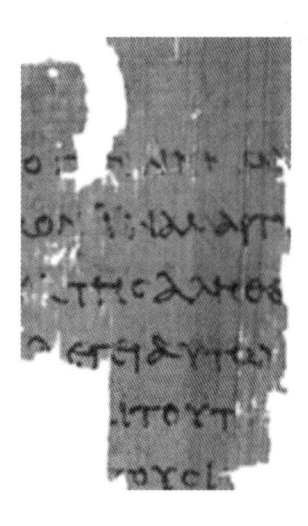

a King I am. For **this I have been born** and (for this) I have come into the **world so that I would** testify to the truth. Everyone who is **of the truth** hears of me my voice." **Said to him** Pilate, "What is truth?" **and this** having said, again he went out unto **the Jews** and said to them, "I find **not one** fault in him."

The Rylands Library Papyrus P52, also known as the St. John's fragment, is a fragment from a papyrus codex, measuring only 3.5 by 2.5 inches (8.9 by 6 cm) at its widest; and conserved with the Rylands Papyri at the John Rylands University Library (Gr. P. 457), Manchester, UK. The front (recto) contains parts of seven lines from the Gospel of John 18:31–33, in Greek, and the back (verso) contains parts of seven lines from verses 37–38. Since 2007, the papyrus has been on permanent display in the library's Deansgate building.

Although Rylands P52 is generally accepted as the earliest extant record of a canonical New Testament text, the dating of the papyrus is by no means the subject of consensus among scholars. The style of the script is strongly Hadrianic, which would suggest a most probable date somewhere between AD 100 and AD 115 but the difficulty of fixing the date of a fragment based solely on paleographic evidence allows a much wider range, potentially extending from before AD 100.

These, and many other fragments that have been recovered, prove that the original Greek texts of the New Testament were not as the Roman Catholic Church states in its Catechism, "not eyewitness accounts of Jesus' ministry but theological presentations of the stories of Jesus of Nazareth."

We have in our possession, accounts that were copied within several decades of the actual events, the freshest writings and records of any ancient messages.

Sir Alfred Chester Beatty

The Beatty Papyri

Finally, we cannot leave out our own Irish-American "rustic," Chester Beatty.

In 1875, Alfred Chester Beatty was born in New York City and, as a young man, he graduated from Columbia University as a mining engineer. He made his fortune mining in Cripple Creek, Colorado, and other mining concerns the world over. He went on to mine in other places in the American West. He was often called the "King of Copper" for the many copper mines he also owned.

A collector from an early age, he had, by the 1940s, built up a remarkable and impressive collection of Oriental art and books. For Christians, his greatest find was of the New Testament papyri in Egypt dated to the third century. They are housed in part at the Chester Beatty Library in Dublin, Ireland, and in part at the University of Michigan, among a few other locations.

The papyri were most likely first obtained by illegal antiquity traders. Because of this, the exact circumstances of the find are not clear. One account is that the manuscripts were in jars in a Coptic Church or monastery in Egypt.

All of the manuscripts are codices (book form), which was surprising to the first scholars who examined the texts because it was believed that the papyrus codex was not extensively used by Christians until the fourth century. Most of the manuscripts are dated to the third century, with some as early as the second. That's AD 100–300!

The manuscripts employ nomina sacra. One notable example is in P. VI which contains portions of the Old Testament. The name Joshua, which relates linguistically to Jesus, was considered a sacred name and is abbreviated as such.

Since all but two of the eleven manuscripts are dated before the fourth century, they present significant textual evidence for the Greek Bible as it existed in Egypt prior to the Diocletianic persecutions where Christian books are said to have been destroyed and a century or more earlier than the Codex Vaticanus and Codex Sinaiticus.

One of the texts contains ten leaves from the Book of Revelation, documenting chapters 9–17. This manuscript also dates to the third century.

The Chester Beatty discovery means that entire Bibles, in book form in Greek, with sacred abbreviations, were existent within at least 100 years after the apostle John's death in about AD 95. They are quite possibly from the first "book" copies made only one generation away from copies after the original writing. This is extraordinary encouragement that we have "archeologically fresh" words of the disciples who lived with Jesus and saw him with their own eyes. These texts are more "scholarly fresh" than any work of antiquity known to mankind—fresher than copies of Homer's *Iliad* and *Odyssey*, fresher than any copy of any Greek play, philosophy, writing or any Roman history. Fresher than any Egyptian writing, including the famous *Book of the Dead*. We're talking the freshest or earliest of paper writings of antiquity.

The Bible, then, is found to be textually, archeologically, and historically the most proven authentic written document of all time. We Christians should be joyful in knowing we believe in the book which is the most trustworthy of all ancient texts.

(Please see the author's booklet and DVD, *The Light of Truth*, for more information.)

The Christian Missionary Movement

It is not the goal of this book to exhaustively document the English or American missionary movement. There are many excellent books on these subjects. We can only highlight the movement of God through a few of the dedicated, Protestant Christians sent. In fact, they are proof of the "fruit" of the kingdom that Jesus talked about in the verse which began this book. In summary, there can be no doubt in the minds of historians and theological scholars alike that the "rustic" churches of Great Britain and America, in their time, brought, and are bringing, to the world the kingdom of God under his direction. And, they moved out with the Bible as their guidebook and hope.

As time catalogs the future movement of the fruit of the kingdom, let us hope and pray that the "rustic" Christians of the world will prevail and the ecumenical and calcified religions of the past will continue to go the way of all flesh.

The Bible, too, moves on. Sometimes the glut of versions and applications boggles the Christian mind. However, discussion over these is welcome because it will shed the light of truth to the believer and through the true church of Jesus Christ. The following are some important and progressive dates in Christian kingdom work, sponsored by Jesus' chosen, rustic people. Compare the positive effect of these over the negatives of the so-called "established religions" of the world.

Each of these has had a positive, life-giving, family-nurturing, people-loving influence.

1841
David Livingstone opens Africa to Christian missions (fights slavery trade)
1844
YMCA founded in London by Sir George Williams (fights child labor)
1846
World Evangelical Alliance formed in London
1849
Charles G. Finney holds evangelistic campaigns in England
1851
YMCA comes to Montreal and Boston

1854
International Missionary Conference in New York: "Converting the World to Christ;" Illinois Institute (Wheaton College) founded by Jonathan Blanchard
1857
NYC Fulton Street Revival grows from 6 to 10,000 laymen in six months
1859
Second Evangelical Awakening in England, more than 1 million converts
1859–Satan's Challenge
Charles Darwin's *On the Origin of Species by Means of Natural Selection* published (challenge to Christianity)
1865
Salvation Army founded by William Booth in England; China Inland Mission (Overseas Missionary Fellowship) founded by J. Hudson Taylor
1869
Boston Missionary Training School (Gordon College) founded by A. J. Gordon
1873–74
Moody/Sankey revivals reach more than 3 million people in Scotland and England
1886
Chicago Evangelization Society (Moody Bible Institute) founded
1887
Two societies formed: The Christian Alliance and The Evangelical Missionary Alliance (later known as The International Missionary Alliance)
1888
C&MA begins ministry in China
1888
Student Volunteer Movement for Foreign Missions coins slogan: "The Evangelization of the World in this Generation;" Centenary Conference on Foreign Missions in London, 1,576 missionaries from 140 agencies attend
1895
Africa Inland Mission (AIM) founded by C&MA missionary, Peter Cameron Scott
1899
Gideons International organized by three businessmen in Janesville, Wisconsin
1900
NYC World Missionary Conference, 200,000 attendees
1904
Welsh Revival, ministry of Evan Roberts, 100,000 converts in six months

1906
Azusa Street meetings in Los Angeles, California, led by William Seymour, launches Pentecostal movement
1908
Billy Sunday begins citywide campaigns, 1 million converts by **1930**
1910
Edinburgh World Missions Conference begins twentieth-century ecumenical movement;
Sunday School Council of Evangelical Denominations established
1917
Interdenominational Foreign Missions Association (IFMA) founded
1925–Satan's Challenge
Scopes Monkey Trial: John T. Scopes convicted of teaching evolution in a public school (Scopes was convinced to enter suit by the newly formed ACLU)
1927–Satan's Challenge
Russian communist government destroys thousands of churches and kills thousands of Christians; Anti-Christian movement in China forces 5,000 Protestant missionaries to leave its shores
1931
First major international Protestant radio station, HCJB "Voice of the Andies," founded by Reuben Larson (C&MA) and Clarence Jones
1933
The Navigators discipleship program started by Dawson Trotman (Trotman and Billy Graham instrumental in purchasing Glen Eyrie Conference Center in CO, 1953)
1934
Wycliffe Bible Translators, Inc. founded by William Townsend Cameron
1937
Child Evangelism Fellowship, Inc. organized by Jesse Overholtzer
1939
Back to the Bible International founded by Theodore Epp; Old Fashioned Gospel Hour with Charles Fuller reaches 10 million listeners every Sunday
1939-1945 Satan's Challenge
Hitler invades God's chosen Britain and threatens God's America
1941
InterVarsity Christian Fellowship, USA organized
1941–Satan's Challenge
Imperial Japan attacks God's chosen rustic nation, America
1944
National Association of Evangelicals (NAE) & Evangelical Foreign Missions Association (EFMA) founded; National Religious Broadcasters and World Relief Corp. established

1945
Theologian Dietrich Bonhoeffer is executed at Buchenwald by Nazis; his writings survive;
Youth for Christ International founded; Mission Aviation Fellowship organized by three former World War II pilots to bring aid to missionaries in third world
1950
World Vision founded by Bob Pierce;
Billy Graham Evangelistic Association established
1951
Campus Crusade for Christ International organized by Bill Bright
1952
President Harry Truman signs National Day of Prayer resolution
1956
Five missionaries killed by Huaorani (Auca) Indians in Ecuador
1957
Two million attend Billy Graham NYC crusade, 55,000 decisions reported
1960
Christian Broadcasting Network (CBN) begun by Pat Robertson;
Youth With A Mission (YWAM) founded by Loren Cunningham
1962
Evangelism Explosion International, organized by D. James Kennedy
1963
Theological Education Extension (TEE) begins in Guatemala;
author C. S. Lewis dies at 64; (wrote *Mere Christianity* and *The Chronicles of Narnia*)

This chronology just scratches the surface of Protestant, Christian work during the 130 years leading up to our generation. There is so much more, if one has the eyes to see and the ears to hear.

Modern Bible Translations

In America today, there are many applications of the English Bible. The four versions that I recommend for Bible reading and study are:

The New King James Version—which keeps the lyrical style of the text and has been updated with the latest textual and archeological information.

The New International Version—which is the latest, most widely accepted version as the most readable "concept for concept" text.

The New American Standard Version—which is the best "word for word" version for Bible exposition from the pulpit, etc., but a bit challenging for lengthy reading.

The Christian Standard Bible–which is the latest, greatest blending of concept for concept and word for word version and an excellent family reading Bible.

These versions can be found in dozens of applications and there are emphases for all age ranges and specific study groups.

(Please see appendix 2 for more information on these.)

Conclusion

Christians have the same call today as all of the saints of the kingdom that we have read about in this book. We also have the same temptations to run after false gods and add to the gospel in order to escape from danger or feed our lusts, as others in this book did. This sinful behavior kills the Bible and its message of salvation for those lost from God. We must never forget that we are commissioned by the risen Christ Jesus to be truthful witnesses everywhere and always. Jesus has always chosen ordinary folks whom he trusted with the truth to spread the Gospel. We lie when we are ashamed of the Gospel or when we appear open to a pluralist view that all religions are equally valid ways to salvation.

Today, we "rustic Christians" must continue to fight for the freedoms of religion that millions have died for. The main weapon in that war is our Bible. And our true Commander-in-Chief has won many battles against the enemy. We live in a world where people are engaged in an endless pursuit of self fulfillment and entitlement. They want to kill the Bible by either defamation, destruction, or ignoring it as legend and fiction while venerating made-up traditions. The metropolitan culture of our cities and suburbs is decadent and decaying. Worse still, many of our churches are more into helping people fully enjoy this life while neglecting the implications of eternity. Their leadership is interested in moralizing virtue and trivializing sin. Pastors psychologize the Scriptures to make the message of Christ more user-friendly, which marginalizes the cross of Christ. These activities must be held up to the light of truth and exposed for the pablum they are.

Every Christian's Job

Have you ever thought about what a Christian's job really is? What are we really supposed to do as Christians, at the core of it? Yes, we are to be following the teachings of Christ. But how do we focus on that in our daily lives? The "until death do us part" job of every Christian is to <u>expend oneself in service to others</u> by the methods and in the name of Jesus Christ as we know him from the Bible. This "expending" is the model that God, Jesus Christ, and the Holy Spirit follow in their interaction with us.

"For God so loved the world that he gave his one and only son..." (Jn. 3:16a NIV).

"[Father]...I have brought you glory on earth by finishing the work you gave me to do..." (Jn. 17:4 NIV).

"In the same way, the Spirit helps us in our weakness. We do not know what we ought to pray for, but the Spirit himself intercedes for us." (Rom. 8:26 NIV).

"Expending" our lives is the job. If you are a rustic Christian, here is how you can explain your story. It is revealed in two non-English words every Christian should know: *doxa* and *esjoir*.

One of the most famous, historical Christian confessions, The Westminster Confession, states that the purpose of mankind is two-fold:

1. To glorify God
2. To enjoy him forever.

These two purposes beg the questions, "How do we glorify God?" and "How do we enjoy him?"

DOXA

The word we know as *glory* in English is translated from the Greek word *doxa*. *Doxa* means 'the true reputation of.' So, to glorify God is to reflect what his true reputation is. His true reputation reflected in our lives allows us and others to be close to him and to his love and power. As our lives reflect his true reputation, we represent him to the world and serve those who are in need, in his name and under his banner. All the information we need for this is in the Bible. That is why so many have tried and continue to try to kill its influence in our lives. Sadly, most religions are the best tools in accomplishing this task for the evil ones.

We rustic Christians reflect God's true reputation when we are doing what Jesus taught us to do in the four Gospels of the New Testament: Matthew, Mark, Luke, and John.

ESJOIR

At its core, the word *enjoy* means more than just to get pleasure from. It comes, originally, from the Latin, down through the French language, in the form of the word *esjoir* (pronounced "es suar"), which means to "combine with." So, to enjoy God, is to combine with him. Our methods and purpose are to constantly be about combining our lives with the life of God, and to do it forever.

God constantly "expends" his energy toward us in sacrificial love. He purposed that we would "be" and "be one with him" from the beginning of the world and personified that purpose in the life, work, and sacrifice of Jesus Christ, his son. Jesus and our Father God sends the Holy Spirit to join their Spirit with ours as we follow the will and example of the Father— the sacrificing of ourselves in helping others throughout life.

This continuing activity in our daily lives reveals God's "true reputation," what he is really like, and allows us to daily esjoir or "combine with" his Spirit.

Jesus Christ, our best picture of what God, the Father of all in the universe, is like, tells us:

"Whoever believes in me, does not believe in me only, but in the one who sent me. When he looks at me, he is seeing the one who sent me" (Jn.12:44–45 NIV).

"Jesus answered, 'I am the way and the truth and the life. No one comes to the Father except through me. If you really knew me, you will know my Father as well. From now on, you do know him and have seen him.' (John 14:6–7 NIV).

As we study the life of Jesus and follow his teachings, we show doxa, the true reputation and we esjoir, combine with his Spirit. And this combining is not until death do us part; it is forever and ever beyond time. And, it's our primary job. Everything else flows from this understanding.

Whether this is your first day on the job or if you have been a Christian for decades, this is the core of your job description. Memorize it. Make it your "doxa," your reputation. Relax in it and make it your esjoir, your enjoyment in combination with God for a lifetime and beyond.

It is our hope that all who have read these pages will realize their true identity as Christians, rise up and be released from the bondage of religions of slavery, renewing their dedication to God's kingdom work in the world. Who is on God's side, the side of truth? We know Myles Coverdale had his answer. Coverdale translated the following verses of Isaiah while in exile and, upon arriving in England, spoke them to the first truly free English-speaking Bible readers.

Myles Coverdale

Isaiah 50:10–11 (KJV) asks, "Who is among you that feareth the LORD, that obeyeth his voice of the servant, that walketh in darkness, and hath no light? Let him trust in the name of the LORD, and stay upon his God. Behold all ye that kindle a fire, that compass yourselves about with sparks: walk in the light of your fire and in the spark that ye have kindled" (KJV). Does your heart burn within you as Jesus breaks his "bread" for you? Is there a Spirit-spark that kindles a heart's fire that you and others can walk in because of its light?

May this study have opened your eyes and your heart to go forth and know that your Bible is true, was bought with a great price, and is the story of the One True God, Jehovah, and his only Son, Jesus the Christ, our Savior and Lord, forevermore. May you not only have been encouraged in the miraculous history lesson of the Holy Scriptures in English, but may you also recognize he has a life plan for YOU and your ministry to enlarge his kingdom on earth. Oh, Christian, become yet another faithful link in the scarlet chain of Bible teachers the rustic remnant has always been. It is our mandate from the Lord! The time is shorter than it has ever been before. Remember, as you go and teach, that our risen Savior has, by His sacrifice, gained dominion over all things; all thrones, all high places have been placed beneath his feet until the end of the world.

How to Remain "Rustic" in Christ's Realm

Remaining rustic is crucial for our spiritual health. However, it is dangerous in this world. As we have looked through history together, haven't we seen that there is always a minority and never the majority who carry on the work of the true kingdom of Christ? Haven't we seen that they have always been persecuted, even by those who were supposedly Christians? It is still so today and will be until Jesus comes again. Until that time, we must all daily take up our cross and follow him to the best of our ability. We must remember what Paul told the Ephesian church:

"You are no longer strangers and aliens, but you are fellow citizens with the saints and members of the household of God, built on the foundation of the apostles and prophets. Christ Jesus himself being the cornerstone, in whom the whole structure, being joined together, grows into a holy temple in the Lord. In him you also are being built together into a dwelling place for God by the Spirit" (Eph. 2:19–22).

What magnificent words! Jesus has adopted us into his household of eternity and his household of now. Do we truly understand what this means? God, the Creator of the Universe, is our Father. He who put the world in space and the stars in place, he who creates out of nothing and who holds everything is our Father! It is unfathomable, but the Bible says it is true. The Bible calls us to remember the apostles and prophets as our foundation, and all the rustics who stepped out on faith to further Christ's kingdom. This is not an option, it is a statement of being. We stand on this foundation now, today.

God is the Father, Jesus is the head of our household. The Spirit gives us the power, right now, to create his family dwelling place. The apostle Peter calls us living stones in the Father's house. Yet, we are more than this, we are brothers and sisters by holy blood. This gives each of us flowing energy toward our bold destiny as long as we persevere and do not falter.

"For just as the body is one and has many members, and all the members of the body, though many, are one body, so it is with Christ" (1 Cor. 12:12).

Paul, seeing through the inspired glass clearly, says that every Christian is an organic, Spirit-filled part of the whole person of Jesus Christ in the world. This state of being is continually constructed in us through the relationships God gives us with other marvelous members of his body. We should never minimize the gathering of the saints, all of us working together. Consider where you are weak and who God has brought, or will bring, to infuse the body with life and strength in that area for the common good of the kingdom. Consider where you are strong and how that strength can aid the body toward triumph for the kingdom.

Also know that, though you are a magnificent work through him who birthed you in the Spirit, you are also in a state of physical entropy; you are not long for this world, maybe years, maybe decades, not long. Time will not slow down. There are no "do-overs." And you must work while the daylight lasts. Christians should not engage in "body-building" for admiration, profit, amusement, or advancement in religion. In everything we do we must ask ourselves, "Does this action advance the kingdom?" Work for the night is coming when we will work no more on this earth. Steadily work, remembering this:

God, in his wisdom, did not prepare Jesus' church body to meet our goals, but to fulfill his! Your bold destiny has never been yours alone, but also the King's. I implore you not to leave this book, this holy spiritual ground upon which you stand, and run ahead to grasp your kingdom work but to move on your knees, through prayer, for how to eventually walk and build and become a son or a daughter after God's own heart. Jesus used a great term in the Beatitudes (see Matt. 5:9). He used the term that the Greek language of the New Testament called *Toyosdeh*. And, he specifically paired it with being a peacemaker. *Toyosdeh* means "a complete holder of," an adult that is the "spitting image of" your Father in heaven. It is an active description, as in how the Father sent Jesus to make peace with humankind. This is your commission, to have the spiritual attitude of God, if you have the courage to take it.

But, I challenge you to become the true image of Jesus and the Father by opposing those selfish, compromising, fantasy-building, false, religions in every form. By now, you know what I am speaking of. You realize that Jesus did not start a "religion" but a true Jesus movement best known as "People of the Way," which is "a rustic people dedicated to the true-truth" of reality in God's world. Every religious founder of every other major religion says, "I'm a prophet who has come to show you the way to find God." Only Christianity has a founder who has the audacity to say, "I am God, and I have come to find you." Jesus admitted this fifteen times, in public, during his earthly ministry. This must be the basis of our worldview. It is found only in the Bible.

We must also be of the Grace Narrative. For those who need a refresher, the Grace Narrative is that Jesus Christ came to earth to accomplish our salvation, but he didn't do it through his strength. He did it through his adopted weakness. He came as a man and died on the cross. By the same token, we only get this gift of salvation when we admit our failure. This is what all man-made religions don't seem to understand. The truth is that we must say that we are failures and admit to God that we need mercy and grace. Then, in him, we are accepted, not because of our performance, but his. The truth for a real Christian is being saved by grace not by works. <u>Then</u>, we work to love others because of our gratitude.

We must also remember that Christianity is not feel-good therapy. We have shown that the Bible flows from history and what God has done in relation to humankind through history. If we can't accept the historical Bible with all the evidences of its efficacy by now, we must let go of every document of antiquity as unproven or falsified by later-day proponents who wish their hopes to be reality. We must challenge false beliefs as God gives us the strength and opportunity to do so. We must not sit by and do nothing while worldly, revisionist, and atheistic attitudes about truth are infiltrating our communities, churches, and families. We must not embrace ecumenical charity, collegiality, and unity at the expense of Jesus' reality. Finally, we must be prepared to die for the truth.

When Jesus stood before Pilate, the Roman governor said, "You are a king, then!" Jesus answered, "You are right in saying I am a king. In fact, for this reason I was born, and for this I came into the world, to testify to the truth." The Greek language construct in the Gospel of John for "the truth" is *i Aletheias*. It means "the reality." Jesus is the King of the reality of God's sovereignty. Truth has no meaning apart from a fixed source. His name is Jehovah God, and his best revelation to us is Jesus Christ. Every truth claim apart from this is preposterous. We must be soldiers of Christ in The Way of pulling down ideological strongholds and casting down the lies of the Evil One.

In this book we have not examined in detail non-Christian worldviews, but they have their part in discouraging the Bible by their tenants. A discerning eye will read the Hindu Vedas and discover many absurdities, like a civilization of humanity living on the sun and incorrect statements about the moon and the planets, etc. Priests of Hinduism admit that the Vedas were not written to teach truth. They are mantras to be memorized and chanted. Their worth is in the sound, not the meaning. In the *Bhagavad Gita*, the god Krishna encourages Arjuna to kill his cousins and teachers. The Lord Krishna advises Arjuna not to have pity for those he is to kill because the soul really never dies. He says, "Wise men feel no pity either for what dies or what lives" (Bhagavad Gita II, 12–13).

In 1999, loyal Hindus burned Christian missionary Graham Stains and his two young sons to death by surrounding their Jeep, dousing it with kerosene, and lighting it. Stains had been working with leprosy victims for thirty-four years. He wanted to give them hope within a society that shunned them. Apparently this was an insult and he was killed. Why? Because the avatars of Indian epics, like Krishna, command that the status quo, or dharma, must be preserved.

Buddhism mainly has teachings that sprout from Hinduism. Buddhism is a works-based religion practiced mostly in China's mountain areas and the rural areas of the East that says that everything and everybody is God. (Which really means that nobody and nothing is God.) The overriding Buddhist principle or law is that we should always do our best to avoid harming others. (That's why there aren't very many Buddhist terrorists.) The largest sect of Buddhism is Zen Buddhism, which is a mixture of Confucianism, Taoism, and Buddhism. Following their religious laws increases Zen or happiness in the world. There are three basic precepts to following the law of Zen:

1. Avoid all evil thoughts and actions.
2. Attain good thoughts and do right actions.
3. Develop "wisdom" so that all humanity is benefitted.

Sounds great, doesn't it. But, who defines where the lines are drawn? The Buddhist himself.

Buddhism does not strictly teach that an individual person continues to exist after death. It believes that we are all a part of an endless cycle and we continue on as part of cosmic life (or an energy form). Many elitists, atheists, and agnostics in the West find Buddhism attractive because it provides an opportunity for supposed spiritual depth without following up with obedience to authority required by belief in a deity.

Islam is based on the writings of an illiterate sheikh with the help of an outcast monk, who name-dropped enough Bible names and characters to appear to give it credence. The Koran is Arabic esoteric poetry with commentaries of intellectual elitism. (i.e., If you're not an imam, you can't get it, so just let the imams tell you what to do.) Islam is based on what is called the Five Pillars–the five essential duties in worship of Allah. Muslims believe that in order to go to paradise or heaven, they must regularly perform certain religious duties. Additionally, they must be perceived by their religious leaders to do these acts and rites in an attitude of total submission. The local Imams decide who is in proper submission and, so, hold a "Sword of Damocles" of sorts over all Muslim followers. They report to the regional imams and their police force for punishment of any infractions. Nice work if you can get it. We know all too well that Islam is a religion of selfishness and violence. It is a hierarchy of slavery.

Muhammad boldly claimed for years that he had ascended into the seventh heaven, and there before "the effulgent majesty of the Almighty" he was informed that he was being sent with the sword to compel all the people in the world to cast away their other religions and accept the Koran and Allah.

The Koran says: "A night spent in arms [fighting] is more precious in the sight of God than months of fasting and prayer. Whosoever dies in battle, his sins are forgiven. In the Day of Judgment, his wounds shall be resplendent as vermilion, and odoriferous as musk. In the Muslim's paradise, seventy-two damsels of sparkling beauty shall minister to the most humble of the faithful" (i.e., those who die in battle).

*See the author's booklet, *Help, We've Fallen and We Can't Get Up* which is available on killingthebible.com, for more information on false religions and false narratives within so-called Christianity and New-age religions.

What About Non-Religious Proponents?

Sceptics and so-called intellectuals will come against us with all their post-modern jargon. The true Christian must understand that the "modernists" in the early part of the twentieth century came to stand for the rejection of the past as a guide to the present. They then endeavored to regenerate morality on the basis of eternal truths based on scientific theory and philosophizing. The goal was to eject from society the historic religion of the past because religion was divisive. As we have seen, that seems reasonable considering all the evil that has been done in the name of religion. Religions <u>have</u> been divisive. Even true Christianity is divisive, but for the purpose of shedding a light on sin which separates us from God. This divisiveness is one of love. When history was ejected as irrelevant, what was left for the "modernists" was the "individual will" making its own rules.

Since then, what post-modernists have done is to take modernism to the next level. In their individualistic thinking, instead of asking what the ideal for human behavior is, the post-modernist wants to know what the prevailing average of human behavior is. The result is that the tyranny of the average holds sway. The average, comfortable self has become the unifying ideal. Therefore, for them, the Christian concept of an all-saving fixed truth divinely established to meet the crying needs of the human condition is unacceptable. When a true Christian brings the Bible into the conversation, modernists attempt to destroy it with its own truth. (Remind you of Satan in the Garden of Eden?) They kill the Bible by stirring up compassion. They say the Bible is wicked in not relegating to all individuals their rights, no matter the sin. The rallying cry is, "Do not judge!" Congregants in our churches have been told that the greatest virtue is charity. Thus the post-modernist call for compassion is sometimes a means of brainwashing us into ignoring our historical biblical standards. Please don't fall for this hogwash.

I have endeavored to give the reader the knowledge within these pages to begin to stand up to the killers of the Bible. Please do not squander it by closing this book and saying, "Well, wasn't that interesting." It is more than that. It is ammunition in the spiritual realm that God has delivered to you for stamina in the faith. I invite you to join the true Jesus movement based on your new reality. I encourage you to pray about joining the work of one of the ministries listed in this chapter. They have stood the test of time. They (for the most part) are Bible based and practice the true faith of Jesus Christ. Above all, remember to

REMAIN RUSTIC in the LORD'S SERVICE!
AMEN.

Sources

1. *Early Manuscripts and Modern Translations of the New Testament* (Comfort), 4.

Images

Two examples of the pottery that held some of the Dead Sea Scrolls documents found at Qumran.

*From Wikipedia, the free encyclopedia

Appendix 1
Historical Outline of Killing the Bible

In the following outline, we see the movements of God, followed by rebellion of men. At which time, God gives them over to sin and degradation. However, God always has a remnant that remains close to him and is allowed to provide the re-birth of a people who continue to bring the kingdom of God on earth. We also see the Bible as it forms from the Holy Spirit but through those dedicated to God, until the apostle John penned the last verse of Revelation in about the year AD 90 and his letters in about AD 92–95. In this list, we are focusing on the British Isles. In the <u>remnant</u> you will see your heritage as an American Christian.

The Ancients

Old Testament Noahic remnant families become the Cymry of Ancient Britain.

GOD MOVES
The ancient druidic religion is protected as a perfect framework for conversion to Christianity.

GOD GIVES THEM OVER
Many druids chose selfishness and power-mongering, perverting the worship of God.

REMNANT
The Cymric Celts (descendants of Gomer, Japeth, and Noah) continue to walk with God and know some Hebrew and Greek and "ways of the East." They worship one God and believe that he works in the world.

First–Third Centuries

GOD MOVES
Joseph of Arimathaea, Simon Zelotes, and their small group bring Christianity to the British Isles and the Cymric Celts convert.

GOD GIVES THEM OVER
Compromise with the Romans makes the populace slaves to their brutality, and Satan forms bands of heretics in order to kill the Bible in its cradle.

REMNANT
The Ceile-de and the Irish church face the Romans, love them, and convert many.

BIBLE
The Bible, God's Word, is complete and used in its original languages of Hebrew, Greek, and Aramaic. Genesis to Revelation is endorsed by the true church of the Celts.

Fourth–Fifth Centuries

GOD MOVES
British/Roman Constantine and his theological elders legalize Christianity throughout the world.

GOD GIVES THEM OVER
The Roman Church begins to enslave the populace through religion, i.e., church and state. The first steps are made to religiously kill the Bible.

REMNANT
The Welsh and Scottish Culdees stay true to Christianity of the first century.

BIBLE
Roman Church makes a Bible in Latin that is corrupted from the original languages, sometimes by ignorance, often by design.

Sixth–Eighth Centuries

GOD MOVES
The northern British, Welsh, and Scotts build a society under true biblical principles.

GOD GIVES THEM OVER
The Roman Church brings in wealth, cathedrals, and hierarchy which the kings of Britain compromise with. The Vikings come to plunder the wealth and the people.

REMNANT
Silurian Celts and Culdees stay the course through persecution of the powerful, the so-called Church and the evil Vikings.

BIBLE
Bible picture books of the Celts, Scots, and Scandinavians keep the Greek original meanings of Holy Scripture.

Ninth–Eleventh Centuries

GOD MOVES
King Albert the Great, consolidates the kingdom of the British under God in Christ. He and his court begin to translate the Bible into English for the people of England.

GOD GIVES THEM OVER
Descendant kings compromise with Rome and European Viking Emperors, while getting caught up in the Crusades and the Islamic Wars. Temporal fears overcome Bible teaching, and the power-mongers take over most of the world.

REMNANT
Welsh Celts, Scottish Culdees, and Irish Proto-protestants stay true and even convert many Vikings to Christianity, including their kings and queens.

BIBLE
The Roman Church invents penance, purgatory, Mariology, and angelology in order to consolidate power over the people and fight the Islamist hoards. They weave the lies into the new Latin Bible, effectively killing the influence of the Word. However, the Celtic peoples of the British Isles remain pure.

Twelfth–Fourteenth Centuries

GOD MOVES
Anglo-Saxons, Vikings, and British Patriots unite to fight Roman Church domination in the British Isles.

GOD GIVES OVER
The popes and their vassal kings of England and Europe power-monger to enrich themselves and cover their lies. The people suffer continued violence, usurpation, and plague.

REMNANT
The "highlander Scotts and Celts" remain true to Christianity. They begin to be called Lollards by the Catholics from Rome.

BIBLE

The Bible in any language is forbidden to the people by Rome and her vassals. Even the Latin bible is restricted from the lower Catholic priests in fear they will divulge the truth of Holy Scripture to the people.

The priest, Wycliffe, translates the Latin Vulgate Bible into thirteenth-century English for the people to read. He is excommunicated by Rome.

FIFTEENTH–SIXTEENTH CENTURIES

GOD MOVES

British patriots from the Highlands and former Roman priests solidify England under kings and queens who honor God, even if with "feet of clay."

GOD GIVES THEM OVER

Popes and evil kings of England and France oppress the people under Roman Church dominion. These are primarily the Tutor kings (Henrys I–VIII and Mary Tudor.) Their actions effectively kill the Bible for most of the subjects of their reigns.

REMNANT

The Lollards, the English martyrs, and those of the Protestant Revolt.

BIBLE

English Bible champions smuggle English Bibles into the hands of Christians. These are the days of former Roman priests who become protestant evangelists, Tyndale, Luther, and Calvin. The Celtic Welsh, Scottish Lollards, and English pastors get the English Bible to the English people.

SEVENTEENTH–EIGHTEENTH CENTURIES

GOD MOVES

British Christian separatists and the highlanders of Wales, Scotland, and Ireland stay the course and hold to the separation of church and state, with the true Christians running the highlander local governments. The Pilgrims (1620) sail to America for religious liberty. Thousands of Christians move to North America, giving her names like Nova Scotia (New Scotland), Plymouth, and New England. America is born of revolution against tyranny and the state church.

GOD GIVES THEM OVER
The British church and state begin to harass and jail Christian British highlanders and their followers. Those who would stay in England during these times must have state religion, which, at times, persecutes Protestants by compromising with and supporting Roman Catholic hegemony. The Islamists fight their way into Europe to the gates of Vienna, Austria, and southern France because so-called Christians are fighting between themselves for power and control. The Islamists continuing aim is to conquer the world for Allah.

REMNANT
The Scottish Highlanders, Welsh Celts, and northern British form the local churches as Protestant and Bible-based. John Knox confronts the compromisers and persecutors. The Pilgrims, Methodists, Baptists, and Anglicans flood the New World.

BIBLE
The Puritans, and others, bring the Geneva Bible with them to the new world, and it is the Bible most used for the first one-hundred years of the United States. The Geneva is the first study Bible and children of the colonists, including our first statesmen, are taught from God's word. The American Declaration of Independence and Constitution are based on biblical principles.

Late Eighteenth and Nineteenth Century

GOD MOVES
Freedom is won by the Americans against the British oppressors. A "new world order" is set up which the Founding Fathers intend to be under God rather than under fallen men of the church (popes) or the state (kings). It is intended to be a republic, not a monarchy, an oligarchy, or an unruly and chaotic democracy. Missionaries begin to be sent to the world in the name of Christ Jesus. British Christians begin to rise from their slumberous compromise with pseudo-Christians.

GOD GIVES THEM OVER
Compromises with the British monarchy, the French Democrats, the Spanish Catholics, and the Islamic pirates cause the new republic to falter and make fearful choices that will hinder freedom in America during future decades.

REMNANT
Christians throughout rural or rustic America come to the realization of their heritage and have a series of "Great Awakenings." Rural churches become solid and patriotic.

BIBLE
The King James Bible is edited and amended by true scholars and is blended with the Geneva Bible study notes for Americans. The Revised Standard Bible is created at the turn of the century for ease of understanding of the Holy Scriptures.

Twentieth Century

GOD MOVES
America becomes the bulwark of Christianity above any other nation. Consequently, it has the hand of God on it. Christian missionaries flood the world for Christ and take the Bible into lands and languages of the populace overseas.

GOD GIVES THEM OVER
The state, the academics, and the atheistic scientists take leadership of the institutions of the people. Atheism, post-modernism, and materialism kick God out of the schoolroom, the capitol, and the state-houses. Global war plagues the world that has lost its zeal for the one true God and trusts in the goodness of mankind.

REMNANT
Christian evangelists and the rural church keep the notions of God and country throughout the century. They continue to move out into all nations to proclaim the gospel and the sovereignty of Jesus Christ. They reject evolution, the lie of humanism, and the rampant capitalism of the materialists.

BIBLE
The Bible is studied by scholars from Hebrew, Greek, and Aramaic backgrounds. Biblical archeology proves many skeptics wrong when they question the stories of the Old Testament and New Testament. Dozens of versions and paraphrases flood the U.S. populace and stimulate discussion. Evangelism is spurred by the NASB, NIV, ESV and HCSB versions of the English Bible; all excellent guides to the holy life and the mission of God to bring His kingdom to the earth.

21st Century

GOD MOVES
God is still moving. In the early years of the current century, the Roman Church is seeking to rise. The Islamists and their terror campaigns are rising. God still has His hand on America's 'rustic' people who will not yield to selfishness and power-mongering from within or without the country.

GOD CAN GIVE US OVER
God cannot sanction the sinful direction of the American leaders, in the church or out of it, who selfishly look to every power but him for salvation. Already many of our children are lost to him because we have compromised with evil and ceased to teach them their special place in God's sovereign plan.

REMNANT
There is a remnant today who are going back to the basics of our heritage and Bible belief. The sophisticated elite snicker and shun the rustics of our cities and towns. But God has always had a people, and he seeks to bless us as we look to him.

BIBLE
The Bible is our rock and our true history. As we read, study, and enact its principles, we will overcome until that day we will see his face.

Many Christians believe that the twenty-first century will be the final chapter in the current earthly passage and that we will see the second coming of Christ within this time. We cannot say, but what we have shown by this list is that, throughout time, God has always moved on the earth, men have been given over to their human selfishness, and a remnant people of God have been sustained by him for his purposes of bringing his kingdom upon the earth. The Bible has been, and continues to be, the guidebook for our salvation and our life as God's people. We neglect it, and our history as providential people, to our doom. We embrace it to our heavenly credit.

APPENDIX 2
POPULAR BIBLE VERSIONS

Americans responded to England's ERV Bible by publishing the nearly-identical American Standard Version (ASV) in 1901. It was also widely-accepted and embraced by churches throughout America for many decades as the leading modern-English version of the Bible.

In 1971, it was again revised and called New American Standard Version Bible (often referred to as the NASB). This New American Standard Bible is considered by nearly all evangelical Christian scholars and translators today, to be the most accurate, word-for-word translation of the original Greek and Hebrew Scriptures into the modern English language that has ever been produced.

In 1973, the New International Version (NIV) was produced, which was offered as a "dynamic equivalent" translation into modern English. The NIV was designed not for "word-for-word" accuracy, but rather, for "phrase-for-phrase" accuracy, and ease of reading even at a junior high school reading level. It was meant to appeal to a broader (and in some instances less-educated) cross-section of the general public. It has become the best-selling modern-English translation of the Bible ever published.

In 2002, a major attempt was made to bridge the gap between the simple readability of the NIV, and the extremely precise accuracy of the NASB This translation is called the English Standard Version (ESV) and is rapidly gaining popularity for its readability and accuracy. The twenty-first century will certainly continue to bring new translations of God's Word in the modern English language.

In 2006, the Holman Christian Standard Bible, the HCSB, was created and is considered by scholars to be one of the best translations of all.

English is the most read, the most spoken, the most proliferated language in the world.

More Chinese now speak English than British and Americans.

English Bibles and English commentaries should be taken to the world in greater numbers.

English Bible history should be revealed to all Christians in America.

Appendix 3
Islam and her Tenants

The following is the Muslim justification for causing followers to continually pray and, when they pray, to bring offerings so that their prayers would be seen as sincere and effective. In this, they are "saved each time" for Allah:

Prophet Muhammed is reported to have said, "The first duty that Allah, the Supreme, has ordained upon my nation is that of offering prayer, and indeed prayer is the first thing that will be taken account of on the Day of Resurrection." as well as "Whoever keeps the prayer established, has kept his religion established—and whoever leaves Prayer has demolished religion (i.e. left the fold of Islam)." While the Qur'an makes it clear that the purpose for creation is to worship Allah alone, and that the most excellent way of praying is to offer Salaah standing before Allah in devout obedience. The Islamic *Adhaan* (call for prayer) which is recited at time of each prayer contains two verses (each recited twice), "*Hayya'ala-Salaah*" and "*Hayya'ala-Falaah*" which translate as "Come to Salaah" and "Come to success" respectively, indicating that by performing Salaah, one may attain eternal success.

In a Hadith reference, Abdullah ibn Mas'ud narrates, "I asked Allah's Messenger, Prophet Muhammed: "O Messenger of Allah, which deed is most beloved to Allah?" He said: "Prayer at the appointed time." I said: "Then what?" He said: "Kindness to parents." I said: "Then what?" He said: "Jihad (struggle) in the way of Allah."

"Prophet Muhammed is also reported to have likened the Salaah to five daily baths that cleanse a persons sins; Abu Huraira narrates that, "I heard Allah's Apostle saying, "If there was a river at the door of any one of you and he took a bath in it five times a day, would you notice any dirt on him?" They said, "Not a trace of dirt would be left." The Prophet added, "That is the example of the five prayers with which Allah blots out [annuls] evil deeds."

The Qur'an has also pointed out that believers perform Salaah only to earn the pleasure of Allah and not to impress anyone else, calling anyone who does so a hypocrite. Moreover, those who abandon Salaah are warned of dire consequences, while only those who humbly submit themselves to Allah alone are said to have ease in offering it. In Surah Al-Ma'arij, Allah uses the word *halu'an* to describe the restless and impatient nature of man, stating that whenever he is afflicted with trouble he lacks patience and trembles in despair. This occurs due to shortcomings in his faith, whereas when he is given in abundance he becomes ungrateful towards Allah. He is also arrogant and uncaring towards those less fortunate than him. The Qur'an then assures the observance of Salaah as a way to preserve hope in times of grievance and humbleness as well as humility in periods of bountiful life. Salaah thus has the power to erase the roots of evil deeds which bring barriers in the society giving birth to racial as well as financial discriminations and sinful intentions.

APPENDIX 4
The Fruit of Islamism

Further Proof that Islam is of the Evil One, the Prince of this world.

In 1206, the young Mongol leader Temujin was declared the ruler of all the Mongols; he took the name Genghis Khan(or Chinguz Khan). By the time he died in 1227, Genghis Khan controlled Central Asia from the Pacific coast of Siberia to the Caspian Sea in the west.

After Genghis Khan's death, his descendants divided the empire into four separate khanates: the Mongolian homeland, ruled by Tolui Khan; the Empire of the Great Khan (later Yuan China), ruled by Ogedei Khan; the Ilkhanate Khanate of Central Asia and Persia, ruled by Chagatai Khan; and the Khanate of the Golden Horde, which would later include not just Russia but also Hungary and Poland.

Each Khan sought to expand his own portion of the empire through further conquests. After all, a prophecy predicted that Genghis Khan and his offspring would one day rule "all the people of the felt tents." Of course, they sometimes exceeded this mandate—nobody in Hungary or Poland actually lived a nomadic herding lifestyle. Nominally, at least, the other Khans answered to the Great Khan.

In 1251, Ogedei died, and his nephew Mongke, Genghis's grandson, became the Great Khan. Mongke Khan appointed his brother Hulagu to head the southwestern horde, the Ilkhanate. He charged Hulagu with the task of conquering the remaining Islamic empires of the Middle East and North Africa.

Throughout history, few names have inspired such terror as "Tamerlane." Born in 1337, Timur-i Lang (Tamerlane, Timur the Lame), was the brutal Mongol ruler of Samarkand who cut a wide swath of destruction across Persia and the Middle East. Timur founded the Timurid Dynasty and became infamous for building pyramids out of the skulls of his slain enemies.

That was not the Central Asian conqueror's actual name, though. More properly, he is known as Timur, from the Turkic word for "iron."

Amir Timur is remembered as a vicious conqueror, who razed ancient cities to the ground and put entire populations to the sword. On the other hand, he is also known as a great patron of the arts, literature, and architecture. One of his signal achievements is his capital at the beautiful city of Samarkand, in modern-day Uzbekistan. A complicated man, Timur continues to fascinate us some six centuries after his death.

Timur's Early Life

Timur was born in 1336, near the city of Kesh (now called Shahrisabz), about fifty miles south of the oasis of Samarkand, in Transoxiana. The child's father, Taragay, was the chief of the Barlas tribe. The Barlas were of mixed Mongolian and Turkic ancestry, descended from the hordes of Genghis Khan and the earlier inhabitants of Transoxiana. Unlike their nomadic ancestors, the Barlas were settled agriculturalists and traders.

Ahmad ibn Muhammad ibn Arabshah's fourteenth-century biography, *Tamerlane or Timur: The Great Amir*, stated that Timur was descended from Genghis Khan on his mother's side.

Disputed Causes of Timur's Lameness

The European versions of Timur's name—"Tamerlane" or "Tamberlane"—are based on the Turkic nickname *Timur-i-leng*, meaning "Timur the Lame." Timur's body was exhumed by a Russian team lead by archaeologist Mikhail Gerasimov in 1941, and they found evidence of two healed wounds on Timur's right leg. His right hand was also missing two fingers.

The anti-Timurid author Arabshah says that Timur was shot while stealing sheep. More likely, he was wounded in 1363 or 1364 while fighting as a mercenary for Sistan (southeastern Iran) as stated by contemporary chroniclers Ruy Clavijo and Sharaf al-Din Ali Yazdi.

Transoxiana's Political Situation

During Timur's youth, Transoxiana was riven by conflict between the local nomadic clans and the sedentary Chagatay Mongol khans who ruled them. The Chagatay had abandoned the mobile ways of Genghis Khan and their other ancestors, and taxed the people heavily in order to support their urban lifestyle. Naturally, this angered their citizens.

Note: This information was found on-line at www.wikipedia.com and other sources cited following and can be found by searching under any of the references below.

In 1347, a local amir ("prince") named Kazgan seized power from the Chagatay ruler Borolday. Kazgan would rule until his assassination in 1358. After Kazgan's death, various warlords and religious leaders vied for power. Tughluk Timur, a Mongol warlord, emerged victorious in 1360.

Young Timur Gains and Loses Power

Timur's uncle Hajji Beg led the Barlas at this time, but refused to submit to Tughluk Timur. The Hajji fled, and the new Mongol ruler decided to install the seemingly more pliable young Timur to rule in his stead. In fact, Timur was already plotting against the Mongols. He formed an alliance with the grandson of Kazgan, Amir Hussein, and married Hussein's sister Aljai Turkanaga. The Mongols soon caught on; Timur and Hussein were dethroned and forced to turn bandit in order to survive. In 1362, the legend says, Timur's following was reduced to two: Aljai, and one other. They were even imprisoned in Persia for two months.

Timur's Conquests Begin

Timur's bravery and tactical skill made him a successful mercenary soldier in Persia, and he soon collected a large following. In 1364, Timur and Hussein banded together again and defeated Ilyas Khoja, the son of Tughluk Timur. By 1366, the two warlords controlled Transoxiana. Timur's wife died in 1370, freeing him to attack his erstwhile ally Hussein. Hussein was besieged and killed at Balkh, and Timur declared himself the sovereign of the whole region. Timur was not directly descended from Genghis Khan, so he ruled as an amir, rather than as khan. Over the next decade, Timur seized the rest of Central Asia, as well.

Timur's Empire Expands

With Central Asia in hand, Timur invaded Russia in 1380. He helped the Mongol Khan Toktamysh retake control, and also defeated the Lithuanians in battle. Timur captured Herat in 1383, the opening salvo against Persia. By 1385, all of Persia was his. With invasions in 1391 and 1395, Timur fought against his former protege in Russia, Toktamysh. The Timurid army captured Moscow in 1395. While Timur was busy in the north, Persia revolted. He responded by leveling entire cities and using the citizens' skulls to build grisly towers and pyramids.

By 1396, Timur had conquered Iraq, Azerbaijan, Armenia, Mesopotamia, and Georgia.

Timur Conquers India, Syria, and Turkey

Timur's army of 90,000 crossed the Indus River in September 1398 and set upon India. The country had fallen to pieces after the death of Firuz Shah; Bengal,

Kashmir, and the Deccan each had separate rulers. The Turkic/Mongol invaders left carnage along their path; Delhi's army was destroyed in December, and the city ruined. Timur seized tons of treasure and ninety war elephants, and took them back to Samarkand.

Timur looked west in 1399, retaking Azerbaijan and conquering Syria. Baghdad was destroyed in 1401, and 20,000 of its people slaughtered. In July of 1402, Timur captured Turkey and received submission from Egypt.

Timur's Final Campaign and Death

The rulers of Europe were glad that the Ottoman Turk sultan Bayazid had been defeated, but they trembled at the idea that "Tamerlane" was at their doorstep. The rulers of Spain, France, and other powers sent congratulatory embassies to Timur, hoping to stave off an attack. Timur had bigger goals, though. He decided in 1404 that he would conquer Ming China. (The ethnic-Han Ming dynasty had overthrown his cousins, the Yuan, in 1368.)

The Timurid army set out in December, during an unusually cold winter. Men and horses died of eposure, and the sixty-eight-year-old Timur fell ill. He died in February, 1405 at Otrar, in Kazakhstan.

Timur's Legacy

Timur started life as the son of a minor chieftain, much like his putative ancestor Genghis Khan. Through sheer intelligence, military skill, and force of personality, Timur was able to conquer an empire stretching from Russia to India, and from the Mediterranean Sea to Mongolia.

Unlike Genghis Khan, however, Timur conquered not to open trade routes and protect his flanks, but to loot and pillage. The Timurid Empire did not long survive its founder, because he rarely bothered to put any governmental structure in place after he destroyed the existing order.

While Timur professed to be a good Muslim, he obviously felt no compunction about destroying the jewel-cities of Islam and slaughtering their inhabitants. Damascus, Khiva, Baghdad...these ancient capitals of Islamic learning never really recovered from Timur's attentions. His intent seems to have been to make his capital at Samarkand the first city of the Islamic world.

Contemporary sources say that Timur's forces killed about 19 million people during their conquests. That number is probably exaggerated, but Timur does seem to have enjoyed massacre for its own sake.

Timur's Descendants

Despite a death-bed warning from the conqueror, his sons and grandsons immediately began to fight over the throne when he passed away. The most successful Timurid ruler, Timur's grandson Uleg Beg, gained fame as an astronomer and scholar. Uleg was not a good administrator, however, and was murdered by his own son in 1449. Timur's line had better luck in India, where his great-great-grandson Babur founded the Moghul Dynasty in 1526. The Moghuls ruled until 1857, when the British expelled them. (Shah Jahan, builder of the Taj Mahal, is thus also a descendent of Timur.)

Timur's Reputation

Timur was lionized in the West for his defeat of the Ottoman Turks. Christopher Marlowe's *Tamburlaine the Great* and Edgar Allen Poe's "Tamerlane" are good examples. Not surprisingly, the people of Turkey, Iran, and the Middle East remember him rather less favorably.

In post-Soviet Uzbekistan, Timur has been made into a national folk hero. The people of Uzbek cities like Khiva, however, are skeptical; they remember that he razed their city and killed nearly every inhabitant.

After Tamerlane

Between 1206 and 1526, much of India was ruled by the Delhi Sultanate, which was established by the heirs of Muhammad Shahab ud-Din Ghori, victor in the Second Battle of Tarain. In 1526, the ruler of Kabul, a descendent of both Genghis Khan and Timur (Tamerlane) named Zahir al-Din Muhammad Babur, attacked the much larger Sultanate army. Babur's force of some 15,000 was able to overcome Sultan Ibrahim Lodhi's 40,000 troops and 100 war elephants because the Timurids had field artillery. Gun-fire spooked the elephants that trampled their own men in their panic. Lodhi died in battle, and Babur established the Mughul ("Mongol") Empire, which ruled India until 1858, when the British colonial government took over.

Sources

Clavijo, "Narrative of the Embassy of Ruy Gonzalez de Clavijo to the Court of Timour, A.D. 1403-1406," trans. Markham (1859).

Encyclopedia Britannica on-line.

Marozzi, *Tamerlane: Sword of Islam, Conqueror of the World* (2006).

Saunders, *History of the Mongol Conquests* (1971).

In the Other Corner:
The Mamluk Dynasty of Egypt

While the Mongols were busy with their ever-expanding empire, the Islamic world was fighting off Christian Crusaders from Europe. The great Muslim general Saladin (Salah al-Din) conquered Egypt in 1169, founding the Ayyubid Dynasty. His descendants used increasing numbers of Mamluk soldiers in their internecine struggles for power.

The Mamluks were an elite corps of warrior-slaves, mostly from Turkic or Kurdish Central Asia, but also including some Christians from the Caucasus region of south-eastern Europe. Captured and sold as young boys, they were carefully groomed for life as military men. Being a Mamluk became such an honor that some free-born Egyptians reportedly sold their sons into slavery so that they, too, could become Mamluks.

In the tumultuous times surrounding the Seventh Crusade (which led to the capture of King Louis IX of France by the Egyptians), the Mamluks steadily gained power over their civilian rulers. In 1250, the widow of Ayyubid sultan as-Salih Ayyub married a Mamluk, Emir Aybak, who then became sultan. This was the beginning of the Bahri Mamluk Dynasty, which ruled Egypt until 1517.

By 1260, when the Mongols began to threaten Egypt, the Bahri Dynasty was on its third Mamluk sultan, Saif ad-Din Qutuz. Ironically, Qutuz was Turkic (probably a Turkmen), and had become a Mamluk after he was captured and sold into slavery by the Ilkhanate Mongols.

Prelude to the Show-down

Hulagu's campaign to subdue the Islamic lands began with an assault on the infamous Assassins or Hashshashin of Persia. A splinter group of the Isma'ili Shia sect, the Hashshashin were based out of a cliff-side fortress called the *Alamut*, or "Eagle's Nest." On December 15, 1256, the Mongols captured Alamut and destroyed the power of the Hashshashin.

Next, Hulagu Khan and the Ilkhanate army launched their assault on the Islamic heartlands proper with a siege on Baghdad, lasting from January 29 to February 10, 1258. At that time, Baghdad was the capital of the Abbasid caliphate (the same dynasty that had battled the Chinese at Talas River in 751), and the center of the Muslim world. The caliph relied on his belief that the other Islamic powers would come to his aid rather than see Baghdad destroyed. Unfortunately for him, that did not happen.

When the city fell, the Mongols sacked and destroyed it, slaughtering hundreds of thousands of civilians and burning down the Grand Library of Baghdad. The victors rolled the caliph inside a rug and trampled him to death with their horses. Baghdad, the flower of Islam, was wrecked. This was the fate of any city that resisted the Mongols, according to Genghis Khan's own battle plans.

In 1260, the Mongols turned their attention to Syria. After only a seven-day siege, Aleppo fell, and some of the population was massacred. Having seen the destruction of Baghdad and Aleppo, Damascus surrendered to the Mongols without a fight. The center of the Islamic world now drifted south to Cairo.

Interestingly enough, during this time the Crusaders controlled several small coastal principalities in the Holy Land. The Mongols approached them, offering an alliance against the Muslims. The Crusaders' erstwhile enemies, the Mamluks, also sent emissaries to the Christians offering an alliance against the Mongols. Discerning that the Mongols were a more immediate threat, the Crusader states opted to remain nominally neutral, but agreed to allow the Mamluk armies to pass unhindered through Christian-occupied lands.

Hulagu Khan Throws Down the Gauntlet

In 1260, Hulagu sent two envoys to Cairo with a threatening letter for the Mamluk sultan. It said, in part: "To Qutuz the Mamluk, who fled to escape our swords. You should think of what happened to other countries and submit to us. You have heard how we have conquered a vast empire and have purified the earth of the disorders that tainted it. We have conquered vast areas, massacring all the people. Whither can you flee? What road will you use to escape us? Our horses are swift, our arrows sharp, our swords like thunderbolts, our hearts as hard as the mountains, our soldiers as numerous as the sand."

In response, Qutuz had the two ambassadors sliced in half, and set their heads up on the gates of Cairo for all to see. He likely knew that this was the gravest possible insult to the Mongols, who practiced an early form of diplomatic immunity.

Fate Intervenes

Even as the Mongol emissaries were delivering Hulagu's message to Qutuz, Hulagu himself received word that his brother Mongke, the Great Khan, had died. This untimely death set off a succession struggle within the Mongolian royal family.

Hulagu had no interest in the Great Khanship himself, but he wanted to see his younger brother Kubilai installed as the next Great Khan. However, the leader of the Mongol homeland, Tolui's son Arik-Boke, called for a quick council (*kuriltai*) and had himself named Great Khan. As civil strife broke out between the claimants, Hulagu took the bulk of his army north to Azerbaijan, ready to join in the succession fight if necessary.

The Mongolian leader left just 20,000 troops under the command of one of his generals, Ketbuqa, to hold the line in Syria and Palestine. Sensing that this was an opportunity not to be lost, Qutuz immediately gathered an army of roughly equal size and marched for Palestine, intent on crushing the Mongol threat.

The Battle of Ayn Jalut

On September 3, 1260, the two armies met at the oasis of *Ayn Jalut* (meaning "The Eye of Goliath" or "Goliath's Well"), in the Jezreel Valley of Palestine. The Mongols had the advantages of self-confidence and heartier horses, but the Mamluks knew the terrain better and had larger (thus faster) steeds. The Mamluks also deployed an early form of firearm, a sort of hand-held cannon, which frightened the Mongol horses. (This tactic cannot have surprised the Mongol riders themselves too greatly, however, since the Chinese had been using gunpowder against them for centuries.)

Qutuz used a classic Mongol tactic against Ketbuqa's troops, and they fell for it. The Mamluks sent out a small portion of their force, which then feigned retreat, drawing the Mongols into an ambush. From the hills, Mamluk warriors poured down on three sides, pinning the Mongols in a withering crossfire. The Mongols fought back throughout the morning hours, but finally the survivors began to retreat in disorder.

Ketbuqa refused to flee in disgrace, and fought on until his horse either stumbled or was shot out from under him. The Mamluks captured the Mongol commander, who warned that they could kill him if they liked, but "be not deceived by this event for one moment, for when the news of my death reaches Hulagu Khan, the ocean of his wrath will boil over, and from Azerbaijan to the gates of Egypt will quake with the hooves of Mongol horses." Qutuz then ordered Ketbuqa beheaded.

Sultan Qutuz himself did not survive to return to Cairo in triumph. On the way home, he was assassinated by a group of conspirators led by one of his generals, Baybars.

Aftermath of the Battle of Ayn Jalut

The Mamluks suffered heavy losses in the Battle of Ayn Jalut, but nearly the entire Mongol contingent was destroyed. This battle was a severe blow to the confidence and reputation of the hordes, which had never suffered such a defeat. Suddenly, they did not seem invincible.

Despite the loss, however, the Mongols did not simply fold their tents and go home. Hulagu returned to Syria in 1262, intent on avenging Ketbuqa. However, Berke Khan of the Golden Horde had converted to Islam, and formed an alliance against his uncle Hulagu. He attacked Hulagu's forces, promising revenge for the sacking of Baghdad.

Although this war among the khanates drew off much of Hulagu's strength, he continued to attack the Mamluks, as did his successors. The Ilkhanate Mongols drove towards Cairo in 1281, 1299, 1300, 1303, and 1312. Their only victory was in 1300, but it proved short-lived. Between each attack, the adversaries engaged in espionage, psychological warfare and alliance-building against one another.

Finally, in 1323, as the fractious Mongol Empire began to disintegrate, the Khan of the Ilkhanids sued for a peace agreement with the Mamluks.

A Turning-Point in History

Why were the Mongols never able to defeat the Mamluks, after mowing through most of the known world? Scholars have suggested a number of answers to this puzzle.

It may be simply that the internal strife among different branches of the Mongolian Empire prevented them from ever throwing enough riders against the Egyptians. Possibly, the greater professionalism and more advanced weapons of the Mamluks gave them an edge. (However, the Mongols had defeated other well-organized forces, such as the Song Chinese.)

The most likely explanation may be that the environment of the Middle East defeated the Mongols. In order to have fresh horses to ride throughout a day-long battle, and also to have horse milk, meat, and blood for sustenance, each Mongol fighter had a string of at least six or eight small horses. Multiplied by even the 20,000 troops that Hulagu left behind as a rear guard before Ayn Jalut, that is well over 100,000 horses.

Syria and Palestine are famously parched. In order to provide water and fodder for so many horses, the Mongols had to press attacks only in the fall or spring, when the rains brought new grass for their animals to graze on. Even at that, they must have used a lot of energy and time finding grass and water for their ponies.

With the bounty of the Nile at their disposal, and much shorter supply-lines, the Mamluks would have been able to bring grain and hay to supplement the sparse pastures of the Holy Land. In the end, it may have been grass, or the lack thereof, combined with internal Mongolian dissension, that saved the last remaining Islamic power from the Mongol hordes.

Sources

Reuven Amitai-Preiss. *Mongols and Mamluks: The Mamluk-Ilkhanid War*, 1260-1281, (Cambridge: Cambridge University Press, 1995).

Charles J. Halperin. "The Kipchack Connection: The Ilkhans, the Mamluks and Ayn Jalut,*Bulletin of the School of Oriental and African Studies*, University of London, Vol. 63, No. 2 (2000), 229–245.

John Joseph Saunders. *The History of the Mongol Conquests*, (Philadelphia: University of Pennsylvania Press, 2001).

Kenneth M. Setton, Robert Lee Wolff, et al. *A History of the Crusades: The Later Crusades*, 1189–1311, (Madison: University of Wisconsin Press, 2005).

John Masson Smith, Jr. "Ayn Jalut: Mamluk Success or Mongol Failure?," *Harvard Journal of Asiatic Studies*, Vol. 44, No. 2 (Dec., 1984), 307–345.

Appendix 5
A New People for God

By W. Michael McCormack
Scripture Text—Jeremiah 31:22b and Jeremiah 31:31–34

Speaking of the coming of Christianity into the world, Jeremiah got a word from the Lord.

"The Lord will create a new thing on earth—a woman will surround a man" (NIV '84).

In the Hebrew language this sentence has a double meaning:

The created "new thing on the earth" would be a Messiah (Savior) that would be in the womb of a woman.

The created "new thing on the earth" would be a people who would replace the adulterous and divorced Israel.

This interpretation is hard to see until we analyze the Hebrew words and their context. The key word in the verse is *surround*. This Hebrew word is *cabob*. It's root meaning is "to revolve around." There is another Hebrew word which means to surround in order to protect. This word is *ezer*. Sounds nothing like cabob does it? So, this verse, in context, is saying that God has decided to create a new entity on earth to supersede a rebellious and inadequate Israel. How do we know that the context is this? If we back up in Holy Scripture a few chapters, we will see that God says, "Thy bruise is incurable, and thy wound is grievous" (30:12 KJV). This means that Israel will be sent into captivity and, after a time, will be brought back into the land, BUT they will be brought back for one purpose: to bring forth the "new thing on the earth."

This new thing will be the new people of God, Christians under the rule and guidance of the Messiah. We see the prediction of this in Jeremiah 31:31–34 as God continues his word to Jeremiah and explains further this saying, "a woman will surround a man." By this point in Scripture, we have seen that Israel has often been related to as the "wife" of God, but she has been adulterous time and again, disavowing the marriage relationship. This "wife,", though loved, can never bring total healing, because "she" would not have it. God bemoans this but gives her over to her enemies. A new people will now be "wed" to God for the purpose of bringing to the earth new offspring who will be God's chosen children. As in any new marriage, a new covenant is stated for these people in relation to God, our Husband:

"The days are coming," declares the Lord, "when I will make a new covenant with the people of Israel and with the people of Judah. It will not be like the covenant I made with their ancestors when I took them by the hand to lead them out of Egypt, because they broke my covenant, though I was a husband to them," declares the Lord.

"This is the covenant I will make with the people of Israel after that time," declares the Lord.

"I will put my law in their minds and write it on their hearts. I will be their God, and they will be my people. No longer will they teach their neighbor, or say one to another, 'Know the Lord,' because they will all know me, from the least of them to the greatest," declares the Lord. For I will forgive their wickedness and will remember their sins no more" (Jeremiah 31:31–34 NIV).

God is the only personage who can truly "forgive and forget." When he says that he will forgive this people's wickedness, the Hebrew word in the text is translated, "iniquity" which means something is "twisted" so that no proper use for it can be had. He is talking about what we call the human condition of "The Fall." This state of human condition as a "twisted people" was not able to be overcome by the Israelites as a people. They had forfeited their designation as a holy priesthood, separated for God's purposes. So, a new people would now get the designation. What would be their sign of holy priesthood? It is given in the text. The law, the agreements of the New Covenant, will be written on their hearts and they will desire to be God's royal priesthood, following the love in their hearts, given by Messiah. This requires just a bit more interpretation about the human condition of "twistedness."

The state of existence in the human condition means that we are on a constant search for a way to enter into the process of our redemption. We know, in our hearts, that we are iniquitous, twisted to the point of no proper use, and our spirits desperately want to be of proper use. We are on a constant search for a way to enter into the process of our redemption (our straightening out before God). All the world's religions are witnesses to this. But the religious of the world are in something of a catch-22 or conundrum. Our human condition causes us to fail to see the simple reality that God has already provided the great "Straightener," Jesus, the Messiah. So, we strive and strain to attain our own redemption through good works, religious status, co-dependent relationships, crystals, etc.

However, the only way to proper use of US is to gain a redemptive relationship before God. The Bible tells us, and shows us, over and over that the only way to do this is to give up our struggle and accept his free gift of redemption through Jesus Christ, his Son sent for this purpose. And, precisely here is where we must go back to the original verse in Jeremiah 31:22 where we have the picture of something God "cooked up." The verse specifically says, "woman shall surround man." If we can translate that *woman* means the new wife (people) of the new covenant and the *man* is *geber*, a valiant man or warrior who is God's mighty man, then, once again, this word in the middle becomes key. We have already seen that the word *surround* in this verse means to revolve around. The word *cabob* brings forth the picture of what we, today, would call a "shish-Kabob." The "proper use" of meat on a shish kabob is to place it on the skewer and revolve it around the heat that cooks and purifies it for proper consumption. The new verse, therefore, means:

"My new people will revolve around (be rotated over the heat and light of) my Valiant Warrior, until well-done (sanctified)." Brings a whole new meaning to the saying, "Well done, good and faithful servant," doesn't it.

As we, Christians, revolve around Jesus and fulfill the Great Commission, to go into all the world under his authority and make disciples of all nations; baptizing them in the name of the Father, Son, and Holy Spirit; and teaching them to obey everything he has commanded, we will have him with us, his law will be on our hearts, he will be our God, and we will be his people–a proper use indeed.

APPENDIX 6
BASIC BIBLE PRECEPTS

Why would people want to kill the Bible? Killing the Bible is necessary for us to feel that we are in charge of our destiny and are adequate in our own right. The Bible will not endorse this fantasy. In a nutshell, the Bible says this:

1. The nature of humans is that humans are made in the image of God but separated from God by our own choice.

2. All humans have sinned against God and cannot restore the relationship on our own.

3. We are all, by nature, children of wrath.

4. No innate self-sufficiency, re-adjustment through education, or filling of a social gap can make us right with God.

5. All human troubles come through this one source of being in a "fallen state" and no eternal troubles can be solved ultimately unless and until the relationship to God, broken through sin, is restored.

6. Disorder and not order is at the core and center of each person's life. All of us have a rebellion problem within us that is of a personal and spiritual nature.

7. In biblical faith, nature and reason are all perverted through sin and humans are gripped in a tetanus-like death, wherein the self turns upon the self. This cannot be willed or worked away. A healing injection from outside oneself is required.

8. The Bible calls for a rescue, NOT a resolve. The Bible says our problem calls for a Messiah, whom God sends to rescue us.

9. The Bible's core, in one verse, is this: "For God so loved the world [us] that he gave his one and only Son, that whoever believes in him shall not perish, but have eternal life" (John 3:16 NIV) This Son is Jesus the Christ.

10. Once we are restored in relationship to God, through accepting the gift of the sacrifice of Jesus alone, we can proceed to fulfilling our social mission here on earth, <u>because we want to</u> and can now do this properly, led by the Holy Spirit who counsels us.

W. Michael McCormack succeeds where others have failed!

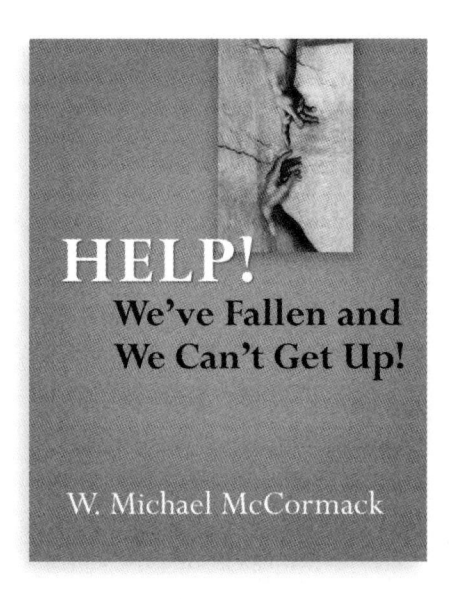

Help! We've Fallen and We Can't Get Up! is an apologetics house-call.

- The Human Condition
- The Big Three: Islam, Judaism, Catholicism
- Are there other Earths?
- New Age Religions
- What About Evolution?
- Can God Exist?
- Work-based Religions

A great deal has been said and written about the human condition and our man-made religions. It has been hard for scholars to put the Christian position in a nutshell that the average person can relate to.

Download this and more at killingthebible.com

W. Michael McCormack reveals what we have of 1st and 2nd Century proof texts of the Bible and where they are today. Not only that, but the true stories of their discovery in Egypt, Israel and the Middle East are fascinating. *The Light of Truth* is the perfect blend of Theology and History. Church members want to know what source material exists or, at least, if we have near copies of the original New Testament writings. Be illuminated by *The Light of Truth* as you never have been before!

The Topics

- How do Bible historians best find the truth?
- Who found Oxyrhynchus and why?
- Do we have copies of the Gospels from the 1st Century?
- Where are these ancient records now?
- How did an American find the oldest copies of the New Testament?

The DVD of *The Light of Truth* is available and comes with a small-group leader's guide.

Get both the digital booklet and the DVD package at killingthebible.com

Plan a special event you will never forget.

***Killing the Bible LIVE* could be coming to a venue near you!**

"W. Michael McCormack reveals the true history of the Christian Church and God's plan to use America. The characters in our Bible history are so colorful. Don't pass up the chance to see your Christian heritage right before your eyes!"

Seminar includes:
- A full day of live performance
- Big-screen media
- Antique Bibles on display
- Inspirational music
- More

Find out that:
- St. Augustine was the father of the inquisition
- Pope Gregory created the Papacy 500 years after Christ
- St. Patrick was a Brit and not an Irishman
- King James knowingly changed his version of the Bible
- Martin Luther had a wife and six kids
- William Tyndale was burned at the stake for translating the bible into English
- Muhammad beheaded 900 men in one day